Yale Language Series

Volumes by John DeFrancis in the Yale Language Series

Beginning Chinese, *Second revised edition*
Character Text for Beginning Chinese, *Second edition*
Beginning Chinese Reader (Parts I and II), *Second edition*
Intermediate Chinese
Character Text for Intermediate Chinese
Intermediate Chinese Reader (Part I)

A series of special memorization exercises with accompanying
tapes is available through the Institute of Far Eastern Studies,
Seton Hall University, South Orange, New Jersey 07079. A
wide variety of supplementary readers and study aids are
available from the University Press of Hawaii (2840 Kolowalu
Street, Honolulu, Hawaii 96822) and Far Eastern Publications (28 Hillhouse Avenue, New Haven, Connecticut 06520).
For complete lists, write directly to these publishers.

BEGINNING CHINESE READER

Part I

by John DeFrancis

WITH THE ASSISTANCE OF
Yung Teng Chia-yee and Yung Chih-sheng

SECOND EDITION

New Haven and London, Yale University Press

21   20

For Chuck

Beginning Chinese Reader

Contents of Part I

UNIT V

UNIT VI

Contents of Part II

UNIT VII

UNIT VIII

ACKNOWLEDGMENTS

I wish to thank the following institutions and individuals for helping make this book possible:

Office of Education, Deparment of Health, Education, and Welfare, for a grant to compile the book.

Seton Hall University, for providing institutional support for my work.

Dr. John B. Tsu, Director of the Institute of Far Eastern Studies, Seton Hall University, for his energetic concern to make available whatever assistance was needed at all of the work.

Mrs. Teng Chia-yee and Mr. Yung Chih-sheng, for their able and painstaking collaboration in writing the book.

Professors Harriet Mills and James Wrenn, for invaluable criticism and advice about the overall of presentation.

The Editorial Committee, consisting of Dr. John B. Tsu, Dr. David L. Kuan, Dr. E-tu Zen Sun, Prof. Eileen Wei, and Dr. Jonathan Mirsky, for suggesting many improvements in the text.

Mrs. Jean L. Feng, for her assiduous search for special combinations of characters.

Mr. Simon T. H. Chang, for his assistance in preparing the ditto draft of the material.

My wife, for repeated readings and typings of the manuscript.

The revised edition owes much to the assistance provided by Mr. Patrick Destenay and Mr. Constantine Milsky, both of the Université de Provence in Aix-en-Provence, France, who generously made available to me their extensive knowledge of recent Chinese linguistic usages obtained by extensive and continuing contacts both in the People's Republic of China and abroad.

I am also indebted to Mrs. Yung Teng Chia-yee for assistance of various kinds, and to Ms. Chih-yu Ho for providing initial drafts of Narrative 6 in Supplementary Lesson 35 and Narrative 4 in Supplementary Lesson 37.

John DeFrancis

Honolulu, Hawaii

PREFACE TO SECOND EDITION

In Beginning Chinese, citing the old adage "When in Rome, do as the Romans do", I stressed the idea that there are different ways of saying things in Chinese, just as in English and other languages, and that students must learn to recognize these different usages and to handle them appropriately in the different situations they are likely to encounter.[1]

This important point applies to the area of reading as well. The differences that exist in spoken Chinese are reflected in writing when conversations are presented in character form. There are further differences between conversational and narrative styles. Within these styles there are still more variations stemming from differences in time, place, and personal preferences. The individual characters themselves may show variation that reflect either the old variants or the new simplifications.

When students attempt to read any original materials in Chinese they will inevitably encounter these variations in the written language and must be prepared to cope with them. The problem here will be even more acute than in speaking Chinese because, while we can more or less restrict what we say, we have little or no control over what usages will be found in what we read. This is true even in the unlikely situation of reading only within extremely narrow limits of time, subject-matter, and authorship, a situation which is neither desirable nor, realistically speaking, attainable. It is, for example, quite preposterous to think that non-Chinese students who are primarily interested in current publications rather than in those of an earlier period can restrict their knowledge of characters only to the simplified forms adopted in the People's Republic of China in 1956. For any depth of understanding, students must read materials of earlier periods and perhaps of non-PRC origin written in regular characters. At the very least the most important reference tools, such as dictionaries, will for some time to come be those in conventional characters.

---

(1)   See the Preface to Second Revised Edition of Beginning Chinese and the extension of these remarks in my paper "Sociolinguistic Aspects of Chinese Language-Teaching Materials," Journal of Chinese Linguistics, III, 3 (September, 1975).

It is not a question of either or. Students must learn both forms and, since it appears easier to learn simplified after regular, this sequence should be followed in initiating one's study of written Chinese.

Beginning Chinese Reader introduces some of the main variant forms of Chinese. It presents, for example, a few terms that are peculiar to the People's Republic of China, some that are restricted to other areas or to earlier periods of time, and many (by far the majority) that are neutral as to time and place. It also provides material in both regular and simplified characters, the regular being presented first and more extensively as the most efficient procedure. Students may, however, emphasize one or another form by learning one actively and the other passively depending on their individual preferences.

The foregoing features are common to both the first and second editions of this book. In the earlier edition, however, a number of terms were not identified as restricted in usage, and the specific phraseology used in some of the Dialogues and Narratives was not always in agreement with the specific situational content.

In this revised edition, although it is assumed that the reader is familiar with Beginning Chinese, including the new material (especially the Notes) added to the second revised edition, some occasional references to special language usage have been added to the present text. More importantly, the content of a number of Dialogues and Narratives has been revised to make sure that language usage and subject matter are in agreement. It is, for example, inappropriate to write of a student not having money to attend school in present-day Peking, though it is quite appropriate to do so in reference to earlier periods of time or to areas outside the PRC.

The main lessons, which are written in regular characters, provide both PRC and non-PRC subject matter and language usage. Non-specific passages, such as unspecified references to 'China', may be appropriapiate only for one or another area of China at some particular point in time. Where a passage is more specific as to time and place an attempt has been made to make it more specifically appropriate both situationally and linguistically.

In the Supplementary Lessons, which are written in simplified characters, the content is more exclusively related to the PRC, or to other areas or periods of time but more or less phrased in PRC terms. For example, some passages referring to members of people's communes introduce new clichés such as "ask them to introduce their work experience to us" and "their life had a raising high". Material of this sort either replaces earlier passages which were not appropriate or extends the amount of reading matter provided in the simplified characters of the Supplementary Lessons.

Although this amount of material appears to be adequate for the additional task of learning simplified characters after the regular forms, students interested in additional reading in simplified characters may derive both pleasure and profit from the series of five supplementary readers which are correlated with the present text. [2]

---

(2) Four are by Yung Teng Chia-yee: The Herd Boy and the Weaving Maid (to follow lesson 30), The Heartless Husband (to follow lesson 36), The Bookworm (to follow lesson 42), and the Poet Li Po (to follow lesson 48). The fifth is by Kristina Lindell: The Student Lovers (to follow also after lesson 48). All were published by the University Press of Hawaii in 1975.

PREFACE TO FIRST EDITION

The present work forms part of three closely integrated sets of texts in spoken and written Chinese prepared at Seton Hall University. The relationship among them can be seen from the following outline:

CONVERSATION SERIES

Transcription Version	Character Version
Beginning Chinese	Character Text for Beginning Chinese
Intermediate Chinese	Character Text for Intermediate Chinese
Advanced Chinese	Character Text for Advanced Chinese

READING SERIES

Beginning Chinese Reader

Intermediate Chinese Reader

Advanced Chinese Reader

The first two sets are different versions of a single series of conversation texts. The third set, the reading series, consists of character texts which, unlike the character version of the conversation texts, are specifically designed as readers and hence are organized on quite different principles. There is, however, a close correlation between the reading series and the conversation series. The precise nature of the correlation is stated in the preface to each of the texts.

Beginning Chinese Reader is the continuation and extension of a work which was initiated in 1952. The first draft of a number of lessons done at that time was correlated with the first edition of Beginning Chinese, which was originally written in 1943-1944 in the romanization created by Professor George A. Kennedy at Yale University but which has since been completely revised using the pinyin romanization. Beginning Chinese Reader is closely correlated with the revised Beginning Chinese.

One of the beliefs underlying this book is that learning to read can be accomplished most efficiently by students who have some prior grounding in speech and who engage in simultaneous oral practice of what is read. The present text, accordingly, has been correlated with Beginning Chinese and is provided with dialogue in combination with narrative or expository material.

A second belief is that a clear distinction should be made between translating Chinese and reading Chinese. Many programs teach the former under the guise of teaching the latter. The ability to read Chinese implies a fluency which does not necessarily characterize the ability to translate Chinese. It follows that a reading textbook should be designed to promote fluency in reading.

A third belief is that fluency in reading, like fluency in speech, requires an enormous amount of practice. There is, however, a much more serious problem in practicing reading. In speaking, teachers and students readily create many new sentences on the general model of those in the textbook, so that even in beginning classes with limited vocabulary and structures, the amount of varied speaking, if written down, would fill several volumes. In reading, on the other hand, improvisation is much more difficult, so that only an infinitesimal amount of variation is added to what is already in a text. Since most texts have only a small amount of material to begin with and since what little there is suffers from a low ratio between number of different characters and amount of reading matter, there is no opportunity in beginning classes for extensive practice in reading comparable to that in speaking. This situation is partly the result of and partly the reason for the approach adopted by many teachers who defer extensive reading in favor of an initial emphasis on learning as many characters as possible. It is my belief that this approach is fundamentally wrong and is the chief reason for the failure of the teaching of reading to accomplish the kind of significant progress which has characterized the teaching of the spoken language since World War II. To remedy this situation, we must provide extensive reading materials, and since such materials cannot be improvised by teachers and students, it is our responsibility as textbook writers to assume this task.

Beginning Chinese Reader (BCR) is correlated both with Beginning Chinese (BC) and with the Character Text for Beginning Chinese (CTBC).

For the greatest efficiency in the use of these books, certain lessons of the two texts in characters should be studied after related lessons in the transcription text:

BCR	and	CTBC	after	BC		BCR	and	CTBC	after	BC
1-3						13-18		13		13
4		1		1		19-24		14		14
5-6		2		2		25-30		15		15
		3		3		31-36		16		16
7		4		4		37-42		17		17
8		5		5				18		18
		6		6		43		19		19
9		7		7		44		20		20
10		8		8		45		21		21
		9		9		46		22		22
11-12		10		10		47-48		23		23
		11		11				24		24
		12		12						

As can be seen, lessons 1 to 3 of Beginning Chinese Reader have no prerequisite in Beginning Chinese. They can be studied independently, say, during the introduction to the sounds of Chinese when it would be possible to study the thirty characters in lessons 1 to 3 as pure pictographs without regard to their pronunciation. For the remaining lessons, by taking up a lesson in BCR after the indicated lesson in Beginning Chinese, the amount of new material which must be studied is kept at a minimum. Beginning Chinese Reader purposely contains very little new with respect to grammar. Furthermore, of the 400 characters in BCR, except for 33 new characters* introduced in order to be able to take up topics more pertinent to a reading text, the remaining 367 all occur in BC. Of these 367, all but the 22 in lessons 1 to 3 are presented in BCR after they have appeared in the correlated lessons of BC. This means that even if the character version of BC has not been studied, the syllable representing a particular character has with

* These are the characters numbered 2, 3, 5 in lesson 1; 3, 6, 9 in lesson 2; 1 and 4 in lesson 3; and 10 in lessons 13-41 of BCR.

few exceptions already been encountered. To be sure, BCR goes far beyond BC in its use of the characters, which appear in new combinations and new functions.

This book is divided into two parts. The division into separate volumes is purely a practical matter necessitated by the decision to use large characters to make learning as easy as possible for the beginning student. The book consists of forty-eight main lessons arranged in eight units of six lessons each. The number of new characters is limited to ten per lesson to allow greater flexibility. The first five lessons in each unit contain new material; the sixth is a review lesson. In addition to these regular lessons there are forty-four supplementary lessons on simplified characters. These are numbered to match the numbers of the regular lessons. (The supplementary materials lack lessons 1 and 2 and 6 and 7.)

Appendices provide various summary charts for the characters introduced in this book, a brief introduction to Chinese writing, and a stroke order chart for all characters (including those in the supplementary lessons). In addition an index of the individual characters and combinations of characters is provided and is arranged alphabetically according to the pinyin system of transcription used in this book.

Most of the regular lessons, that is, all but the review lessons and the first few introductory lessons, have the same basic subdivisions, as follows:

New Characters

Special Combinations

Exercises

Illustrative Sentences (Chinese)

Dialogues

Narratives

Illustrative Sentences (English)

Miscellaneous

The most common miscellaneous exercises include the following:

Buildups. Modeled after similar exercises in Beginning Chinese, these are designed to show the structure of a phrase or sentence by introducing successive groups of characters. This sort of exercise is particularly needed in the very beginning of character study, but it has been carried as far as unit IV, which is correlated with Beginning Chinese, lesson 14, which contains practice on difficult dependent clauses, in order to provide help in mastering this particularly troublesome feature of written Chinese.

Pitfalls. These exercises present pairs of sentences which superficially seem to have much in common but generally differ in structure. The examples are designed to sharpen the student's ability to recognize the different structural patterns in which some characters occur.

Each lesson begins with the introduction of ten new characters which are presented first in large size in brush-written form. Each character is then repeated in smaller size, followed by its citation pronunciation, that is, the pronunciation when spoken in isolation. (The student must be prepared for changes in pronunciation, such as loss of tone, when characters enter into combinations.) Characters are defined briefly when first introduced.* Not all meanings are given at this time. In general the meanings given are limited to those which actually apply to the character as it is used in the lesson. Additional meanings are noted in subsequent lessons whenever a character is used in a new sense. Such reintroduced characters are numbered 11, 12, etc. All the meanings applied to each character in this book can be found by referring to the index. More complete definitions and discussions can be obtained by consulting dictionaries and other reference works, although it is hardly advisable to try to memorize all this information without practicing the use of a character in each of its meanings.

The selection of the 400 characters introduced in this book has been based on three main criteria, namely correlation with Beginning Chinese, importance for the Western student, and frequency of use. As noted earlier, all but 33 of the characters also occur in the character version of the conversa-

---

* It should be noted that there are often alternative forms of characters, one sometimes preferred over another, to express a particular meaning. Our defining a character in a particular way means only that it is sometimes used in this sense, not necessarily that it is the only or the most common way of expressing the idea in question. A case in point is our definition of character 7 in lesson 23 as 'a watch.' Several members of the Editorial Committee have objected to our using this character in the meaning indicated, on the grounds that the "proper" form of the character contains the "metal radical." This does not invalidate our handling of the matter, which is supported by the fact that several current Hong Kong newspapers, among others, regularly use the simpler character in their advertisements for watches.

tion text, which means that there is a high degree of overlap between the texts. As for the criteria of importance, this is not a simple function of frequency, especially for Western students, whose reading problems can by no means be viewed solely in the light of the reading habits of native Chinese. Hence some high-frequency characters, including several used in the literary style, which Western students normally study at a more advanced stage, have been set aside for later use, and a few characters of relatively low frequency, such as the ones for 'edit' and 'volume' or 'part' of a book, have been introduced so that we can begin as early as possible to treat of things of interest to Western students.

By far the most important criterion, however, is that of frequency of use. In the application of this criterion reliance was placed not on guesswork or subjective judgment but rather on studies involving actual counts of characters appearing in general literature. Chief among these works is the important study by Chén Hèqín, a graduate of Teachers College in New York who at one time was Commissioner of Education in Shanghai. In his study * Chén counted running text of over 900,000 characters appearing in various books, periodicals, and other sources. The number of different characters, he found, was a little under 4800. Chén's data reveal a startling picture of the relative frequency of Chinese characters. The 400 most frequently used characters comprise 73.1 per cent of the total text. The least frequently used half of all the different characters comprise a mere 2.5 per cent of the total text. His data can be summarized by the following table and chart:

number of different characters	order of frequency	per cent of total text	cumulative per cent of total text
400	1- 400	73.1	73.1
400	401- 800	12.4	85.5
400	801-1200	5.8	91.3
400	1201-1600	3.3	94.6
400	1601-2000	1.9	96.5
400	2001-2400	1.0	97.5
2319	2401-4719	2.5	100.0

* Chén Hèqín, Yŭtĭwén yìngyòng zìhuì [Characters used in Vernacular Literature] (Shanghai, 1928).

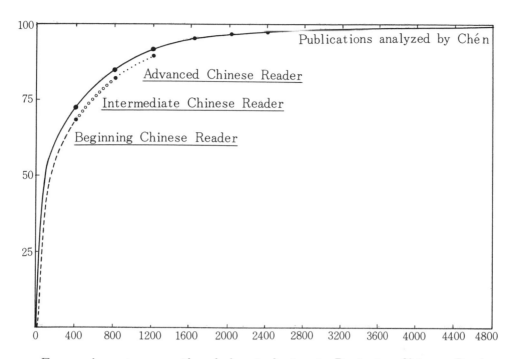

Every character considered for inclusion in <u>Beginning Chinese Reader</u> (and also in <u>Intermediate Chinese Reader</u> and <u>Advanced Chinese Reader,</u> now in the process of being written) was checked against Chén's frequency list. With the exceptions noted earlier, only those characters which ranked high in his list were accepted for inclusion. The resulting close degree of correspondence between the characters selected for inclusion in these textbooks and the characters found by Chén to be of highest frequency can be seen from the accompanying chart, in which the data of the preceding table are presented in graphic form and compared with similar data for the textbooks. As the graph indicates, the 400 characters in <u>Beginning Chinese Reader</u> comprise 68.2 percent of the total text counted by Chén. This figure is higher than for the same number of characters in any other series of textbooks. (The 400 characters to be used in <u>Intermediate Chinese Reader</u> and the like number of characters to be used in <u>Advanced Chinese Reader</u> will raise the figure to about 85 and 90 per cent respectively.)

Another distinctive feature of this book is the application of what might be called "the permutability principle" in the study of Chinese characters. One of the unique features of Chinese writing is that the characters can be combined in many different ways. Basic to acquiring skill in reading is a familiarity with the processes of character-compounding in Chinese. Such familiarity is best acquired by mastering several compounds for a limited number of characters rather than, as is frequently attempted, by learning one or two compounds for many characters. In the preparation of this text all possible combinations of the characters studied were first systematically searched out. An enormous number of combinations were found, but only a few of the most important were used. In all there are 1,250 combinations, an average of slightly over three compounds per character, which is more than twice the ratio for comparable texts.*

The combinations presented in each lesson are limited to those which can be formed with the characters introduced in the same or in previous lessons. The combinations draw on the same range of meanings as those introduced for these characters in the same or previous lessons. In those cases in which new combinations involve new meanings for characters already studied, these characters are, as mentioned above, reintroduced directly after the ten new characters.

Special attention should be paid to the Illustrative Sentences, which demonstrate the use of all new characters, combinations of characters, and special usages. Although the basic grammar of this text does not exceed that of Beginning Chinese, even within the limits of the patterns presented in that work, there is possibility for many variations which might cause difficulties for a beginning student. The illustrative sentences are designed to anticipate possible trouble spots in the remaining exercises. In order to make sure that they are thoroughly understood, they are accompanied by English translations which are placed at the end of the lesson, separated from the Chinese, so that the material can be used as an exercise in translating

---

* In this connection it should be noted that there are :
  - 494 characters in Character Text for Beginning Chinese
  - 33 characters in BCR which are not in CTBC
  - 527 characters in BCR and CTBC combined
  - 265 combinations in CTBC
  - 1051 combinations in BCR which are not in CTBC
  - 1316 combinations in BCR and CTBC combined

In other words, in comparison with Character Text for Beginning Chinese, there are only 33 new characters in Beginning Chinese Reader, but there are 1051 new combinations.

from Chinese to English or from English to Chinese.

There are several reasons for including dialogue materials in a book intended as a reader. The first is to provide the students with audiolingual support of what they read, such additional support being particularly needed for the terms introduced in BCR but not in the correlated conversation text. The second is to prepare the way for the transition to the material contained in Advanced Chinese, a conversation text which presupposes an active command of the contents of both Beginning Chinese and Beginning Chinese Reader. A third is that dialogue is also part of written Chinese, as in plays, novels, and other forms of literature.

Except for the first unit, there is more narrative than dialogue in each lesson. The relative amount of the latter gradually decreases to the point where in the last lessons it forms less than a fifth of the reading matter. Those who wish to achieve a more passive command of the material can use the dialogues as supplementary reading or even ignore them completely with the assurance that the repetition achieved in the narrative section alone is greater than in any other textbook.

Great pains have been taken in this work to assure adequate repetition and review of the material. Mechanical procedures set up to guard against under-use have made it possible to assure that the following minimum schedule of repetitions has been followed:

Single Characters:

    (1) Five times in the lesson of first occurrence (three times in the narratives, once in the illustrative sentences, and once in the dialogues)

    (2) Twice in the next lesson (here and below not counting possible occurrences in the dialogues)

    (3) Once after a gap of one or two lessons

    (4) Once in the unit-final lesson

    (5) Once in the first half and once again in the second half of all succeeding units

Special Combinations

    (1) Three times in the lesson of first occurrence (once each in the illustrative sentences, dialogues, and narratives)

(2) Once in the next lesson (here and below not counting possible occurrences in the Dialogues)

(3) Once after a gap of one or two lessons

(4) Once in the Unit-final lesson

(5) Thereafter at varied intervals determined by the difficulty and importance of individual combinations

In a few cases where it was not possible to follow this schedule precisely (e.g. in the first few and last few lessons), special procedures were devised to assure adequate repetition. In addition, review lessons repeat all characters and compounds introduced in the unit as well as numerous others that provide special difficulties and hence require special attention. The final lesson, lesson 48, is a cumulative review of all characters introduced in the book. Some idea of the amount of repetition can be gathered from the fact that although there are only 400 different characters there are about 120,000 characters of running text.

It should be emphasized that this extensive repetition is aimed at learning much more than 400 characters per se. Learning to recognize 400 characters is no great intellectual feat. If this were all that was involved, much less repetition would be adequate, but achieving a facile mastery over the use of these characters in their various combinations and contexts is an accomplishment of a much higher order. For that, the repetition presented here marks only the beginning of what must be an unremitting effort to consolidate and extend control over these basic building blocks of written Chinese.

It is possible, however, that for some classes there may be more repetition and review than is needed. In such cases it might be possible to skip the review lessons. The dialogues have been designed to be independent of the narratives and, as noted above, can also be omitted if there is no interest in achieving a spoken command of the contents. The decision as to whether to make these and other possible omissions (e.g. of a fraction of the narratives) must rest on the degree of mastery sought for and achieved. For a really facile command it is doubtful that there is an excess of repetition and review. It is well to bear in mind that the longest lessons in this book can be read by a native Chinese in well under half an hour. Our objective should be some such degree of facility.

Beginning textbooks in all languages inevitably encounter difficulties in preparing students to cope with what will be encountered in the real world of writing and publication. The difficulties are particularly great in Chinese, and the road becomes longer and harder before the student gets to the point where he can handle unedited material. A distinctive feature of the present text is the attempt to hasten the student's progress by bringing in as early as possible material closely simulating or fully derived from actual writings.

Toward this end the ordinary special combinations of characters have been supplemented by names of actual people, places, and organizations and titles of books and journals. Most of these are to be found in the section headed Who's Who and What's What. The items listed in this section should be distinguished from fictitious but plausible names and titles which do not occur in this list but appear throughout the book. Such fictitious items have been created on the model of real ones. Thus all given names of people are real, that is have actually been used by people in real life or in literature, but other than those specifically listed they are only fictitiously linked with particular surnames.

In the further search for realism various forms of written Chinese have been introduced in addition to the dialogues and narratives which comprise the bulk of the exercises. Such additional materials include poems, correspondence, tables of contents, booksellers' booklists, maps, and various other kinds of writing, Most important, perhaps, are the items presented under the title Excerpts from Actual Publications. As early as lesson 18, with as few as 150 characters, it has been possible to find a few short excerpts from a play by China's leading dramatist. Additional characters make possible quoting verbatim passages (with occasional deletions) from the works of such outstanding writers as Dr. Sun Yatsen, Mao Tse-tung, Lü Hsün, Hu Shih, and others. Special attention should be paid to these passages. They are the real thing.

PROBLEMS IN READING CHINESE

The Chinese system of writing is the most difficult in the world. One indication of this is the fact that the State Department allots students of Chinese twenty-four to thirty months of full-time study to attain the level of proficiency which it expects of students of French after six to nine months. The hard truth of the difficulty of Chinese should not be obscured, as is frequently done, by creating the impression that written Chinese consists chiefly of charming pictographs or by equating recognition of a certain number of characters with ability to read Chinese. In many ways the Chinese language is unique and fascinating, but it can seriously challenge one's staying power in the lengthy and arduous effort needed to master the writing system. For the Western student the task of learning to read Chinese involves a number of special problems; it is well to be aware of these at the outset.

CULTURAL BACKGROUND

When most Chinese read in their own language, they do so against a solid background of Chinese culture. Even preschool children are familiar with many of the peculiarities of their kinship system, with the stories of ancient heroes and villains, and with all kinds of information which Westerners learning Chinese are likely to know either not at all or only in a sketchy manner.

The beginning student of Chinese clearly cannot acquire the needed cultural background by extensive reading in Chinese. He can and should, however, make progress in this direction by reading about China in English. The more he knows about China, the easier it will be for him grasp the implications of what he reads in Chinese.

COMMAND OF THE LANGUAGE

Besides being familiar with their own cultural background, the Chinese approach the task of learning to read already armed with a full command of their own language in the spoken form. Most Western students of Chinese undertake the study of characters with much less knowledge of the spoken language than a Chinese child of three or four years. Often they are in the position of having to learn simultaneously spoken words, grammatical structures, and characters. There is considerable disagreement among specialists in the teaching of Chinese about how to handle this problem in learning to read Chinese. Most specialists believe that even if the main goal is learning to read, this is most quickly and most efficiently achieved by learning a certain amount of the spoken language first. How much time should be spent first on exclusive study of speech is a matter of dispute. My own belief, reflected in the way this book has been written, is that learning to read should follow learning to speak but that it need not lag very far behind.

SPOKEN VERSUS WRITTEN CHINESE

Rarely do people write exactly as they speak. The gap between speech and writing is perhaps greater in Chinese than in any other language in the world. Spoken Chinese is polysyllabic, but written Chinese, especially in the classical literary style, tends toward such terseness that it is frequently labeled monosyllabic. Wide differences between speech and writing still exist despite the fact that since the 1920s, and increasingly so in recent years, the emphasis in Chinese writing has been on a "plain language" style which more and more approximates actual speech. In addition to stylistic differences in writing there are also important differences stemming from the sometimes widely divergent dialects of Chinese, some of which are as far apart as English and Dutch. Although writers of different dialect backgrounds try to approximate a general standard in their writing, even current literature a- bounds in special terms and turns of phrases which are dialectical in origin. In general, written Chinese is much more of a hodge-podge than the standard spoken language based on the Peking dialect.

One of the major difficulties encountered by students of Chinese stems from the inadequate attention given to the differences between spoken and written Chinese. A beginning in this direction is made in this text by pre- senting material in both the conversational and the written style. Although no attempt is made to stress dialectical peculiarities, nonstandard use of certain characters, and other features of written Chinese which Western students must eventually learn to cope with, they are not totally avoided, and a few are introduced when it seems appropriate and natural. Thus the special dialect form for 'a betrothal' is introduced because it is used in the account (lesson 48) of his mother's betrothal by Hu Shih, himself one of the leaders of the 'plain language' movement.

KNOWING CHARACTERS

In discussions about the teaching of reading, a frequently heard question is "How many characters do you know?" This popular numbers game is generally played in an exceedingly amateurish manner which ignores the fact that the simple question is actually quite complex. Of equal importance are such neglected questions as "How many combinations of characters do you know?" "How many grammatical constructions have you learned?" and "How much actual reading have you done?" Too often "knowing" a character is equated with having been exposed to it in a textbook, regardless of whether the text merely imparts a recognition acquaintance or provides a richer understanding of the way in which a character enters into combinations, performs varied functions in a sentence, or has acquired particular cultural connotations. Such an extended understanding enables us to "know" a symbol even where there is nothing there to "recognize," as in the sentence "George Washington was the first----of the United States." There are in fact varying degrees of knowing characters. One of the most difficult tasks in Chinese is acquiring an adequate knowledge of the richness of usages and meanings attached to individual characters, a richness far exceeding that of individual words in English.

TYPOGRAPHIC DIFFICULTIES

On the printed page the Chinese characters appear as little square symbols of equal size. Although each symbol represents a single syllable of sound, it provides little or no accurate information as to how it is pronounced.

Nor can one tell at a glance whether a character is related to one before it or one after it or whether it is being used in a special way, like capitalized or italicized words in English.

The way in which uniform spacing between characters complicates the problem of relating characters to each other can be illustrated by taking a roughly comparable situation in English in which all the syllables are similarly separated by an equal amount of white space. In English we might have at least momentary trouble with the sentences

     (1) He'll be down right a way.
     (2) He'll be down right mean.

Sentence (1) would normally be written as "He'll be down right away," and sentence (2) as "He'll be downright mean." The conventional grouping of the syllables into words makes the meaning of the sentences immediately clear. In Chinese with its uniform spacing between characters (and hence between syllables), the reader who lacks a firm command of the language is at a special disadvantage. I do not believe that the solution to this problem is the un-Chinese device of putting related adjacent characters closer to each other. Even less do I approve of the unaesthetic and unnecessary device of combining characters and transcription in the rebus method. The solution lies instead in extensive practice in reading Chinese as close to the way it is actually written and printed as possible.

Since all characters are of equal size, Chinese lacks the distinction between small and capital letters that is so useful in English. The headline PLAN TO RAZE WHITE HOUSE has three possible meanings which can readily be distinguished by the normal use of capitals and small letters:

     (1) Plan to raze White House
     (2) Plan to raze White house
     (3) Plan to raze white house

The lack of capitalization has led many students of Chinese to translate a term which is really a proper name, a practice comparable to rendering Oxford as 'the ford for oxen.' The difficulty can be overcome or at least reduced if practice is provided on proper names—personal names, place-names, names of institutions, organizations, and so on.

Situations in which English makes use of italics, as in titles of books, are sometimes handled in Chinese by underlining (or in vertical texts, side-lining) the characters in question. Even today this is by no means the universal practice, and in earlier texts such devices were hardly ever used. The problem which results from the lack of italics (and capitals) can be illustrated in English with the following sentence :

How did you like the man in the iron mask?

This could mean either 'How did you enjoy meeting the man wearing the iron mask?' or 'How did you enjoy reading The Man in the Iron Mask?' Some terms occur particularly often in titles, a point which is illustrated in English by expressions like 'History of⋯', 'Essay on⋯', 'Life of⋯', and so on. Practice with phrases of this sort can help the student improve his ability to identify names and to translate titles in Chinese.

INTERRELATIONSHIP OF PROBLEMS

We have just discussed only a few of what are actually many interrelated problems in learning to read Chinese. This interrelationship itself comprises an additional problem. In the joining of characters to form a connected text, idiomatic distinctions are often added which are not covered by ordinary textbook notes and definitions. Such subtleties as literary style, level of discourse or narration, special turns of phrases, ideas half-expressed or implied, and so on are all important to Chinese writing, even Chinese writing in an elementary text such as this. The ability to handle all these matters goes beyond a knowledge of characters, combinations, and structures and requires a feeling for the language as a whole. Such a feeling, involving as it does the total of all the interrelated problems in learning Chinese, can only be acquired by the total act of reading.

SUGGESTIONS FOR STUDY

Since Chinese programs differ widely in number of classroom hours, size of class, and other variables, there are many possible ways in which this text might be studied. In general it is suggested that the correlation indicated earlier between Beginning Chinese and Beginning Chinese Reader be followed as closely as possible. This means studying characters only after the related material has been learned in transcription form. Furthermore, although some characters can be taken up at the very beginning of the program, they should be introduced slowly in the beginning and more rapidly later as a firm base is achieved in the spoken language. Such a procedure is especially called for in the case of most high school classes.

In some programs, especially those in college, it would be possible to introduce characters at a faster rate without undue interference with learning to speak. This can be done by following up a lesson in Beginning Chinese with the related lessons in both Character Text for Beginning Chinese and Beginning Chinese Reader.

There are 400 characters in Beginning Chinese Reader and 494 in Character Text for Beginning Chinese. The combined total of different characters in the two texts is 527. Of these, 367 occur in both texts, 33 occur only in Beginning Chinese Reader, and 131 occur only in Character Text for Beginning Chinese. The large overlap in characters between the two texts means that an enormous amount of reading matter is available for a limited number of characters. Moreover, experience has shown that the Character Text for Beginning Chinese is practically self-teaching.

In some accelerated programs seeking the most rapid introduction to written Chinese, the attempt is sometimes made to dispense with conversation altogether. I do not think this is advisable because even though the initial progress in characters will be more rapid than in the case of programs which start with speech and gradually effect a transition to reading, the lack of a firm audiolingual base is likely to have a retarding effect on subsequent progress.

A possible compromise is to retain the initial emphasis on speech but to effect a more rapid transition to reading. This compromise might take the course of studying Beginning Chinese through lesson 16 together with related materials in the two character texts and then concentrating on Beginning Chinese Reader. There are two reasons for making the cutoff at lesson 16. First, the main structures requiring the most extended conversational practice occur in the first sixteen lessons. Second, three subsequent lessons (17, 19, and 21) deal with eating situations and hence contain some vocabulary items which have less utility for general reading. On the other hand, of the 342 characters in lessons 1 to 16 of Character Text for Beginning Chinese, all but 40 occur in Beginning Chinese Reader as well (all but 15 occur in Intermediate Chinese Reader), and of these only one (that in lesson 2 representing the exclamation 'Oh!') ranks very low in frequency and might be considered as having very little use.*

In all programs it is advisable to spend a good deal of time, at least at the beginning stage, in learning how to write characters. Some teachers place much emphasis on the ability to write characters from memory. Others are content if students can copy characters correctly and are aware of their component elements. Regardless of the approach, it is advisable to pay special attention to the writing of the first thirty characters. These are of particular importance since they are all radicals.

The study program for each lesson should start with a brief classroom discussion of the composition, pronunciation, meanings, and use of each new character. Apart from a general introduction to the subject, stroke order need not be discussed for each character since this is covered by the Stroke-Order Chart. The component parts and similarities in structure of various characters should be pointed out as an aid toward memorization. In considering the meaning and use of a character, special attention should be paid to its appearance in the special combinations and also in the illustrative sentences. Since the latter often involve points of special difficulty, they

---

* The combined total of different characters in lessons 1 to 16 of Character Text for Beginning Chinese and lessons 1 to 48 of Beginning Chinese Reader is 440, of which 302 are common to both, 98 occur only in the Reader (mainly in lessons 37 to 48), and 40 occur only in the Character Text.

should be gone over carefully and should be thoroughly understood before the student goes on to the remaining exercises.

As an aid to memorizing individual characters and special combinations, a set of flashcards covering these items has been prepared. In addition a set of Practice Sheets has been prepared as an aid to writing the individual characters. Also available are tape recordings covering the sentences and connected text. * Listening to the recordings while silently reading the text can be an important help not only in learning new terms but also in learning to read with the speed and rhythm of a native Chinese rather than with the haphazard pauses characteristic of a beginning student. This is not simply an aesthetic matter but is vitally related to gaining fluency in reading.

Regardless of the program adopted, it is recommended that classroom time not be taken up with line by line translation of the material in this text. In the interest of covering as much ground as possible students should be required to assume the responsibility of reading the material outside of class. If the groundwork has been adequately prepared the student should be able to undertake this task. Class time should be taken up only with presenting new material and dealing with problems encountered by students in the course of preparation. Spot checks on points known to be difficult should provide the teacher with an adequate check of student accomplishment. This can be achieved either by asking for English translation of key passages, or by using the dialogue material for conversation in Chinese about the contents of both the narratives and the dialogues.

Above all it must be borne in mind that the aim is to read Chinese, to read it with fluency, and not merely to translate. In seeking this objective it is appropriate to take a cue from the common saying among language teachers that "Language learning is over-learning." The same idea can be applied to reading.

In learning to speak, the primary emphasis is on achieving facility in uttering sentences rather than simply in memorizing lists of words. Simi-

*The flashcards, Practice Sheets and other supplementary aids may be obtained from Far Eastern Publications (Yale University, New Haven, Conn. 06520) and the tape recordings from the Institute of Far Eastern Studies, Seton Hall University, South Orange, New Jersey. 07079.

larly in reading the object is to read diverse materials with speed and comprehension rather than simply to "know" an impressive number of individual characters or to be content with the agonizing translation or decoding which far too often passes for reading. Fluency in reading can only be achieved by extensive practice on all the interrelated aspects of the reading process. To accomplish this we must READ, READ, READ.

Beginning Chinese Reader provides such practice in extensive exercises which combine diversity with repetition. It thus provides a means whereby the difficult task of learning to read Chinese is at least made easier if not--what is really impossible--made easy.*

---

*For further remarks on the problem of reading Chinese see my "Why Johnny Can't Read Chinese," Journal of the Chinese Language Teachers Association, I, 1 (February, 1966), 1 − 20.

UNIT I

Lesson 1

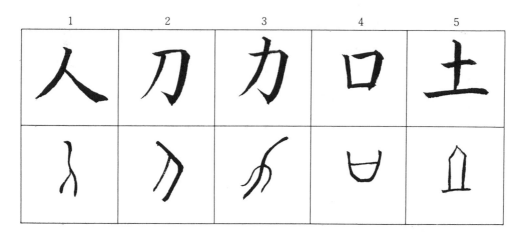

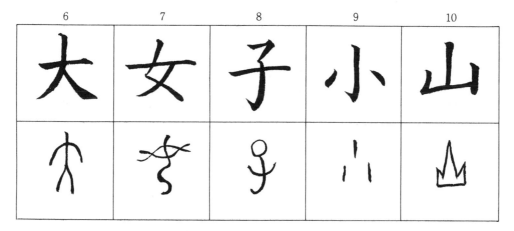

1. 人 rén   man, person (The pictographic form represents a walking man.)

2. 刀 dāo   knife (In the pictograph the upper part apparently represents the handle of the knife, and the lower part the blade, with the tip shown open instead of closed.)

3. 力 lì*   strength, power, force (The early form appears to be a

---

* Asterisks designate items which are restricted in use, that is either bound forms (i.e. occurring only in close combination with another character) or forms limited to a particular style or usage. Where the grammatical category or usage of an item is not clear from the definition, it is indicated by an abbreviation, such as (N), after the definition. For the abbreviations used, see the first page of the Index.

drawing of a hand and arm.)

4. 口 kǒu*   mouth, entrance, opening (The modern form is only slightly modified from the early drawing of an opening.)

5. 土 tǔ   earth, soil (The pictograph represents the Altar to the Soil, which was a central feature in traditional Chinese religious practice.)

6. 大 dà   big, large (The early form is a stick drawing of a man with outstretched arms.)

7. 女 nǚ*   woman, female (The drawing is of a kneeling woman.)

8. 子 zǐ*   son (The pictograph shows a human being with a large head, i.e. a child.)

9. 小 xiǎo small (The early form consists simply of three small dots.)

10. 山 shān mountain, hill (The pictograph clearly represents mountain peaks.)

Special Combinations

Here are a few simple combinations which illustrate character-compounding in Chinese.

1. 大刀 dàdāo   big knife, sword
2. 女人 nǚren   woman
3. 人力 rénlì   manpower
4. 山口 shānkǒu   mountain pass (used especially in place-names)
5. 土人 tǔrén   an aborigine, a native

Lesson 2

1	2	3	4	5
工	心	手	日	月
工				

6	7	8	9	10
木	毛	水	火	牛

1. 工　gōng　　work, labor (The pictograph represents a carpenter's square.)

2. 心　xīn　　heart (The sketch is of a heart inside the chest cavity.)

3. 手　shǒu　　hand; (used also as noun-forming suffix)(The pictograph shows a formalized drawing of a hand.)

4. 日　rì *　　sun (The drawing shows the sun with added dot.)

5. 月　yuè *　　moon (The drawing is of a crescent moon.)

6. 木　mù *　　tree, wood (The pictograph is a stylized drawing of a tree.)

5

7. 毛 máo   feather, fur, body hair (This, too, is a stylized drawing.)

8. 水 shuǐ   water (The drawing represents running water.)

9. 火 huǒ   fire (The pictograph appears to be a stylized representa-
tion of flames.)

10. 牛 niú   ox, cow (The drawing concentrates attention on the curved
horns.)

Special Combinations

1. 工人 gōngren   worker
2. 火山 huǒshān   volcano
3. 山水 shānshuǐ   landscape
4. 手工 shǒugōng   handicraft
5. 水口 shuǐkǒu   mouth of a stream (used especially in place-names)
6. 水力 shuǐlì   water power
7. 水牛 shuǐniú   water buffalo
8. 水手 shuǐshǒu   sailor (literally 'water hand')

Lesson 3

1	2	3	4	5
田	目	見	角	言
田	(pictograph)	(pictograph)	(pictograph)	(pictograph)

6	7	8	9	10
車	長	門	馬	魚
(pictograph)	(pictograph)	(pictograph)	(pictograph)	(pictograph)

1. 田   tián   field, farmland (The pictograph represents the square divisions of irrigated fields.)

2. 目   mù*   eye (The pictographic origin of this character is very clear.)

3. 見   jiàn   see (The drawing shows <u>rén</u> 'man' with big <u>mù</u> 'eye.')

4. 角   jiǎo*   horn (The drawing is of an animal head with curved horns.)

5. 言   yán*   word, speech (The modern form appears to show a mouth with words issuing from it, but the early form is a drawing of a mouth and trumpet-like flute. The character was used as a phonetic loan word for <u>yán</u> 'speech.')

7

6. 車 chē   cart, vehicle (The drawing is of a chariot.)

7. 長 cháng   long (The pictograph appears to be a drawing of a man with long hair.)

8. 門 mén   door, gate (The figure represents a double door.)

9. 馬 mǎ   horse (For a discussion of the evolution of this character, see Beginning Chinese, p. 446.)

10. 魚 yú   fish (For a discussion of this character, see Beginning Chinese, p. 446.)

Special Combinations

1. 大門   dàmén   big gate, main gate
2. 火車   huǒchē   train
3. 馬車   mǎchē   horse-drawn cart
4. 馬力   mǎlì   a horse's power, horsepower
5. 人力車 rénlìchē ricksha
6. 水田   shuǐtián irrigated fields, paddy

Exercise 1. Practice in Map Reading

The following is a list of actual place-names. Most of the places are small and only of local significance, but one, number 1 below, is the site of an important hydroelectric complex. Transcribe the names, locate them on the accompanying map, and give the coordinates for each.

1. 水口山	8. 馬山口	15. 長水	22. 大田
2. 毛目	9. 大牛山	16. 大目山	23. 長山
3. 牛角山	10. 長門	17. 小水口	24. 土門
4. 木馬	11. 大水口	18. 山門	25. 角山
5. 大魚山	12. 車門山	19. 大山口	26. 大人山
6. 牛田	13. 馬水口	20. 小山	27. 長子
7. 日月山	14. 牛山	21. 馬山	28. 小水

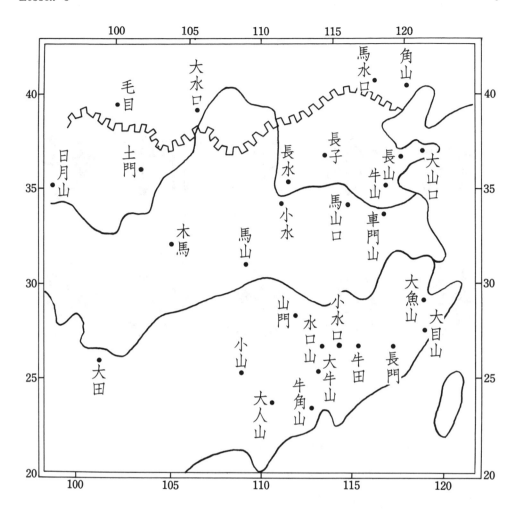

Lesson 4

1	2	3	4	5
我	你	他	們	好

6	7	8	9	10
都	很	也	嗎	呢

1. 我   wǒ   I, me
2. 你   nǐ   you
3. 他   tā   he, him, she, her, it
4. 們   men   (pluralizing suffix)
5. 好   hǎo   good, well
6. 都   dōu   all, both
7. 很   hěn   very
8. 也   yě   also
9. 嗎   ma   (question particle)
10. 呢   ne   (question particle)

Special Combinations

1. 我們   wǒmen   we, us
2. 你們   nǐmen   you (plural)
3. 他們   tāmen   they, them

10

Exercise 1. Illustrative Sentences (Chinese)

1. 我們都好.

2. 你呢?

3. 你們都好嗎?

4. 他們也很好.

Exercise 2. Dialogues

1. 田: 你好嗎?

   馬: 我好. 你呢?

   田: 我也好.

2. 毛: 他們都好嗎?

   田: 他們都很好.

3. 馬: 我們都很好. 你們呢?

   毛: 我們也很好.

4. 田: 他們好嗎?

   馬: 他們好.

5. 毛: 他好嗎?

   田: 他很好.

6. 馬: 我很好. 你們呢?

   毛: 我們也都很好.

Exercise 3. Illustrative Sentences (English)

1. We're all fine.

2. And what about you?

3. Are you all well?

4. They're very well, too.

Lesson 5

1	2	3	4	5
白	高	先	生	不

6	7	8	9	10
是	中	美	英	國

1. 白　bái　(1) white ; (2) (a surname)

2. 高　gāo　(1) tall, high ; (2) (a surname)

3. 先　xiān*　first

4. 生　shēng　(1) give birth to ; (2) be born ; (3) (suffix used in terms referring to scholars)

5. 不　bù　not, no

6. 是　shì　be, is, are

7. 中　zhōng*　middle

8. 美　měi　beautiful

9. 英　yīng*　brave

10. 國　guó　country, nation

11. 馬　mǎ　(a surname ; see lesson 3)

12. 毛　máo　(a surname ; see lesson 2)

13. 田　tián　(a surname ; see lesson 3)

12

Special Combinations

1. 中國　Zhōngguo　China
2. 美國　Měiguo　America, the United States
3. 英國　Yīngguo　England
4. 先生　xiānsheng　(1) gentleman; (2) teacher; (3) Sir; (4) Mr.

Note on the Enumerative Comma

In addition to the ordinary comma (,) Chinese has another which might be called the enumerative comma (、). The latter is used to join two or more items, most often nominal expressions, which are enumerated in a series. The following pair of otherwise identical sentences illustrates the difference in meaning conveyed by the use of the two commas:

毛先生, 高先生也好嗎？　　Mr. Mao, is Mr. Gao also well?

毛先生、高先生也好嗎？　　Are Mr. Mao and Mr. Gao also well?

Note that the use of the two commas makes it possible to distinguish sentences which are otherwise identical in writing but which are recognized in speech by quite different intonations. Note also that the items joined by an enumerative comma have the same syntactical function in a sentence and can be handled as a single syntactical unit. In the above example, the enumerated items function as a compound subject.

Exercise 1. Illustrative Sentences (Chinese)

1. 你是美國人嗎？
2. 馬先生是中國人不是？
3. 我是田水心. 你是…？
4. 白心田、毛力都是英國人嗎？

Exercise 2. Dialogues

1. 高：白先生是英國人不是？
   馬：不是．他是美國人．

2. 毛：我是毛小山．你是⋯？
   田：我是田力子．

3. 白：你們都是中國人嗎？
   高：是．我們都是中國人．

4. 田：他是毛力不是？
   白：不是．他是高長山．
   田：他是美國人嗎？
   白：不是．他是英國人．

5. 白：高先生，你好？
   高：很好．白先生，你呢？
   白：我也好．

6. 毛：田子心、馬長山都是美國人嗎？
   白：不都是．田先生是美國人．馬

先生是英國人.

Exercise 3. Illustrative Sentences (English)

1. Are you an American ?
2. Is Mr. Ma Chinese ?
3. I'm Tian Shuixin. (And) you're … ?
4. Are Bai Xintian and Mao Li both English ?

Lesson 6

Exercise 1. Review of Single Characters

Listed below are the fifty characters studied in this unit. Give the pronunciation and meaning of each.

1. 呢	9. 長	17. 先	25. 美	33. 不	41. 見	49. 牛
2. 手	10. 嗎	18. 山	26. 女	34. 門	42. 是	50. 們
3. 白	11. 口	19. 也	27. 毛	35. 田	43. 馬	
4. 魚	12. 角	20. 木	28. 很	36. 水	44. 力	
5. 刀	13. 月	21. 我	29. 工	37. 都	45. 火	
6. 日	14. 你	22. 目	30. 生	38. 土	46. 好	
7. 他	15. 高	23. 英	31. 小	39. 國	47. 人	
8. 言	16. 心	24. 大	32. 車	40. 子	48. 中	

Exercise 2. Review of Special Combinations

All combinations studied in this unit are listed here in scrambled order. Practice pronouncing and translating the combinations until you can run through the list quickly.

1. 火車	7. 先生	13. 馬車	19. 水牛	25. 水手
2. 工人	8. 女人	14. 英國	20. 馬力	26. 人力車
3. 他們	9. 水田	15. 人力	21. 山水	
4. 山口	10. 手工	16. 中國	22. 大門	
5. 水力	11. 水口	17. 大刀	23. 你們	
6. 美國	12. 火山	18. 我們	24. 土人	

Exercise 3. Distinguishing Partially Similar Combinations

Practice pronouncing and translating the following groups of already studied combinations until you can run through them swiftly without being thrown off by the changes in meaning, pronunciation, or function which some characters acquire when used in different positions or when compounded with different characters. Be careful. In order to sharpen your understanding and test your mastery, traps have been set deliberately by including in some groups one or more terms which at first glance look like the others but which are actually quite different.

A. Same Character in Initial Position

1	2	3	4	5
大刀	山口	水口	馬力	火山
大門	山水	水牛	馬車	火車
		水田		
		水力		
		水手		

B. Same Character in Final Position

1	2	3	4	5
人力	山口	土人	馬車	英國
水力	水口	女人	火車	中國
馬力		工人		美國

C. Same Character in Different Positions

1	2	3	4
火山	女人	山水	土人
山水	人力	水手	人力

Exercise 4. Dialogues

1. 高：他們都是美國人嗎？

   田：不都是．白先生是美國人，
   毛先生是英國人．

   高：馬先生呢？

   田：他也是英國人．

2. 馬：你是田先生嗎？

   田：是．我是田子水．

   馬：你是不是英國人？

   田：不是．我是美國人．

3. 白：你們都好嗎？

   毛：都很好．你們呢？

   白：我們也很好．

4. 馬：高先生不是英國人嗎？

   田：不是．他是美國人．

5. 毛：他們是中國人嗎？

   田：是．他們都是中國人．

UNIT II

Lesson 7

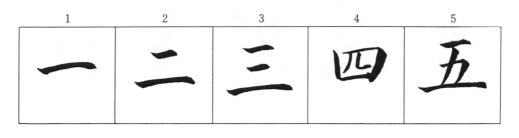

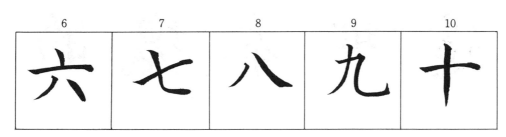

1. 一 yī one
2. 二 èr two
3. 三 sān three
4. 四 sì four
5. 五 wǔ five

6. 六 liù six
7. 七 qī seven
8. 八 bā eight
9. 九 jiǔ nine
10. 十 shí ten

Exercise 1. Practice on Numbers 11 to 99

1. 八十五
2. 四十七
3. 二十四
4. 十 一
5. 九十六
6. 三十四

7. 七十二
8. 五十四
9. 七十一
10. 十 六
11. 二十七
12. 九十九

13. 四十四
14. 八十二
15. 六十一
16. 二十五
17. 十 九
18. 四十七

19. 五 十
20. 三十三
21. 六十八
22. 二十三
23. 二十一
24. 六十九

Lesson 8

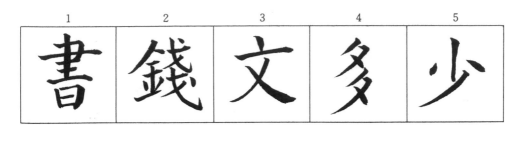

1. 書 shū book
2. 錢 qián (1) money ; (2) (a surname)
3. 文 wén* (1) writing ; (2) literary ; (3) (a surname)
4. 多 duō much, many
5. 少 shǎo few, little
6. 這 zhè, zhèi this
7. 那 nà, nèi that
    nǎ, něi which? what?
8. 本 běn (1) root, origin, foundation ; (2) volume (of books)
9. 塊 kuài (1) lump, piece ; (2) dollar (M)
10. 的 de (subordinating particle)
11. 毛 máo dime

Special Combinations

1. 多少? duōshao ? how many ? how much ?
2. 日本 Rìběn Japan

22

3. 日文　Rìwén　　Japanese (language and literature)

4. 中文　Zhōngwén　Chinese (language and literature)

5. 英文　Yīngwén　English (language and literature)

Exercise 1. Buildups

In this exercise go over each buildup once or twice slowly while observing closely how the various characters or groups of characters fit together. Then read through each buildup several times aloud, taking care to read in groups of characters and to increase your speed with each successive reading.

書

三本書

1. 這三本書

白先生

是白先生

是白先生的

2. 這是白先生的

英文

英文書

3. 你的英文書

中文書

那本中文書

那本中文書多少錢？

4. 你那本中文書多少錢？

Exercise 2. Pitfalls

In this exercise go over the material carefully and make sure you understand what it is that makes the phrases or sentences different in meaning. Read each group through several times aloud until you can read each phrase or sentence fluently, with the appropriate grouping of characters.

1. 那本書.

那本書？

2. 他是美國人.

他是那國人？

3. 那也是中文書嗎？

他也是中國人嗎？

4. 那是毛先生不是？

那是毛先生的書.

5. 那本書是他的.
   那本書是他的？
   那本書是他的嗎？

Exercise 3. Illustrative Sentences (Chinese)

1. 他不是日本人嗎？

2. 這本日文書多少錢？

3. 這不是我的，是<u>文</u>先生的.

4. <u>錢</u>先生的中文書很多.

5. 那本英文書三塊五毛錢.

6. <u>白</u>先生是那國人？…他是美國
   人…<u>高</u>先生呢？

7. <u>田見文</u>是我們的手工先生.

8. 那不是我的，是<u>錢</u>先生的.

9. 這是三本中文書、一本日文書.

10. 我的中文書很少.

Exercise 4. Dialogues

1. 錢：你們都是中國人嗎？

文：不都是．我是中國人，他是日
　　本人．

2. 馬：這本書多少錢？
　　高：那本？
　　馬：這本英文書．
　　高：六塊七毛一．

3. 毛：他的中文書多不多？
　　田：很多．
　　毛：日文書呢？
　　田：日文書也不少．

4. 白：那也是中文書嗎？
　　文：不是．是日文書．
　　白：也是田先生的嗎？
　　文：是，也是他的．

5. 田：你這本英文書很好．多少錢？
　　毛：二十九塊八毛四．

6. 文：你是錢先生嗎？
　　錢：是．我是錢見文．你是……？

文：我是文國本.

Exercise 5. Narratives

1. 白先生是美國人. 他的書很多. 英
   文的、中文的都不少. 日文的很少.

2. 你們是日本人，日文書很多. 我們
   是美國人，英文書很多.

3. 這十塊四毛錢是我的. 那一塊二毛
   錢是他的. 那五塊錢呢?

4. 這本書七毛錢. 那本書八毛錢. 都
   是很好的書.

5. 這九塊錢不是我的，也不是他的，
   是白先生的.

6. 那六本書都很好.五本是田先生的,
   一本是我的.

Exercise 6. Illustrative Sentences (English)

1. Isn't he Japanese?
2. How much is this Japanese book?

3. This isn't mine; it's Mr. Wen's.

4. Mr. Qian has a great many Chinese books.

5. That English book is $ 3.50.

6. What is Mr. White's nationality?... He's an American ....What about Mr. Gao ?

7. Tian Jianwen is our handicrafts teacher.

8. That's not mine; it's Mr. Qian's.

9. These are three Chinese books and one Japanese (book).

10. I have very few Chinese books.

Lesson 9

1	2	3	4	5
會	説	話	没	有

6	7	8	9	10
還	就	兩	甚	麽

1,	會	huì	(1) can; (2) know, know how to; (3) likely to
2.	説	shuō	say, speak, speak of
3.	話	huà	speech, talk, language
4.	没	méi	not
5.	有	yǒu	(1) have; (2) there is, there are
6.	還	hái	additionally, in addition, still, still more
7.	就	jiù	(1) only, just; (2) precisely, indeed; (3) immediately
8.	兩	liǎng	two
9.	甚	shén ?*	what?
10.	麽	mo	(question particle)
11.	白	bái *	clear, obvious, easy to understand, plain

Special Combinations

1.	説話	shuō huà	speak, talk
2.	白話	báihuà	vernacular language, vernacular style

3. 白話文　　báihuàwén　　literature in the vernacular language

4. 文言　　　wényán　　　literary language, literary style, classical style

5. 文言文　　wényánwén　　literature in the classical style

6. 小説　　　xiǎoshuō　　（1）fiction;（2）novel

7. 甚麼?　　shénmo?　　what?

8. 是的　　　shìde　　　yes, that's so

9. 不是的　　búshìde　　no, that's not so

10. 也…也…　　yě…yě…（1）both…and…;（2）neither…nor…(before negative verbs)（See Supplementary Notes）

11. 就是　　　jiùshi（1）is precisely;（2）only;（3）is only;
（4）that is,namely, i.e.;（5）even ;（6）even if

Exercise 1. Buildups

多少?　　　　　　　　　　　　　　　　很多

多少錢?　　　　　　　　　　　　　　　很多書

1. 多少錢一本?　　　　　　　　　　　很多中文書

　　　　　　　　　　　　　　　　　　有很多中文書

　　　　　　　　　　　　　　　4. 我有很多中文書

一塊

一塊三毛

2. 一塊三毛五

　　　　　　　　　　　　　　　　　　　　　小説

　　　　　　　　　　　　　　　　　　文言小説

甚麼?　　　　　　　　　　　　　　有文言小説

甚麼書?　　　　　　　　　　　　就有文言小説

有甚麼書?　　　　　　　　　　就有一本文言小説

還有甚麼書?　　　　　　　5. 我就有一本文言小説

3. 你還有甚麼書?

中國

有   中國話

没有   説中國話

他没有   會説中國話

他没有錢   也會説中國話

6. 他没有錢嗎？   7. 他也會説中國話

Exercise 2. Pitfalls

1. 一本書兩塊錢.   3. 這本書是他們的.
   一本書兩塊四.   這本書是文言的.

2. 那是甚麼？   4. 他的中文書很小.
   那是甚麼書？   他的中文書很少.

Exercise 3.   Practice in Map Reading

The following are names of actual places in China. Transcribe the names,
locate them on the accompanying map, and give the coordinates for each.
Places marked with a large dot are district towns. (The district or county
is a major administrative unit in China.)

1. 三水	7. 木馬	13. 高門	19. 八美	25. 五馬山
2. 文山	8. 英山	14. 毛目	20. 白山	26. 白水口
3. 大田	9. 文水	15. 八角	21. 毛牛	27. 七子山
4. 美山	10. 兩門	16. 九山	22. 兩女	28. 大魚山
5. 白水	11. 大有	17. 大中	23. 八大	29. 水口山
6. 中山	12. 四會	18. 錢山	24. 土門	30. 白馬山

Exercise 4. Illustrative Sentences (Chinese)

1. 他就會英文嗎?

2. 他就是會說中國話.

3. 他就是<u>錢</u>先生.

4. 那本小說是白話的是文言的?

5. <u>白</u>先生還有不少中文小說.

6. 中文書，白話文的、文言文的我都有．

7. 他也是三水人嗎？

8. 這兩本書都是你的嗎？…不是的，
   是文先生的．

9. 他也不是美國人也不是英國人．

10. 那是甚麼？…那是大刀．

11. 中國没有火山．…美國呢？…美國
    有．

12. 馬長有說這本書很好．…也不很好．

13. 你是美國人嗎？…是的，我是美國
    人．

14. 就是白先生會說中國話．

15. 這是甚麼書？是小說嗎？

Exercise 5. Dialogues

1. 馬：你是白文山先生嗎？
   白：是．我就是白文山．

馬：你是英國人嗎？

白：不是．我是美國人．

馬：你會説中國話嗎？

白：我會説中國話．

5 馬：日本話呢？

白：我不會．

2. 田：毛先生，這兩本書很好．是你
　　　的嗎？

毛：是的．那兩本書是我的．

田：多少錢一本？

5 毛：那兩本書三塊九．

田：你就有這兩本書嗎？

毛：不．我還有．

田：你還有甚麼書？

毛：我也有中文書也有英文書．

10 田：你有文言小説嗎？

毛：我就有白話小説，没有文言小
　　　説．

3. 白：<u>錢</u>先生，那本書是甚麼書？

錢：那是一本文言小説.

白：好不好？

錢：很好.

5 白：多少錢一本？

錢：四塊六毛五.

白：你還有甚麼書？

錢：我還有很多白話小説.

白：日文小説你有嗎？

10 錢：没有. 我就有中文小説，還有
兩本英文小説.

4. 錢：你們都是大田人嗎？

文：不是的. 他是大田人，我是英
山人.

5. 毛：那本中文書是文言文呢是白話
文呢？

馬：是白話的，不是文言的.

Exercise 6. Narratives

1. <u>高</u>先生是中國人．他會説英國話，
也會説日本話．他有很多中文書、
英文書，還有不少日文書．中文書，
文言文的、白話文的他都有．我這
兩本英文小説就是<u>高</u>先生的．

2. <u>白文山</u>、<u>馬一心</u>、<u>田月文</u>都是美國
人．他們都會説中國話．中文書也
很多．文言文、白話文的書他們都
有．

3. 我没有馬車，就有馬．<u>錢</u>先生也有
馬車，也有馬．

4. <u>白力</u>先生是美國人．他不是英國人．
他會説中國話．他有很多中文書，
還有不少英文書．

5. 他們都是文山人．我不是．我是大
田人．

6. 那兩本書是甚麼書？是甚麼人的？
   是不是高先生的？有人說，那兩本
   書是高先生的.

7. 馬先生說："那二十多本書是甚麼
   書？是不是都是你的？"我說："不
   是的. 都是田先生的. 就有兩本是
   我的."

8. 這本書一塊二毛錢，那本書也是一
   塊二毛錢. 兩本書是兩塊四毛錢.

9. 我就有中文書，没有日文書. 毛大
   文有中文書，也有日文書.

10. 先生說："你們都有書嗎？"我們
    說："是的，我們都有書."

Exercise 7. Illustrative Sentences (English)

1. Does he only know English?
2. He can speak only Chinese.
3. He is (indeed) Mr. Qian.

4. Is that novel in the vernacular or literary language?

5. Mr. White also has quite a few Chinese novels.

6. I have Chinese books in both the vernacular and the literary language.

7. Is he a native of Sanshui too?

8. Are these two books both yours?···No, they're Mr. Wen's.

9. He's neither American nor English.

10. What's that?···It's a sword.

11. There are no volcanoes in China. ···What about the United States?···
    The United States has (volcanoes).

12. Ma Changyou says this book is very good.··· Actually it's not very good.

13. Are you an American?···Yes, I'm an American.

14. Only Mr. White knows how to speak Chinese.

15. What (sort of) book is this? Is it a novel?

Supplementary Notes

也 yě "also" is used before a negative in three different ways: (1) in the meaning "also not": 他没有錢．···我也没有．"He doesn't have any money ... Neither do I". (2) in the meaning "neither ... nor ..." when occurring in pairs: 我也没有錢也没有書．"I have neither money nor books". (3) in the meaning "actually not" when countering a previous assertion: 他的書很多．···也不很多．"He has a lot of books ... Actually he doesn't have many".

Lesson 10

1	2	3	4	5
能	想	要	看	念

6	7	8	9	10
學	買	賣	太	姐

1. 能 néng able (to), can

2. 想 xiǎng (1) think, think about, think of, think that; (2) desire, want to; (3) plan to

3. 要 yào (1) want; (2) request, order (something); (3) will; (4) if

4. 看 kàn (1) look at, see; (2) read; (3) have the view that, think that

5. 念 niàn (1) read aloud, chant; (2) read, study (a book or subject); (3) study at (a school)

6. 學 xué (1) study; (2) branch of learning, -ology (as in "biology"); (3) school (in compounds)

7. 買 mǎi buy

8. 賣 mài (1) sell, sell for (so and-so much money)

9. 太 tài* (1) great; (2) too, excessively; (3) very, extremely

10. 姐 jiě* (1) older sister; (2) (unmarried) young lady

11. 角 jiǎo angle, corner

12. 子 zi* (noun suffix)

38

Special Combinations

1. 本子　　běnzi　　notebook
2. 刀子　　dāozi　　knife
3. 姐姐　　jiějie　　older sister
4. 小姐　　xiáojie　　(1) young lady ; (2) Miss
5. 太太　　tàitai　　(1) married woman, wife ; (2) Mrs.
6. 買賣　　mǎimai　　buying and selling, trade, business (used chiefly in Taiwan)
7. 買賣人　　mǎimairén　　merchant (used chiefly in Taiwan)
8. 學生　　xuésheng　　student, pupil
9. 小學　　xiǎoxué　　elementary school
10. 中學　　zhōngxué　　middle school, high school
11. 大學　　dàxue　　college, university
12. 小學生　　xiǎoxuésheng　　middle school student
13. 中學生　　zhōngxuésheng　　middle school student
14. 大學生　　dàxuésheng　　college student
15. 三角　　sānjiǎo　　(1) triangle ; (2) trigonometry
16. 三角學　　sānjiǎoxué　　trigonometry
17. 文學　　wénxué　　literature
18. 看書　　kàn shū　　read (a book)
19. 念書　　niàn shū　　study (used chiefly in Taiwan)
20. 還是　　háishi　　(1) still, after all ; (2) or
21. 要是　　yàoshi　　if
22. 甚麼的　　shénmode　　and so forth, etc.
23. 想要　　xiǎngyào　　(1) would like to have (followed an noun) ; (2) would like to (followed by a verb)

Who's Who and What's What

From time to time under this heading will be noted the names of actual persons, places, books, organizations, and other names worth knowing. These items are to be distinguished from other names, fictitious (as far as we know) but plausible, which are introduced in the exercises but which are not listed with the real names in this section.

1. 中山　Zhōngshān　(1) Sun Yatsen, founder of the Chinese Republic; (2) town in Kwangtung Province named after Sun Yatsen.　(On the name Zhōngshān see Beginning Chinese, p. 84, note 10, and p. 380, footnote. For the location of Zhōngshān, see map p. 31.)

2. 中山先生　Zhōngshān Xiānsheng　Mr. Sun Yatsen (honorific form)

3. 中山大學　Zhōngshān Dàxué Sun Yatsen University (in Canton)

4. 中大　Zhōng-Dà (short for Zhōngshān Dàxué)

Exercise 1. Buildups

文學
學文學
1. 我學文學

毛先生
是毛先生
這是毛先生
2. 這是毛先生的書

很好
書很好
3. 這本書很好

學生
我是學生
4. 我是中山大學的學生

很好
説的很好
他説的很好
5. 他中國話説的很好

Exercise 2. Pitfalls

1. 他念文學.
他念中學.

2. 他是大學生.
他是好學生.

3. 他還是念書.   4. 他賣三本書.
　　他也是學生.   他賣三塊錢.
　　　　　　　　　　　　　　　　　書賣三塊錢.

Exercise 3. Illustrative Sentences (Chinese)

1. 我要學中國文學.

2. 他姐姐也是中山大學的學生嗎？

3. 他是小學生還是中學生？

4. 要是我有錢我就買那本小說.

5. 書、本子、甚麼的他都賣.

6. 馬太太也是中山人嗎？…是的. 他
　 也是.

7. 你看我學三角學好不好？

8. 要是那本小說賣二十塊錢我想沒有
　 人買.

9. 錢小姐的書有中文的也有英文的.
　 就是沒有日文的.

10. 我們的買賣不太好.

11. 他們都説那本小説很好. 我想要買
一本.

12. 我能説中國話，不能看中文書.

13. 他想要車，不要馬.

14. 他還是念中學嗎？

15. 他們也賣魚嗎？

Exercise 4. Dialogues

1. 白：你是高文英先生嗎？

高：是. 我就是高文英. 你是…？

白：我是白大文. 你是英國人是美
國人？

5 高：我是英國人.

白：你是學生嗎？

高：我是中山大學的學生.

白：你是大學生，你學甚麼？

高：我學文學.

白： 學中國文學嗎？

高： 我也學英國文學也學中國文學．

白： 你能看中文書嗎？

高： 能看．

2. 高： 馬太太，你好？

馬： 我好． 你好嗎，高小姐？

高： 好． 馬先生好嗎？

馬： 好． 你還是念書嗎？

高： 是的． 我還是念書． 我學英文
呢．

3. 文： 你是買賣人嗎？

錢： 不是的． 我是工人． 毛長文是
買賣人．

文： 田小山呢？

錢： 他是水手．

4. 毛： 小姐，你要甚麽書？

白： 你們有小說嗎？

毛：有．你想要甚麼小說？

白：<u>美人魚</u>這本小說有嗎？

毛：有．

白：賣多少錢一本？

5 毛：兩塊六毛四．還要買甚麼？

要是買本子、刀子、甚麼的我

們也有．

白：我不買．

5. 高：<u>中山</u>先生是不是中山人？

馬：是的．<u>中山</u>先生是中山人．

6. 錢：你是中學生，還是小學生？

田：我念小學．我是小學生．

錢：你姐姐呢？

田：他念中學．他是中學生．

5 錢：你姐姐念三角學嗎？

田：是的．他念三角學．

錢：你呢？

田：我不念三角. 小學没有三角學.

Exercise 5. Narratives

1. 我是英國人，是中山大學的學生.
我姐姐也是中大的學生. 我們都學
文學. 我們能説中國話，也能看中
文書. 我就能看白話文. 我姐姐能
看白話文，也能看文言文.

2. 毛力要賣一本英文書. 他那本書想
賣三十塊錢. 我想三十塊錢没有人
買.

3. 馬子言是工人. 錢能是水手. 他們
都會説日本話.他們也能看日文書.

4. 我們是中山人. 我念小學. 我是小
學生.我姐姐是中學生.我姐姐念中
文、英文、三角學、甚麼的. 先生
都説我姐姐是好學生.

5. 我没有錢．我想我不能念大學．要是能念大學，我就學文學．

6. <u>錢美英</u>小姐是中國人．他會説英國話，也能看英文書．他是中學的學生．他學中國文學，也要學美國文學．

7. <u>毛一文</u>是美國人．他中文很好，能看中文書．他中國話不太好．他説他還想學中國話．

8. <u>田</u>先生是買賣人．他賣書，也賣刀子、本子、甚麼的．他的買賣很好．

9. <u>高</u>太太書不少．中文書、英文書、日文書都有．他的中文書有文言的也有白話的．我這五本書都是<u>高</u>太太的．

10. 我姐姐念大學．他有很多文學書．

文言的、白話的他都有，還有小說、
甚麽的.

11. 我說這兩塊錢是<u>白</u>先生的. <u>白</u>先生
說：“不是的. 這兩塊錢不是我的，
是<u>馬</u>先生的.”

12. <u>毛</u>太太說：“那本小說很好. 我想要
買一本. 多少錢？一塊錢？一塊錢
不多. 好，我買一本.”

Exercise 6. Illustrative Sentences (English)

1. I'd like to study Chinese literature.
2. Is his older sister also a student at Sun Yatsen University?
3. Is he an elementary school student or a middle school student?
4. If I had the money, I'd buy that novel.
5. Books, notebooks, etc.--he sells everything.
6. Is Mrs. Ma also a native of Zhongshan?···Yes, she [also] is.
7. Do you think it's a good idea for me to study trigonometry?
8. If that novel sells for $20, I don't think anybody will buy it.
9. Miss Qian's books include Chinese and English. She just lacks Japanese.
10. Our business isn't too good.
11. They [all] say that that novel is awfully good. I'd like to buy a copy.
12. I can speak Chinese (but) can't read Chinese books.
13. He'd like to have a car, not a horse.
14. Is he still (studying) in middle school?
15. Do they sell fish as well?

Lesson 11

1	2	3	4	5
比	寫	字	典	地

6	7	8	9	10
圖	幾	個	張	外

1. 比　bǐ　　　　(1) compare; (2) compared with; (3) than

2. 寫　xiě　　　　write

3. 字　zì　　　　character, word

4. 典　diǎn*　　　records

5. 地　dì　　　　land, ground, floor

6. 圖　tú　　　　diagram, map, chart, illustration

7. 幾? jǐ? *　　　how many?

8. 個　gè, ge　　(general measure for persons and things)

9. 張　zhāng　　(1) (measure for flat objects); (2) (a surname)

10. 外　wài*　　　outside, foreign

Special Combinations

1. 字典　zìdiǎn　　dictionary

2. 地圖　dìtú　　　map

3. 國文　guówén　Chinese [lit. national] literature (a school course)
(used chiefly in Taiwan)

4. 外國　wàiguo　foreign (country)

5. 人口　rénkǒu　(1) population (2) number of people in a family

6. 人人　rénrén　everybody

7. 中美　Zhōng-Měi　China and America, Chinese and American, Sino-American

8. 中日　Zhōng-Rì　China and Japan, Chinese and Japanese, Sino-Japanese

9. 中英　Zhōng-Yīng　China and England, Chinese and English, Sino-British

10. 英美　Yīng-Měi　England and America, English and American, Anglo-American

11. 寫字　xiě zì　write (characters)

12. 好看　hǎokàn　good-looking

13. 有錢　yǒu qián　(1) have money; (2) be wealthy

14. 有的　yǒude　some (in the sense of 'some but not all')

15. 好的　hǎode　Fine, OK (as isolated utterance)

16. 不要　bú yào　(1) not want (something); (2) don't (negative imperative when followed by a verb)

Exercise 1. Buildups

地
那塊地
買那塊地　　　　　　　　　寫
要買那塊地　　　　　　　　寫的好
我要買那塊地　　　　　　　我寫的好
1. 我要買他那塊地　　　2. 他說我寫的好

地圖
地圖三塊錢
這張地圖三塊錢
3. 我這張地圖三塊錢

是不是？

是字典不是？

是英文字典不是？

是馬先生的英文字典不是？

4. 這是馬生生的英文字典不是？

寫的好

他寫的好

他寫的比我好

他寫的比我好的多

5. 他中國字寫的比我好的多

他有書

他有文學書

他有英國文學書

他有很好的英國文學書

他有三十本很好的英國文學書

6. 他有三十多本很好的英國文學書

Exercise 2. Pitfalls

1. 他念的好.
   他們的好.

2. 他很好看.
   他很想看.

3. 他說我念的好.
   他比我念的好.

4. 他說：" 很好."
   小說很好.

Exercise 3. Illustrative Sentences (Chinese)

1. 我想買錢先生那塊地.

2. 大張的中國地圖賣多少錢？

3. 他說中國話說的比我好的多．

4. 你看那個女學生好看不好看？

5. 中美兩國人口都很多．

6. 那本中日字典不太好．你不要買．

7. 是中國人口多還是美國人口多？…
還是中國人口多．

8. 馬子言、馬子文他們兩個人，一個
是中國人一個是外國人．

9. 中國字就是你一個人寫的好．

10. 人人都說田先生很有錢．

11. 外國人說中國話，有的說的很好，
有的說的不好．

12. 白先生說有一本很好的書，大學國
文，他想買一本念．

13. 中英字典七塊八，刀子六毛五，本
子九毛．

14. 他念中學念的很好.

15. 你說是寫字好呢, 還是念書好呢?

16. 中學生, 學不學國文?

17. 你有幾本中日字典?

18. 我沒有錢, 不能買.

19. 英美兩國的人都說英國話.

20. 「看書」的「看」、「想要」的「想」都有
    「目」字.

Exercise 4. Dialogues

1. 張: 你要買甚麼書?

   田: 有中英字典嗎?

   張: 你看這本好不好?

   田: 就是這本. 幾塊錢?

 5 張: 四塊七.

   田: 我要一本.

   張: 還要甚麼?

   田: 中國地圖.

張：要大張的要小張的？

田：大張的賣多少錢？

張：九塊二．

田：小張的呢？

5 張：三塊五．

田：我要小張的．我還要十個本子．

張：好的．十個本子一塊八毛五．

2. 文：毛子心要買馬先生那塊地．那
　　　塊地好不好？

　　白：很好．那塊地是水田．他的水
　　　牛也要賣．毛先生也買嗎？

5 文：毛子心很有錢．要是馬先生賣，
　　　我想他也買．

3. 張：那個外國學生，中國字寫的很
　　　好．

　　馬：是的，人人都説他寫的好．

　　張：他能看中文書嗎？

馬：我想他能看．他有很多中文書、中文字典、甚麼的．我這張中國地圖就是他的．

4. 錢：那個女學生很好看．他是那國人？

毛：他是日本人．

錢：他會説中國話嗎？

5 毛：會．

錢：他中國話説的好不好？

毛：他説的比我好．

5. 高：你們都是英國人嗎？

文：不是的．我是英國人．他們兩個人是美國人．

高：你們都能看中文書嗎？

5 文：我能看．他們兩個人就會説中國話，不能看書．

高：你們會寫中國字不會？

文：我們都不會寫中國字．

6. 文： 有<u>中學國文</u>嗎？

　　張： 有．你看是這一本嗎？

　　文： 就是這本．多少錢？

　　張： 兩塊二．

　5文： 我要一本．有刀子嗎？

　　張： 沒有．我們就賣書．

7. 田： 英美兩國都是大國嗎？

　　毛： 是的．都是大國．

　　田： 美國人口多還是英國人口多？

　　毛： 還是美國人口多．

8. 錢： 那五個外國人都是美國人嗎？

　　高： 不都是美國人．有的是英國人，
　　　　有的是美國人．

9. 張： 我想買一張地圖．

　　文： 你要買那國地圖，中國地圖還
　　　　是外國地圖？

　　張： 我要買日本地圖．

文：日本地圖我有．你不要買．

10. 田：你們有中日字典嗎？

　　馬：有．

　　田：多少錢一本？

　　馬：三塊二．

5　田：我買一本．

　　馬：好的．

　　田：有<u>中美的人口</u>這本書嗎？

　　馬：那本書没有．

Exercise 5. Narratives

1. <u>毛</u>小姐、<u>田</u>小姐他們兩個人都很好
看．一個是英國人，一個是美國人．
兩個人都是美國大學的學生，都念
中文．他們中文念的都很好，中國
5字也寫的好．他們的字寫的比我好
的多．

2. 張力先生書很多．有的是中文書，
   有的是英文書．他有五十多本很好
   的英國文學書．我那兩本英文小說
   就是張先生的．

3. 馬子言、田見文是兩個中學生．馬
   子言很有錢，田見文没有錢．田見
   文書念的比馬子言好，字也寫的比
   他好．馬子言書念的不太好．他的
   5 書很多．中文書、英文書、日文書、
   中國地圖、外國地圖、中英字典、
   中文字典、甚麼的他都有．田見文
   的英文書都是馬子言的．

4. 那本小說很好．人人都想買．要是
   我有錢我也要買一本．

5. 我姐姐說有一本很好的書，文心，
   他想買．我說我也要買一本．我姐
   姐說："你没有錢．你不要買."

6. <u>張大文</u>很有錢. 是一個買賣人. 他不能看書, 也不會寫字.

7. 我念小學, 是一個小學生. 我有兩個姐姐. 他們都是中學生. 一個國文很好, 一個三角學很好. 我要是念中學, 我也學三角.

8. 中國是一個大國, 美國也是一個大國. 中美兩國都是大國. 中國人口很多, 美國人口也不少.

9. 姐姐要買書, 還要買外國地圖. 我說:"我也要買書." 姐姐說:"你要買甚麼書?" 我說:"我要買英文書, 也要買外國地圖." 姐姐說:
   5 "你要買幾本英文書, 幾張地圖?" 我說:"我想要買一本中學英文書、一張美國地圖." 姐姐說:"好的."

10. <u>中山</u>先生是中山人. 他念小學就念

的很好. 人人説他是一個很好的小
學生.

11. 田先生是大學的學生. 他太太也是
一個大學生. 他們兩個人都想要念
外國大學.

12. 我就有四塊錢. 我是買書呢, 還是買
地圖呢? 要是買書, 能買幾本呢?

Exercise 6. Illustrative Sentences (English)

1. I'm thinking of buying that plot of land which belongs to Mr. Qian.
2. How much do large [sheet] maps of China sell for?
3. He speaks Chinese a lot better than I do.
4. Do you think [lit. see] that girl [lit. girl-student] is good-looking?
5. [The two countries] China and America both have large populations.
6. That Chinese-Japanese dictionary isn't too good. Don't buy it.
7. Which has the greater population, China or America? ···China.
8. With regard to [the two persons] Ma Ziyan and Ma Ziwen, one is Chinese, and the other is a foreigner.
9. Only you [one person] write Chinese characters well.
10. Everyone says Mr. Tian is very rich.
11. As regards foreigners speaking Chinese, some speak it quite well and some speak it badly.
12. Mr. White says there's an excellent book (called) Chinese Literature for Colleges. He'd like to buy a copy to read.
13. The Chinese-English dictionary is $7.80, the knife $0.65, and the note-book $0.90.

14. He did very well in middle school.

15. Do you think [lit. say] it would be better to write characters or to read?

16 Do middle school students study Chinese literature?

17. How many Chinese-Japanese dictionaries do you have?

18. I don't have any money. I can't buy it.

19. The people of England and America all speak English.

20. The <u>kàn</u> of 'read books' and the <u>xiǎng</u> of 'would like' both have the character <u>mu</u>.

Lesson 12

Exercise 1. Review of Single Characters
(See lesson 6, exercise 1)

1. 説	9. 學	17. 圖	25. 九	33. 買	41. 這	49. 少
2. 十	10. 六	18. 話	26. 能	34. 四	42. 還	50. 五
3. 多	11. 典	19. 寫	27. 幾	35. 外	43. 比	
4. 就	12. 書	20. 一	28. 的	36. 甚	44. 文	
5. 要	13. 兩	21. 姐	29. 看	37. 錢	45. 個	
6. 二	14. 没	22. 那	30. 三	38. 字	46. 想	
7. 麼	15. 太	23. 地	31. 張	39. 八	47. 本	
8. 塊	16. 七	24. 有	32. 會	40. 念	48. 賣	

Exercise 2. Review of Special Combinations
(See lesson 6, exercise 2)

1. 本子	14. 小姐	27. 有的	40. 中大	53. 中山大學
2. 中文	15. 好看	28. 説話	41. 中美	54. 小學生
3. 念書	16. 白話	29. 三角	42. 英文	55. 文言文
4. 姐姐	17. 文學	30. 甚麼	43. 中英	56. 中山先生
5. 學生	18. 買賣	31. 人人	44. 就是	57. 也…也
6. 地圖	19. 文言	32. 多少	45. 中學生	
7. 日本	20. 中日	33. 國文	46. 買賣人	
8. 中學	21. 是的	34. 刀子	47. 有錢	
9. 外國	22. 還是	35. 大學	48. 甚麼的	
10. 小説	23. 日文	36. 看見	49. 大學生	
11. 要是	24. 寫字	37. 英美	50. 白話文	
12. 太太	25. 小學	38. 看書	51. 三角學	
13. 中山	26. 人口	39. 字典	52. 好的	

Exercise 3. Distinguishing Partially Similar Combinations

(See lesson 6, exercise 3)

A. Same Character in Initial Position

1	2	3	4	5	6
中國	三毛	小學	大學	中美	英國
中文	三角	小說	大門	中山	英文
中學	三個	小姐	大的	中日	英美
中英	三塊	小的	大刀	中大	

7	8	9	10
文言	日本	買書	人力
文學	日文	買賣	人口

11	12	13	14
有錢	太太	白話文	甚麽書
有的	太大	白先生	甚麽的

B. Same Character in Final Position

1	2	3	4	5
中學	是的	中文	買書	中國
小學	有的	日文	賣書	外國
文學	好的	英文	看書	大國
大學	我的	國文	念書	

6	7	8	9	10
水口	兩本	要是	先生	水力
人口	日本	還是	學生	馬力
山口	幾本	就是		

11	12	13	14	15
說話	刀子	不少	買車	中山
白話	本子	多少	火車	火山

16	17	18	19	20
中美	姐姐	想要	人力車	念文學
英美	小姐	不要	我的車	念大學

C. Same Character in Different Positions

1	2	3	4
日本	日文	好看	小説
本子	文言	看書	説話

5	6	7	8
很多	寫字	中國	大刀
多少	字典	國文	刀子

9	10	11	12
土人	中山	買馬	手工
人口	山水	馬力	工人

13	14	15	16
中英	文學	中美	三角學
英美	學生	美國	學三角

Exercise 4. Narratives

1. 我是一個中學生. 我姐姐是一個大學生. 我姐姐書念的比我好. 他的國文、英文都好. 先生都説他是一個好學生.

2. 馬子水是一個買賣人, 很有錢. 他

說他想買<u>張</u>先生那塊地，還要買<u>文</u>
先生的大水牛．

3. <u>毛見文</u>是美國人．是中山大學的學
生．他說中國話說的很好，能看中
文書，還能寫中國字．

4. <u>張長文</u>的書不少．中文書、英文書、
日文書他都有．他還有一本<u>中英大</u>
<u>字典</u>，很好．要是我有錢我也買一
本．

5. 我念小學．我是小學生．我姐姐念
中學．他書念的比我好．他能念大
學．我想我不能念，我也不想念大
學．

6. <u>高</u>先生的書很多．他有兩本很好的
字典．一本是中英字典，一本是中
日字典．他還有不少地圖．有的是
中國的，有的是外國的．外國的都
是英美兩國的地圖．

7. 中國的人口很多，比英美兩國的人
   口多的多．馬先生想要寫一本中國
   人口．

8. 田長木説：“人人想要有一個好的
   太太．人人想要有一個好看的太太”
   張先生説：“我要好的太太，我不
   要好看的太太．”

9. 馬月英説：“你要買幾本書、幾個
   本子？”我説：“我要買一本書、
   五個本子．”

10. 英國的人口不多．中美兩國的人口
    都比英國人口多．

11. 人人都説我好看．我説：“我不好
    看．我姐姐比我好看的多．”

12. 有一個外國人會説中國話，能看中
    文書．有人説他也能寫中國字．他
    説：“我就會寫「一」、「二」、「三」
    三個字．

13. 他們都是外國人. 兩個是美國人,
一個是英國人. 都會說中國話, 也
都說的很好.

14. 我想買兩本字典——一本中日字典,
一本中英字典. 有人說你那兩本字
典要賣. 我想買.

15. 這張中國地圖多少錢？是一塊五毛
錢嗎？一塊五不多. 我想買兩張.

UNIT   III

Lesson 13

1	2	3	4	5
因	為	所	以	雖

6	7	8	9	10
然	可	了	兒	報

1. 因 yîn*   because
2. 為 wéi*   (1) act as, be; (2) as
        wèi*   for, because of
3. 所 suǒ*   (1) that which, as in suóyǒu (de) 'that which there is',
                    i.e. 'all'; (2) therefore (in suóyi)
4. 以 yǐ*   (1) take; (2) by, with; (3) hence
5. 雖 suí*   although
6. 然 rán*   thus, so
7. 可 kě*   (1) may, be permitted; (2) indeed, however
8. 了 le   (aspect particle)
9. 兒 ér   (1) child; (2) son
        r   (nonsyllabic suffix)
10. 報 bào   newspaper, journal

Special Combinations

1.	兒子	érzi	son
2.	兒女	érnǚ	son(s) and daughter(s)
3.	女兒	nǚer	daughter
4.	門口(兒)	ménkǒu(r)	doorway
5.	這兒	zhèr	here
6.	那兒	nèr	there
		nǎr	where?
7.	因為	yīnwei	because, since
8.	所以	suóyi	therefore, hence
9.	雖然	suírán	although
10.	可是	kěshi	but, however, nevertheless
11.	可以	kéyi	(1) can, may; (2) possible
12.	可能	kěnéng	(1) be possible; (2) possibly; (3) possibility
13.	看見	kànjian	see
14.	以為	yǐwéi	suppose, think (usually 'think incorrectly,' in contrast with xiǎng, which is never used in this sense)
15	不見了	bújiànle	(1) not see any longer; (2) be no longer visible, disappear, be lost
16.	所有的	suóyǒude	all
17.	為甚麼？	wèi-shénmo?	why?
18.	是麼/嗎？	shìma?	Is that so? Really?
19.	可不是(麼/嗎)！	kěbushì(ma)!	Isn't that so! Yes, indeed!

Exercise 1. Buildups

念書   女兒

不念書   三個女兒

我不念書   那三個女兒

1. 我不念書了   2. 他那三個女兒

不少

學生不少

外國學生不少

這兒外國學生不少

中大這兒外國學生不少

3. 我們中大這兒外國學生不少

Exercise 2. Pitfalls

1. 他没有錢.
   他没有來.

2. 我看見了.
   書不見了.

3. 他不會寫字.
   他不會英文.

4. 他二兒子念書.
   兩個兒子念書.

Exercise 3. Illustrative Sentences (Chinese)

1. 他們都不可能念大學.

2. 我的小刀不見了.

3. 他大兒子學買賣，二兒子念中學，
   小兒子念小學.

4. 雖然他是中國人，可是他不會説中
   國話.

5. 我們這兒所有的書、報都是中文的.

6. 他女兒是大學生. 我以為他是中學

生.

7. 他要念大學, 可是没有那個可能.

8. 因為他們的兒女太小, 所以還没念書呢.

9. 我可以看你的中文報嗎?

10. 我的那本中英字典你看見了没有?

11. 他的兒女為甚麼不念書呢?

12. 他是中國人. … 是嗎? 我以為他是日本人呢.

13. 你們門口那個人是馬先生嗎?

14. 他們那兒没有好字典.

15. 他中國話說的很好, 是不是? …可不是嗎!

16. 外國人很少能看中文報.

17. 他有中文書, 可是他不會看.

18. 你為甚麼說這本字典不好?

19. 你買了幾張地圖?

20. 這兒所有的書都是你的嗎？

Exercise 4. Dialogues

1. 張：田太太，你有幾個兒子？
   田：我有三個兒子.
   張：都念書了嗎？
   田：我大兒子、二兒子念書了. 小
       兒子還没念書.

2. 馬：你念中學呢還是念大學呢？
   白：我不念書了.
   馬：為甚麼不念書呢？
   白：因為没有錢,所以我不念書了.

3. 高：我的字典不見了.你看見了嗎？
   文：甚麼字典？
   高：中英字典.
   文：我没看見. 田子山那兒有一本
       是不是你的？
   高：我想可能是我的.

4. 錢： 你看報了嗎？

   白： 我看了.

   錢： 你看中文報了還是看英文報了？

   白： 我看中文報了. 我不會看英文
       報.

5. 毛： 你看見錢小姐了嗎？

   田： 没有, 我没看見他.

   毛： 我以為你看見他了.

   田： 張一文說他看見錢小姐了.

6. 錢： 門口那個小姐是不是毛小姐？

   高： 不是毛小姐. 是白美文小姐.

   錢： 白小姐是中國人是日本人？

   高： 白小姐是中國人.

7. 張： 書都是你的嗎？

   文： 不是的. 有的是我的, 有的是
       馬先生的.

   張： 我可以看嗎？

文：可以，可以．所有的書你都可
以看．

8. 馬：我看見白先生、白太太了．

毛：他們都好嗎？

馬：他們都很好．

毛：他們兒女不少，是不是？

5 馬：可不是嗎！他們有五個兒子四
個女兒．

9. 白：田大生念大學了嗎？

錢：沒有．

白：為甚麼？

錢：因為他沒有錢，所以不能念大
5   學．

白：他要念大學嗎？

錢：是．他雖然沒有錢，可是他還
是想要念大學．

10. 馬：你們有小刀嗎？

毛：没有．我們這兒就賣書、報、
本子、甚麼的．

11. 高：那個外國人是英國人還是美國
人？
張：他是英國人．他雖然是外國人，
可是他中國話說的很好．
5 高：他也會說日本話，是不是？
張：是．因為他太太是日本人，所
以他也會說日本話．

12. 白：你們那兒有中文報嗎？
文：没有．你要看嗎？
白：是的．
文：<u>毛一山</u>有．
5 白：是嗎？他是個外國人．他有中
文報？
文：他雖然是外國人，可是中文書、
報他都有．

Exercise 5. Narratives

1. 張先生、張太太他們有三個兒子、
兩個女兒. 書念的都很好, 所以張
太太説: "我們雖然没有錢, 可是
我們有好兒女."

2. 我是英國人, 是中山大學的學生.
我們中大外國學生不少. 有英國學
生、美國學生, 也有日本學生. 我
雖然是英國人, 可是因為我學中國
5 文學, 所以買了不少中文書、報、
字典、甚麽的.

3. 毛一心、馬長山、高見文都要念大
學了. 因為毛一心、馬長山書念的
好, 所以能念大學. 可是高見文書
念的不太好. 我想他不可能念大學.

4. 白水心小姐很高, 很好看. 中國話
也説的很好. 我以為他是中國小姐.

錢大文說他是日本人. 他說雖然他
是日本人, 可是不會說日本話.

5. 文力有三個兒子. 因為没有錢, 所
以三個兒子都不能念書. 大兒子是
工人, 二兒子學買賣, 小兒子賣報.

6. 白先生是美國人. 他中國話說的很
好. 能看中文書、報, 也能寫中國
字. 他雖然能看中文書, 可是他還
要念中文. 我說: "你是一個外國
人. 書、報都能看了, 字也能寫了.
為甚麼還要念中文呢?"他說:"因
為白話文我可以看, 可是文言文我
不能看, 所以我還要念中文."

7. 我很想看報, 可是這兒所有的報都
是英文報. 我都不能看, 因為我不
會英文.

8. 錢先生有兩個女兒、一個兒子. 他

的兩個女兒書念的很好，兒子書念
的很不好，所以錢先生說：“我的
兩個女兒都能念大學，可是我的兒
子，書念的太不好，不能念大學.”

9. 這兒所有的中學生都有一本中英字
典. 我因為沒有錢，所以不能買.

10. 我的小刀不見了. 我想買. 張有文
說：“你不要買了. 我那兒有.”

11. 我要念大學了，所有的書都要買，
可是我沒有很多錢.

12. 我看見張太太了. 他說他那三個女
兒都不念書了. 因為張先生買賣不
太好，所以沒有錢念書了.

13. 錢先生的門口有一個女人. 有人說
是錢先生的太太. 我說:“是嗎？
錢先生有太太嗎？我還以為他沒有

太太呢！”

14. 人人都説我姐姐字寫的好．我説：
“可不是嗎！我姐姐的字寫的很好．
寫的比我好的多．”

15. 因為我的中國地圖太小，所以我要
買一張中國大地圖．

16. 我是一個外國學生．我念中文．雖
然我念了不少的中文書，可是我還
不能看中文書、報．我想買一本中
英字典．張大文有一本字典要賣．
我想買．

17. 毛小姐書很多．中文書、英文書、日
文書他都有．我姐姐説：“你不會
日文．為甚麼要買很多日文書呢?”
毛小姐説：“我要是有錢所有的書
我都要買．”

18. <u>錢</u>先生是一個工人. 他有一個兒子、
一個女兒. 兒子念大學，女兒念中
學. 書念的都很好. 人人都說<u>錢</u>先
生有兩個好兒女.

19. <u>馬</u>小姐是美國人. 他中國話說的很
好，也能看中文書. 白話的、文言
的他都看. 字也寫的很好.

20. 所有的學生書都買了. 就是我一個
人還沒買呢. 我要買字典、地圖、
國文、甚麼的.

21. 我會了很多中國字. 雖然中國字我
能寫、能念，可是我還不能看書這
<u>張</u>先生說："你買小說看. 我想你
白話文可以看."

22. 我們這兒有不少的外國學生. 有的
中國話說的很好，有的中國話說的
不很好，有的中國話說的很不好.

Exercise 6. Illustrative Sentences (English)

1. None of them can attend college.
2. My little knife has disappeared.
3. His eldest son is learning business (as an apprentice, not in school). His second son is in middle school, and his youngest son is in elementary school.
4. Although he's Chinese, he can't speak Chinese.
5. All our books and newspapers here are in Chinese.
6. His daughter is a college student. I thought she was a middle school student.
7. He wants to go to college, but there is no possibility of his doing so.
8. Their children don't go to school yet because they're too young.
9. May I read your Chinese newspaper?
10. Have you seen my Chinese-English dictionary?
11. Why aren't his children studying?
12. He's Chinese.··· Is that so?   I thought he was Japanese.
13. Is that man in your doorway Mr. Ma?
14. They don't have any good dictionaries there.
15. He speaks Chinese very well, doesn't he? ···Yes indeed!
16. Very few foreigners are able to read Chinese newspapers.
17. He has some Chinese books, but he can't read them.
18. Why do you say that this dictionary isn't very good?
19. How many maps did you buy?
20. Are all the books here yours?

Lesson 14

1	2	3	4	5
家	校	城	邊	在

6	7	8	9	10
上	下	裏	頭	海

1. 家　jiā　　　(1) home, family ; (2) (suffix of agent like English <u>er</u> in teacher)

2. 校　xiào*　　school, college

3. 城　chéng　　(1) city wall ; (2) city

4. 邊　biān　　(1) side, border ; (2) (place-word suffix) ; (3) (a surname)

5. 在　zài　　be at

6. 上　shàng　　(1) go to (a place) ; (2) ascend, go up ; (3) up, upper, above

7. 下　xià　　(1) descend, go down from ; (2) down, lower, below

8. 裏　lǐ, li*　　inside, interior

9. 頭　tóu　　(1) head ; (2) beginning
　　　tou　　(substantive suffix)

10. 海　hǎi　　sea, ocean

11. 長　zhǎng*　　head, chief

Special Combinations

1.	海邊	hǎibiān(r)	seaside, seashore, beach
2.	海口	hǎikǒu	seaport
3.	海外	hǎiwài	overseas
4.	大家	dàjiā	everybody
5.	人家	rénjia	(1) people; (2) other people; (3) other
		rénjiā	human habitation, household
6.	國家	guójiā	nation, state, country
7.	小説家	xiǎoshuōjiā	novelist
8.	文學家	wénxuéjiā	literary man
9.	想家	xiǎng jiā	think of one's home, be homesick
10.	家長	jiāzhǎng	parents
11.	校長	xiàozhǎng	head of a school, principal, president
12.	學校	xuéxiào	educational institution: school, college, university
13.	地下	dìxià	below ground, underground
		dìxia	on the ground, on the or
14.	地下車	dìxiàchē	subway
15.	中心	zhōngxîn	center, pivot, heart of something.
16.	上下	shàngxià	(1) above and below, up and down; superior and inferior; (2) ascend and descend
17.	上下文	shàngxiàwén	context, text above and below(term derived from Chinese vertical writing)
18.	馬上	mǎshàng	immediately
19.	這裏	zhèlǐ	here (written and general Mandarin)
20.	那裏	nàlǐ	there (written and general Mandarin
		nálǐ?	where? (written and general Mandarin)
21.	在外	zàiwài	(1) be extra, not be included; (2) not including
22.	為的是	wèideshì	because, for the reason that, so as to
23.	不然	bùrán	otherwise (usually used with preverbial jiù)
24.	要不然	yàoburán	otherwise (usually used with preverbial jiù)

25. 一塊兒   yíkuàr   (1) together; (2) the same place

26. 還有   háiyǒu   (1) also have; (2) and (before last of a series),
                                        in addition, moreover

Who's Who and What's What

1. 上海   Shànghǎi   Shanghai, China's largest city

2. 張家口   Zhāngjiākǒu   Kalgan or Changchiakou [lit. Zhang Family Pass]
                                   (an important town in northern Hopei Province)

3. 日本海   Rìběn Hǎi   Sea of Japan

4. 地中海   Dìzhōng Hǎi   Mediterranean Sea

Exercise 1. Buildups

下車

在門口兒下車

在學校門口兒下車

1. 在我們學校門口兒下車

上海是海口

上海是大海口

上海是一個大海口

上海是中國一個大海口

2. 上海是中國一個很大的海口

我買書

我買十塊錢的書

我買三十五塊錢的書

3. 我買了三十五塊錢的書

Exercise 2. Pitfalls

1. 他想買.   2. 地下車在那兒?
   他想家.   地中海在那兒?

3. 他說日本話比我說的好.
   他說日本海比地中海大.

Exercise 3. Illustrative Sentences (Chinese)

1. 你說學生中心在那兒?

2. 他家在海邊兒上.

3. 這本書人家都看了. 就是我没看.

4. 我買了十五塊錢的書, 本子在外.

5. 這本字典很好. 要是我有錢, 我馬上就買.

6. 上你們學校, 在那兒上地下車?

7. 他的兒女都不上學了.

8. 你們大家都是學生的家長嗎?

9. 他在家裏頭看書呢.

10. 中心中學的校長是上海人.

11. 那個小說家小說寫的很多.

12. 他說他要念大學. 我心裏想他不可能念大學.

13. 我們大家都很想家.

14. 人家學校都有女學生. 為甚麼我們學校沒有呢?

15. 我念中文為的是要上中國念書.

16. 我、我姐姐、<u>張一文</u>、還有<u>田中一</u>,我們四個人大家在一塊兒念書.

17. 你上那兒?

18. 你的書為甚麼都在地下?

19. 是地中海大還是日本海大?

20. 那本字典要是我姐姐有我就不買了. 不然我就要買一本.

21. 你為甚麼不看上下文?

22. 他女兒在中大念文學.

23. 我們國文先生也是文學家.

24. 那個外國人中國話說的比中國人好.
    …是嗎?

25. 中心小學在那裏? 在城裏頭還是在
    城外頭?

26. 我想要買中英字典、中國地圖、還
    有中學三角學. 你們這裏都有嗎?

27. 在海外的中國大學生多不多?

28. 中國有幾個大海口?

29. 美國、英國、日本這三個國家都有
    地下車.

30. 我在中國念書, 為的是學中國話.
    要不然我就在美國念書了.

Exercise 4. Dialogues

1. 白: 你是不是上海人?

高：我不是上海人．我是張家口人．
　　我在上海上學．

白：上海很大，是不是？

高：上海很大．上海是中國一個大
　　城，也是一個大海口．

2. 邊：你要在學校裏頭買書嗎？

文：不，我不想在學校買．你呢？

邊：我姐姐說在學校買．不然，我
　　也不在學校買．

3. 錢：你那本小說在那裏呢？

田：在<u>國文</u>下頭．

錢：<u>國文</u>下頭不是小說，是一本<u>三</u>
　　<u>角學</u>．

田：要不然就在那本大字典上頭呢．

4. 毛：你上那兒？

馬：我上學生中心．

毛：學生中心在那兒？

馬：就在那個小山上．

毛：你家在那兒？

馬：我家在山下頭海邊兒上．

₅毛：我們一塊兒上學生中心好不好？

馬：好，我很想上那兒看看．

5. 文：你買書了嗎？

張：我買了．你呢？

文：我不買了．

張：人家都買書．你為甚麼不買呢？

₅文：我有書．我不買了．

6. 邊：馬先生是文學家嗎？

毛：是的．他也是小說家．

邊：他寫了多少本小說了？

毛：他寫了二十多本了．

₅邊：是麼？他小說寫的好不好？

毛：寫的很好．我那兒有五六本呢．

7. 高：馬子山，你買了幾本書了？

　馬：我買了六本了，字典在外.

　高：你還要買嗎？

　馬：我還要買兩本. 你呢？

　⁵高：我還沒買呢.

　馬：你為甚麼不買書呢？

　高：我沒錢. 要是有錢，我馬上就買.

8. 白：中國學生在外國還說中國話嗎？

　田：說. 為甚麼不說呢？

　白：人家說所有的中國學生在海外都不說中國話了.

　⁵田：要是看見中國人，他們還是說中國話.

　白：是不是有的中國人不會說中國話了？

　田：可不是嗎！有人不會說了. 毛大文的兒子、女兒、還有張一多的兒子，他們都不會說中國話了.

9. 錢：很多學生家長都在學校門口兒
　　　呢．

　　田：學生就要下學了嗎？

　　錢：是，馬上就下學．

10. 張：你為甚麼不說話了？心裏想甚
　　　麼呢？

　　高：我想家了．

11. 白：我看見錢校長了．

　　文：你在那兒看見他的？

　　白：我在地下車上看見他的．

12. 先生：你們看地圖上地中海在那兒？

　　學生：先生，地圖上沒有地中海．

　　先生：有．你們大家看，在這兒．

13. 毛：那個外國人念了很多中國書了．

　　張：他雖然書念了很多，可是他不
　　　會說中國話．

　　毛：他說他不想說中國話，他念書

為的是看書、看報．

14. 學生：先生，這個字我不會．
    先生：那個？
    學生：這個．
    先生：你看看上下文．

15. 先生：那是甚麼海？
    學生：那是日本海．
    先生：日本那個國家很大嗎？
    學生：日本不大，可是人口很多．
    先生：好．都會了．你們都是好學生．

Exercise 5. Narratives

1. 你看這張地圖上，這就是中國．中
   國是個大國．這就是上海．上海是
   個大海口．人口很多．有工人，有
   買賣人．

2. 一個中國小學生在日本、美國都看

見了地下車. 他心裏想："我們中國
有地下車，美國日本也有."

3. 那個大學在山上. 山下是海. 山上
有一個小城，大學就在城裏頭. 那
兒山水很好看,學生書念的都很好,
所以人人都說那是一個很好的大學.

4. 我的地圖不見了.我想馬上買一張.
我姐姐說他有，我就不買了.

5. 張文海是一個小說家. 他寫了七本
小說，都有「海」字：海上人家，海
外，日本海，火海，海城,海邊上,海
上兒女. 馬國英說："他是不是魚？
要不然為甚麼他的小說都有「海」
字呢？"

6. 我們兩個人雖然都念中文，可是他
比我好. 他可以看書，看報，看小
說了. 我還不能呢.

7. 你看書不要看一兩個字. 要看上下文.

8. 馬校長是上海中學的校長. 他是張家口人. 他的家還在張家口呢.

9. 我以為張有文在學生中心呢, 可是他沒在那裏, 所以我沒看見他.

10. 我看中文報為的是學中文. 不然, 我就看英文報了.

11. 錢文山說日本海比地中海大. 馬長生說地中海比日本海大. 他們看看地圖. 還是地中海大.

12. 我在學校門口看見張先生的兒子了. 他說他不想在那個學校上學了, 因為那裏沒有好先生, 所以他不想念了.

13. 我們三個人, 你、我都很想家. 就是他不想家.

14. 那個外國學生書念的很好. 能看文言書, 也能寫中國字. 他字寫的比我好.

15. 中心小學的校長、先生、學生、還有學生的家長, 大家一塊兒上山. 那個山下頭就是海. 有山, 有水, 很好看. 學生在高山上看大海. 先生、家長, 有的在一塊兒說話, 有的看山水.

16. 張文英是個文學家. 他書多, 學生多, 書寫的也多, 所以人家說他是 "三多先生." 也有人說他是 "三多文學家."

17. 我家在一個小城裏頭. 這裏的人口不多, 買賣也少. 雖然城小人少, 可是學校不少. 大學、中學、小學都有.

18. 這裏的書都是<u>白</u>先生的，可是這本小說在外．是<u>高</u>先生的．

19. 一個小城裏頭有三個大學．都很好，很大，學生也很多．那裏有中國學生、英國學生、美國學生、還有日本學生．那個城可以說是大學城．

20. 我是<u>上海</u>人．<u>上海</u>是個大城．人家都說<u>上海</u>女人很好看，可是有的好看，有的不好看．

21. <u>馬</u>先生是一個中學的三角學先生．他的女兒<u>月英</u>也在那個中學念書．<u>馬</u>先生說："學校裏的學生學三角學學的都很好，就是我的女兒學的不好．"<u>月英</u>說："我就要念大學了．我要念<u>中山</u>大學，要念文學．我在學校裏、在家裏都是看文學的書，不看三角學，所以我學的不好．"

22. 高先生家裏人口很多. 他有一個很好看的太太，有五個女兒也都很好看. 四個女兒是大學生. 就有一個女兒念中學. 所有的女兒書都念的
5 很好. 有人說："你們很多女兒念書，要很多錢呢."高太太說："可不是嗎！"

23. 馬先生有很多刀子.大刀、小刀他都有. 有的是中國刀，有的是外國刀.

24. 我要買文學的書. 姐姐說："你要買幾本？要幾塊錢？" 我說："我要買兩本. 要三四塊錢."姐姐說："好的."我說："我還要買一本字典."
5 姐姐說："我這兒有兩本字典，一本中日字典、一本中英字典. 你不要買字典了."

25. 這個大學有很多外國學生. 你看，

那邊是英美兩國的學生，在一塊兒
看書．這邊是中美兩國的學生在一
塊兒說話．那邊在學校門口還有三
個日本學生．

Exercise 6. Illustrative Sentences (English)

1. Where did you say the student center is?

2. His home is on the seashore.

3. Everyone else has read this book. I'm the only one who hasn't.

4. I bought $15 worth of books, not counting notebooks.

5. This is an excellent dictionary. If I had the money, I'd buy it right away.

6. Where do you get on the subway to go to your school?

7. None of his children go to school any longer.

8. Are all of you parents of students?

9. He's in the house reading.

10. The principal of Central Middle School is a native of Shanghai.

11. That novelist has written a lot of novels.

12. He said he'd like to attend college. I thought to myself that he wouldn't be able to do so.

13. All of us are quite homesick.

14. All the other schools have girl-students. Why doesn't ours?

15. I'm learning Chinese in order to go to China to study.

16. The four of us--I, my sister, Zhang Yiwen, and Tian Zhongyi-- study together.

17. Where are you going?

18. Why are all your books on the floor?

19. Which is bigger, the Mediterranean or the Sea of Japan?

20. If my sister has that dictionary, I won't buy one. Otherwise I'll buy a copy.

21. Why don't you look at the context?

22. His daughter is studying literature at Sun Yatsen University.

23. Our Chinese literature teacher is also a literary person.

24. That foreigner speaks Chinese better than a Chinese··· Is that so?

25. Where's the Central Elementary School? Is it inside or outside the city?

26. I'd like to buy a Chinese-English dictionary, a map of China, and a trigonometry book for middle schools. Do you [here] have them all?

27. Are there many Chinese college students overseas?

28. How many big seaports does China have?

29. [The three countries of] the United States, England, and Japan all have subways.

30. I'm studying in China to learn Chinese. Otherwise I'd study in the United States.

Lesson 15

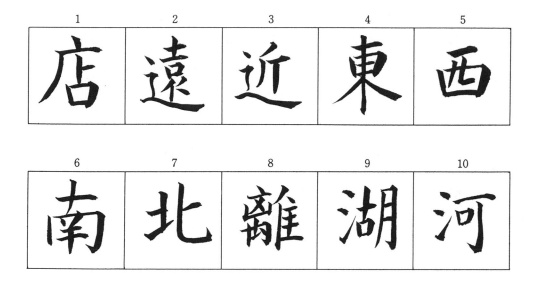

1	2	3	4	5
店	遠	近	東	西

6	7	8	9	10
南	北	離	湖	河

1. 店　diàn*　shop, store

2. 遠　yuǎn　far

3. 近　jìn　near

4. 東　dōng*　east

5. 西　xī*　west

6. 南　nán*　(1) south; (2) (a surname)

7. 北　běi*　north

8. 離　lí*　(distant) from

9. 湖　hú　lake

10. 河　hé　river

11. 口　kǒu　(measure for persons from census point of view)

Special Combinations

1. 地土　dìtǔ　soil, land, territory

101

2. 土地   tǔdì   soil, land, territory

3. 書店   shūdiàn   bookstore

4. 東西   dōng xî   east and west
             dōngxi   thing, object

5. 四邊(兒) sìbiān(r)   (on) four sides, all around

6. 手邊(兒) shǒubiān(r)   at hand, on hand, (readily) available

7. 手上   shǒushang   at hand, on hand, (readily) available

8. 美女   měinǚ   a beautiful woman, a beauty

Who's Who and What's What

1. 河北   Héběi   Hopeh (Province)

2. 河南   Hénán   Honan (Province)

3. 湖北   Húběi   Hupeh (Province)

4. 湖南   Húnán   Hunan (Province)

5. 山東   Shāndong   Shantung (Province)

6. 山西   Shānxi   Shansi (Province)

7. 東北   dōngběi   northeast
            Dōngběi   The Northeast, Manchuria

8. 西湖   xî hú   a western lake
            Xî Hú   West Lake (one of China's foremost scenic spots,
                           near Hangchow)

9. 西山   xî shān   western hills or mountains
            Xî Shān   Western Hills(a popular recreation area near Peking)

10. 東海   Dōng Hǎi   East China Sea

11. 東海大學 Dōnghǎi Dàxué   Tunghai University (in Taiwan)

12. 南海   Nán Hǎi   (1) South China Sea; (2) name of a district in
                           Kwangtung Province

13. 近東   Jìn Dōng   Near East

14. 中東   Zhōng Dōng   Middle East

15. 遠東   Yuǎn Dōng   Far East

16. 遠東大學　Yuǎndōng Dàxué　Far Eastern University (see Beginning
　　　　　　　　　　　　　　　　　　　 Chinese, p. 137, note 9.)

17. 長城　Cháng Chéng　Great Wall

18. 太湖　Tài Hú　　　Tai Lake (between Kiangsu and Chekiang Provinces)

19. 北美　Běi Měi　　　North America

20. 南美　Nán Měi　　　South America

21. 西東大學　Xīdōng Dàxué　　Seton Hall University

Exercise 1. Buildups

　　　　一個人
　　　一個人是東北人
　　他一個人是東北人
1. 就是他一個人是東北人

　　　　　上學
　　　　我上學
　　　我在上海上學
2. 我很小就在上海上學

　　他在書店
　　他在那個書店
　　他在角兒上那個書店
　　他在西南角兒上那個書店
3. 他在西南角兒上那個書店買書

　　他在山上
　　他在小山上
　　他在那個小山上
4. 他在河邊那個小山上

Exercise 2. Pitfalls

1. 你説湖南話嗎？
   你説湖南在那兒？

2. 這是一個中國字.
   這是一個甚麼字？

3. 這兒有張家口人.
   這兒有十九口人.

4. 他是那兒的人.
   他是那兒的人？

Exercise 3. Illustrative Sentences (Chinese)

1. 是不是那個國家土地很大，人口很少？

2. 校長是那兒的人？不是東北人嗎？

3. 他們兩個人，一個是湖南人，一個是山東人.

4. 城四邊都是高山.

5. 我家裏人口很少，就有三口人.

6. 他家在城的西北角上,離城門很近.

7. 這本小説五塊六. 我手邊兒就有五塊錢，所以不能買.

8. 美國西邊山地很多.

9. 就是他一個人是近東人.

10. 你是上海邊書店嗎？

11. 中國人說西湖的美可以比一個美女.

12. 河的兩邊都是山.我家在河邊為的是
山水好看.

13. 東海大學、遠東大學都在中國. 西
東大學在美國.

14. 北美的人口比南美的多的多.

15. 南海、東海、日本海都在遠東.

16. 河南在河北的南邊,在湖北的北邊.

17. 我很想要看長城、太湖.

18. 那是甚麼東西？是刀子嗎？

19. 山西在河北的西邊,在河南的北邊.

20. 這是中國地圖, 没有中東.

21. 遠東的國家人口都很多嗎？

22. 你們那兒的地土好不好？

23. 我想買東西，可是我手上没有錢.

24. 山東、河北、山西都没有水牛.

25. 西山不很高，可是很好看.

26. 這裏都是小書店，西湖書店在外.

27. 他就會説湖南話，不會英文. 那裏
    能念美國大學呢？

28. 我很少看見<u>南</u>先生.

29. 他的中國字那兒能比中國人寫的還
    好？

30. 我家離書店很近，離學校很遠.

Exercise 4. Dialogues

1. 文：你是那兒的人？
   毛：我是河南人.
   文：你家也在這兒嗎？
   毛：不在這兒. 我一個人在這兒.
   5   家裏人都在河南呢.
   文：家裏人口多嗎？

毛： 很多，有十八口人.

文： 你想家嗎？

毛： 我很想家.

2. 張： 西東大學離這兒遠不遠？

南： 不太遠，可是也不很近. 你要
上西東嗎？

張： 是，我想上西東看看.

5 南： 你是不是想在西東念中文呢？

張： 是. 人家都説西東中文、日文
都很好.

南： 是的. 我姐姐就在西東大學念
中文.

3. 毛： 我是東北人. 你是那兒的人？

錢： 我是湖北人. 雖然我是湖北人，
可是我不説湖北話.

毛： 你為甚麼不説湖北話呢？

5 錢： 我不會説，因為我很小就在山
東上學.

4. 田： 先生、學生、家長，都想上山.

白：你説上東山好，還是上西山好？

田：西山人多，東山太遠．要不然
　　上南山？

白：好，南山很好．

5. 邊：那個小姐在那兒念書？

　張：他在遠東大學念書．

　邊：遠大有多少女學生？

　張：很少．就有九十六個女學生．

　⁵邊：是不是你姐姐也在遠大念？

　張：是的，我姐姐也念遠大．

　邊：你姐姐念甚麼？

　張：他念中國文學．

6. 文：我在西湖書店看見一本中英字
　　典，很好．

　馬：你為甚麼不買呢？

　文：我手上没有錢．要是有錢我就
　⁵　買了．

　馬：多少錢？

　文：二十五塊七．

馬：我有三十塊錢．我買好不好？

文：你要是手邊有錢馬上就買．不然就沒有了，因為那個書店就有一本了．我有一本小說你看不看？

5

馬：甚麼小說？

文：山裏的美女．

馬：我不看．

7. 錢：你們學校外國學生多嗎？

毛：很多．中東、近東、遠東的都有．

8. 外國人：中國山地多嗎？

中國人：中國山地很多．

外國人：中國有高山嗎？

中國人：有高山．中國高山都在西邊．

5

外國人：中國長城很長，是不是？

中國人：是，中國長城很長．在河

　　　　北、山西都可以看見.

外國人：是不是上海是一個大海口？

中國人：是，上海是中國一個大海
　　　　口.

9. 邊：你們四個人都是湖南人嗎？

馬：不是. 我們兩個人是湖南人.
　　他們兩個人，一個是山東人，
　　一個是山西人.

10. 高：南美、北美有多少國家？

白：南美、北美都有很多國家.

11. 先生：張國城，你説南海在那兒？

學生：南海在中國東南邊兒.

先生：東海呢？

學生：在中國東邊兒.

12. 白：你想上東海大學念書嗎？

高：是的，我想上東海大學念書，
　　因為張先生説那個大學很好.

白：你上東海大學還是念文學嗎？

高：是，我還念文學．

13. 馬：太湖在那兒？

　　錢：太湖離上海不遠．

　　馬：人家說太湖四邊兒都是水田，
　　　　是嗎？

　5 錢：是的．

14. 毛：南太太，上那兒？

　　南：我上城裏頭買東西．下學了，
　　　　毛小姐？

　　毛：是，下學了．

　5 南：你們學校離這兒很遠,是不是？

　　毛：不遠．就在河邊兒那個小山上．

15. 田：中國東北土地好不好？

　　錢：中國東北地土很好．

Exercise 5. Narratives

1. 離上海不遠有一個很大的湖，是太
　湖．湖的四邊水田很多，湖裏頭還

有很多魚，所以湖邊的人家都説太
湖太好了．

2. 西湖離上海也不遠．雖然比太湖小，
可是山水很好看．有人説西湖的美
可以比一個美女．

3. 中國的長城很長．在河北、山西都
可以看見．因為這個城太長了，所
以説他是長城．

4. 中國的湖南是在一個大湖的南邊．
湖北是在這個大湖的北邊．

5. 中國的山西山地很多，離海很遠．
山東離海很近，東南、東北兩邊都
是海．

6. 中國的東北地土很好．在那裏有很
多山東人，因為山東離東北很近．

7. 白小姐是美國人，在西東大學念中
文．他能看中文書、報，也會寫中

國字.

8. 湖邊書店在湖的北邊. 離遠東大學
很近, 離學生中心也不遠. 很多學
生在那裏看書, 買書.

9. 中國離日本很近. 中日這兩個國家
都在遠東.

10. 英國、日本、南美、北美都有中國
人. 中東、近東就很少了.

11. 我們學校在城外, 離城很遠. 人家
上學、下學都有車. 我沒有. 要是
我手上有錢, 我就馬上買車.

12. 他雖然說不要錢, 可是他心裏想要
二三十塊錢.

13. 那個大學的學生很多. 有河北人、
河南人, 也有山東人、山西人, 還
有湖南的、湖北的. 就是沒有東北
人.

14. 中國土地很大，人口很多. 是遠東一個大國. 東邊有東海，南邊有南海. 就是西、北兩邊没有海.

15. 在學生中心有六七十人，都是大學生. 有東海大學的、遠東大學的，還有八九個美國學生，是西東大學的.

16. 毛小姐在這裏買了很多東西. 他雖然買了很多，可是他説他還要買.

17. 一個學生的家長要見校長. 校長不在學校. 有人説校長在家呢，他家離這裏很近.

18. 張家口離長城很近，離海口很遠.

19. 那個山東人因為他一個人在日本念書，所以他很想家.

20. 我家在東山，他家在西山. 西山離東山很遠，所以我很少看見他.

21. <u>南</u>家有十二口人. 兒女很多，都大了. 他的大兒子是個文學家，二兒子是個小說家，還有很多兒女在海外念書呢.

22. 中國有火車，也有地下車. 英美兩國也有火車，也有地下車.

23. 我想寫一本<u>中國文學</u>. 因為我的書都不在這裏，我手邊沒有書，所以我還沒寫呢.

24. 這裏是工人中心. 有很多工人在這裏看書，看報.

25. 「木、目、心」三個字寫在一塊兒. 「木、目」寫在上邊，「心」寫在下邊. 你說是一個甚麼字？

26. <u>白</u>先生是文學家，也是小說家. 他寫了很多小說. 我想買一本. 我以為這裏的大書店、小書店都可以買，

可是有人説:"有很多人都想買他的
小説. 你要買馬上就買, 不然就没
有了."

27. 南文遠家在河邊. 我家在山上. 我
在山上頭, 能看見河邊, 也能看見
他的家.

28. 小學生、小學生的家長, 大家在一
塊兒看地圖. 有一個小學生説:"這
張地圖上為甚麽没有地中海呢?"家
長説:"你看, 這不是地中海嗎?"

29. 先生説:"你看書要看上下文, 不要
就看一兩個字."學生説:"要是看字
典也看上下文嗎?"先生説:"也要看."

30. 我要念中文.西東大學離我家很近,
可是我是一個中學生, 不能在大學
念書,要不然我就在西東念中文了.

Exercise 6. Practice in Map Reading

Exercise 7. Illustrative Sentences (English)

1. That country has a large territory and a small population, isn't that so ?

2. Where's the principal from? Isn't he a Manchurian ?

3. Of those two men, one is Hunanese, and the other a native of Shantung.

4. There are high mountains all around the city.

5. Our family is very small, just three people.

6. His home is in the northwest corner of the city, close to the city gate.

7. This novel is $5.60. I have only $5 [at hand], so I can't buy it.

8. There is a lot of mountainous territory in the western part of the United States.

9. He is the only one who is a Near Easterner.

10. Are you going to the **Seaside Bookstore**?

11. The Chinese say that the beauty of West Lake can be compared to a beautiful woman.

12. There are mountains on both sides of the river. My house is on the riverside because the scenery (there) is beautiful.

13. Tunghai University and Far Eastern University are both in China. Seton Hall University is in the United States.

14. North America has a much greater population than South America.

15. The South China Sea, the East China Sea, and the Sea of Japan are all in the Far East.

16. Honan is south of Hopeh and north of Hupeh.

17. I'd like very much to see the Great Wall and Tai Lake.

18. What's that thing? Is it a knife?

19. Shansi is west of Hopeh and north of Honan.

20. This is a map of China. It doesn't show [lit. have] the Middle East.

21. Do all the countries of the Far East have large populations?

22. How's your land there?

23. I'd like to buy something, but I don't have any money [at hand].

24. There are no water buffalo in Shantung, Hopeh, or Shansi.

25. The Western Hills aren't very high, but they're very beautiful.

26. All (the bookstores) here are small [bookstores], except for the West Lake Bookstore.

27. All he can speak is Hunanese. He doesn't know any English. How [lit. where] could he study at an American university? (Note this rhetorical use of <u>náli</u>? 'where?'; similarly with <u>nǎr</u>?)

28. I very rarely see Mr. Nan.

29. How can he write Chinese characters better than a Chinese?

30. My home is close to the bookstore but far from school.

Lesson 16

1	2	3	4	5
從	到	來	去	走

6	7	8	9	10
坐	船	路	里	華

1. 從 cóng — from (time or place), since (time)

2. 到 dào — (1) arrive; (2) go to; (3) to

3. 來 lái — come

4. 去 qù — go (to)

5. 走 zǒu — (1) walk; (2) go, leave (IV); (3) go through (a place); (4) away (as a postverb)

6. 坐 zuò — (1) sit; (2) by (such and such conveyance), take ⋯ (as transportation); (3) to seat (so-and-so many people)

7. 船 chuán — boat, ship

8. 路 lù — road, route

9. 里 lǐ — (Chinese) mile

10. 華 huá * — (1) China; (2) (a surname)

11. 本 běn * — this, one's own

12. 口 kǒu — entrance (to a street)

Special Combinations

1. 日報　rìbào　　daily newspaper

2. 月報　yuèbào　monthly journal

3. 學報　xuébào　scholarly journal, learned journal

4. 馬路　　mǎlù　　road, highway, street

5. 路口(兒)　lùkǒu(r)　entrance to a street, intersection

6. 十字路口(兒)　shízì lùkǒur　intersection, right-angle junction of two streets (i. e. like the character 十)

7. 文人　　wénrén　literary man (versus military man, business man, etc.), man of letters, literatus

8. 能力　　nénglì　ability, power, energy

9. 圖書　　túshū　charts and books

10. 走路　zǒu lù　walk, go on foot

11. 坐船　zuò chuán　go by boat

12. 說大話　shuō dà huà　boast, exaggerate

13. 小心　xiǎoxin　be careful, watch out

14. 可見　kějiàn　(1) one can see that, it is obvious that; (2) apparently (referring to a previously mentioned event)

15. (在)心目中　(zài) xīnmùzhōng　in one's mind, in one's thoughts

16. 不到　búdào　not reach, less than

17. 本來　běnlái　originally

18. 近來　jìnlái　recently, lately

19. 一邊⋯一邊　yìbiān⋯yìbiān　on the one hand⋯on the other hand

20. 本地　běndì　(1) this region; (2) local, native

21. 本國　běnguó　this country, ones own country

22. 本人　běnrén　self (I myself, you yourself, he himself)

23. 華里　Huálǐ　Chinese mile

24. 英里　Yīnglǐ　English mile

Who's Who and What's What

1. 中山路 Zhōngshān Lù   Sun Yatsen Avenue (about the equivalent of "Washington Avenue" in America)

2. 大中 Dàzhōng   Great China (in names of places and institutions)

3. 中華 Zhōnghuá   China (formal)

4. 大華 Dàhuá   Great China (in names of places and institutions)

5. 東華 Dōnghuá   East China (in names of places and institutions)

6. 南華 Nánhuá   South China (in names of places and institutions)

7. 華北 Huáběi   North China

8. 華東 Huádōng   East China

9. 華南 Huánán   South China

10. 華西 Huáxî   West China

11. 華中 Huázhōng   Central China

12. 華美 Huá-Měi   China and the United States, China and America, Sino-American

13. 華西大學 Huáxî Dàxué West China Union University (former Christian university, in Chengtu, now merged with Szechuan university)

14. 山東大學 Shāndong Dàxué Shantung University (in Tsingtao, Shantung)

15. 西北大學 Xîběi Dàxué   Northwest University (in Sian, Shensi)

Exercise 1. Buildups

上船

在上海上船

他在上海上船

他在上海上的船

1. 他是在上海上的船

一里路

不到一里路

到書店不到一里路

2. 從這兒到書店不到一里路

毛先生 他賣地
是毛先生 他賣那塊地
他是毛先生 他賣西邊那塊地
3. 他是毛先生的女兒 4. 他賣馬路西邊那塊地

Exercise 2. Pitfalls

1. 他走三里路.　　　　　　　　2. 我從美國來中國.
　他走地中海.　　　　　　　　　我從美國來念書.

3. 在他們學校有兩個人是很有錢的.
　在他心目中那兩個人是很好的人.

Exercise 3. Titles of Newspapers and Journals

Here are the titles of a number of newspapers and journals, some now
defunct, which have been published in China, Hong Kong, or the United States.
Give an appropriate translation for each.

1. 華北日報　　　　　6. 小説月報
2. 上海日報　　　　　7. 華南日報
3. 華東日報　　　　　8. 大華日報
4. 工人日報　　　　　9. 華美日報
5. 南華日報　　　　　10. 大美日報

Exercise 4. Illustrative Sentences (Chinese)

1. 一英里是三華里.
2. 你是走路來的還是坐車來的? … 我
　是走來的.

3. 他心目中就有<u>張</u>小姐.

4. 從英國到中國坐船是不是走地中海？

5. <u>錢</u>先生是本地人，所以他說本地話.

6. 我們在這兒坐下，可以嗎？

7. 大中書店在南華路東口路北，那個大書店就是.

8. 他本人沒來. 他太太來了.

9. <u>文學學報</u>比<u>文學月報</u>好的多.

10. 我在本國念中學，在國外念大學.

11. 我本來想在南華書店買書，可是人家說南華的書太少.

12. 他說大話呢. 我想他沒有能力念大學.

13. 我是在上海上的船.

14. 從這兒到華美書店不到一里路.

15. 他到美國來念書.

16. 我到中國去都是坐船.

17. 你的船太小了. 就能坐兩三個人.

18. 從這兒到大美書店有幾里路？

19. 你不要坐在地下.

20. 華里就是中國里.

21. 大華書店在中山路、中華路的十字路口.

22. 他本來念山東大學. 近來念西北大學了.

23. 我家在華南. 我在華北念的書.

24. 文人書店的圖書不少. 很多華西大學的學生到那兒買書.

25. 在馬路上走要小心.

26. 先生，你說我看東華日報好，還是看上海日報好？

27. 他一邊念書一邊説話. 可見他不是好學生.

28. 華中的土地都很好嗎？

29. 從山西到湖北能走水路嗎？…你看
    地圖，那裏能走水路呢？

30. 你以為他是好人，可是他不是好人.
    可見你不會看人.

Exercise 5. Dialogues

1. 路：從這兒到文人書店有多遠？
   華：不太遠. 不到三里路.
   路：中華書店在那兒？
   華：就在中山路、中華路的十字路
5   口兒上.

2. 華：你上那兒，高小姐？
   高：我到華西大學去.
   華：華西大學很遠. 為甚麼不坐車
       呢？
5 高：我們學校所有的學生都是走路，
       所以我也不坐車.

3. 錢：你從日本來是坐船來的嗎？

馬：是，我是坐船來的。

錢：你為甚麼到這兒來呢？

馬：因為我姐姐在這兒。我來看我

5　　　姐姐。

錢：你姐姐在這兒念書嗎？

馬：是，他在山東大學念書。

4. 白：從你家到東海大學有幾里路？

毛：二十五里路。

白：是英里還是華里？

毛：華里。

5. 先生：<u>南大生</u>，華南離甚麼海近？

學生：華南離南海近。

先生：華東呢？

學生：華東離東海近。

5 先生：華西離甚麼海近？

學生：華西没有海。

6. 路：河南在華中還是在華北？

　　華：河南在華中．河北在華北．

7. 文：你是本地人嗎？

　　錢：我不是本地人．我是東北人．

　　文：你本地話説的很好．你在那個
　　　　學校念書呢？

　5 錢：我在南華中學念書．

　　文：南華中學是一個很好的中學．

8. 高：你們上那兒去？

　　白：我們上西山．

　　高：西山很高，路也不好．你們要
　　　　小心．

9. 張：<u>馬</u>先生來了！坐下，坐下．從
　　　　那兒來？

　　馬：我從書店來．我到西邊兒大華
　　　　書店買書去了．

　5 張：你買甚麼書了？

馬：我的英文字典不見了．買了一
　　本字典，還買了一本小説月報.

張：我也想買書．大華書店的書多
　　不多？

馬：大華書店書很多．他們那兒也
　　賣報.

10. 馬：你看甚麼報？

白：我看中華日報.

馬：是中文的還是英文的？

白：是中文的．我看中文報為的是
　　學中文．你呢？

馬：我看遠東日報.

白：是不是遠東大學的學生都看遠
　　東日報呢？

馬：不，不．有的看，有的不看.
　　我因為遠東日報有很多文學的
　　東西，所以我看遠東日報.

白：華美日報好不好？

馬： 有人說華美日報很好.

11. 張： 田太太，你好嗎？

田： 我好，張太太. 你上那兒去？

張： 我到大中書店去，因為我女兒要買中山學報.

5 田： 張小姐本人為甚麼不去買呢？

張： 他在學校呢.

田： 大中書店在那兒？

張： 在城外頭.

田： 張太太，我在白家門口兒看見白太太了.

10

張： 他近來好嗎？

田： 很好.

12. 毛： 錢大文說張先生馬路東邊兒那塊地要賣，他想買. 他說那塊地很好.

田： 他沒有錢買地.

5 毛： 他說他手上錢很多.

田：我説他没錢．他不可能買．他
　　説大話呢．

13. 高：東華小學在那兒？
　　華：東華小學在西山邊兒上．
　　高：是不是那兒有一個小湖？
　　華：是．
　5 高：小湖四邊兒有買賣嗎？
　　華：没有，就有一個小學校．

14. 馬：錢有文來了嗎？
　　高：他來了．
　　馬：他是來念書嗎？
　　高：不是的．他説他没有能力念書．

15. 南：你説張小姐好看不好看？
　　華：我説他很好看．你説呢？
　　南：我也説他好看．
　　華：學校裏所有的學生也都説他很
　5　　好看．可見他是很好看了．

南：你心目中還有好看的小姐嗎？

華：有．我在西北大學看見一個小
　　姐，比<u>張</u>小姐還好看．大家都
　　說他是美女．

16. 先生：你們不要一邊寫字一邊說話．
　　學生：為甚麼？
　　先生：要是一邊寫字，一邊說話，
　　　　　字就寫的不好．

Exercise 6. Narratives

1. 我從華南來華北．他們從華西來華
　北．大家來到華北都是要看看長城．

2. 我要坐車去大華中學．在中山路西
　口看見了<u>張</u>小姐．他說他也要去．
　我說我們可以一塊兒坐車去．他說
　學校離這兒很近，我們可以走路去．
　5 我說：" 好 "．我們就在路上一邊走，
　一邊說話，我們就走到大華中學．

3. 那個十字路口車太多了. 你要是走到那裏, 你要小心.

4. 上海的「大馬路」是上海的中心. 馬路上車多人多,馬路兩邊都是買賣.

5. 一個中國人、一個外國人一塊兒坐船到上海去. 那個外國人雖然會說中國話,可是說的不太好. 到了上海,有人說:"你們是坐火車來的嗎?"

5 那個中國人說:"不是, 是走水路來的." 那個外國人心裏想:"我們是坐船來的, 為甚麼他說是走來的呢? 還有,水上那裏有路可以走呢?"

6. 南華書店圖書很多. 有中文的、英文的, 還有日文的. 可是我要買南美、北美地圖, 他都沒有. 他們說就賣本國地圖.

7. 河北、山東、山西都在華北. 河南、湖北、湖南都在華中. 上海在華東.
太湖、西湖也在華東. 張家口在華北.

8. 山東大學、 西北大學都是華北很好
的大學. 都有外國學生在那裏念中
文.

9. 一個日本人從英國坐船到他本國日
本去. 在路上他看見了地中海, 也
看見了中國的南海、 東海, 就是沒
看見日本海.

10. 在中國有<u>中國日報</u>是英文的. 很多
中國人看, 為的是可以學英文. 在
美國有<u>華美日報</u>是中文的. 也有美
國人看, 為的是可以學中文.

11. 我家離西山很近, 不到二里路. 我
到西山都是走路去.

12. 在<u>田</u>校長心目中那兩個人都是好人,

可是那兩個人一個沒有能力，一個
就會說大話．可見田校長不會看人．
因為田校長本人是好人，他以為他
們都是好人．

13. 錢東華是上海人．有人說他不會說
上海話．他說："我是上海本地人.
我念小學、中學、大學都在上海.
為甚麼不會說上海本地話呢？"

14. 火車上的人都坐下了，就有一個女
人沒坐下．有一個小學生說："小姐,
你為甚麼不坐下呢？"那個女人說：
"你看！我坐在那裏呢？"小學生說：
5 "你在我這裏坐．我就要下車了."

15. 東華書店離大中書店很近．這兩個
書店都沒有英文書，就有中文書.

16. 一華里就是一中國里．中國里比英
國里小．中國里三里是一英里.

17. 學生中心，書、報很多. 我們在那裏看報. 我看<u>中華月報</u>，他看<u>華西大學學報</u>.

18. 他本來是上海人. 因為在湖南念書，所以會說湖南話.

19. 中華書店本來沒有外國圖書. 近來也有了. 我在那裏買了兩本英文小說、一張美國地圖.

20. <u>張大生</u>是個文人. 他的文學很好，字也寫的好.

21. 我在門口看見<u>張</u>太太了. 他說他的兒子、女兒都要到美國念書了. 我說："是嗎？你兒女要到外國了，<u>張</u>先生也不在家. 就是你一個人在家了."<u>張</u>太太說："可不是嗎！"

22. 我在東海大學念書，我姐姐在遠東

大學念書. 我們兩個人都念中國文
學.

23. <u>華英</u>家在中國的東北. 他説那兒地
土很好, 有很多大山. 他家的四邊
都是山.

24. 我坐船從湖南到上海去. 到了上海,
我手上的錢都不見了. 我手邊就有
兩毛錢了, 所以不能買東西.

25. 有一個美國小姐很好看. 大家都説
他是美女. 他雖然是美國人, 可是
中國話説的很好. 他在西東大學念
中文. 可能到中國去念中國文學.

26. 中國華北土地很大. 山東、山西、
河北都在華北. 要是從河北到山東
可以坐船, 也可以坐火車. 要是從
河北到山西就能坐火車,不能坐船.

27. 我家在華北. 我在上海學英文. 我家離上海太遠了. 我姐姐說："不要在上海學英文了. 太遠了. 華北有很多學校. 為甚麼要在上海學英文呢？"

28. 我到南華書店去買書. 走到中華路西口看見<u>邊大文</u>了. 他說他也到南華去買書, 所以我們兩個人一塊兒到書店去. 書店離這裏很近. 到了書店, 我買字典、地圖、本子、甚麼的. <u>邊大文</u>就買了一本三角學.

29. <u>張心遠</u>是河北人. 他說人人都說華東的山水很好看, 他很想到華東去看山水, 還想看看西湖. 他說他要在西湖裏坐坐小船.

30. 中山大學在中國東南. 那裏學生不少, 也有很多外國學生. 遠東學生、中東學生, 都很多. 就是近東學生少.

Exercise 7. Practice in Map Reading

Exercise 8. Illustrative Sentences (English)

1. An English mile is three Chinese miles.

2. Did you come on foot or by car?···On foot.

3. All he has in his mind is Miss Zhang.

4. In going from England to China by boat, does one go through the Mediter-ranean?

5. Mr. Qian is a local man, so he speaks the local dialect.

6. May we sit down here?

7. The Great China Bookstore is at the eastern entrance to South China Road, on the northern side of the street. That big bookstore is it.

8. He didn't come himself. His wife came.

9. Journal of Literature is a lot better than Literature Monthly.

10. I attended middle school in my own country and attended college abroad.

11. I originally planned to buy some books at the South China Bookstore, but people say it has too few books.

12. He's boasting. I don't think he has the ability to attend college.

13. I embarked at Shanghai.

14. From here to the Sino - American Bookstore is less than a mile.

15. He's coming to America to study.

16. When I go to China, I always go by boat.

17. Your boat is too small. It can seat just two or three people.

18. How many miles is it from here to the Great-America Bookstore?

19. Don't sit on the floor.

20. A hua mile is simply a Chinese mile.

21. The Great China Bookstore is at the intersection of Sun Yatsen Avenue and China Road.

22. He originally studied at Shantung University. Recently he's been studying at Northwest University.

23. My home is in South China. I studied in North China.

24. The Literary People's Bookstore has quite a few books. A lot of West China University students go there to buy books.

25. Be careful when walking along the highway.

26. Sir, do you think it would be better for me to read the East China Daily News or the Shanghai Daily?

27. He talks while he studies. You can see that he's not a good student.

28. Is all the soil in central China quite good?

29. Is it possible to go from Shansi to Hupeh by water [lit. travel water road]?···Look at the map. How would it be possible to go by water?

30. You thought he was a nice person, but he isn't. Obviously you can't evaluate [lit. see] people.

Lesson 17

1	2	3	4	5
第	次	號	條	今

6	7	8	9	10
明	天	年	又	民

1. 第　dì　　(ordinal prefix)

2. 次　cì　　(measure indicating a time or occasion)

3. 號　hào　(measure indicating number in a series, such as days of the month)

4. 條　tiáo　(measure for slim objects, roads, fish, oxen, etc.)

5. 今　jīn *　the present, now

6. 明　míng *　(1) clear, obvious; (2) next (before tiān 'day' or nián 'year')

7. 天　tiān *　(1) sky, heaven; (2) day

8. 年　nián *　year

9. 又　yòu *　(1) again (before verbs); another (before number, e.g. 又 一天 'another day')

10. 民　mín *　people

11. 頭　tóu *　(1) first (when followed by a number or a measure); (2) beginning (lit. head) of a street, lesson, etc.

Special Combinations

1. 今天　　jīntian　　today

2. 明天　　míngtian　　tomorrow

3. 白天　　báitiān　　daytime

4. 天天　　tiāntiān　　every day

5. 今年　　jīnnián　　this year

6. 明年　　míngnián　　next year

7. 去年　　qùnián　　last year

8. 年年　　niánnián　　every year

9. 年月日　niányuèrì　date (used in writing)

10. 上次　　shàngcì　　(1) last time ; (2) previously

11. 下次　　xiàcì　　(1) next time ; (2) later on

12. 頭次　　tóucì　　first time

13. 有一天　yǒu yìtiān　one day, once, once upon a time

14. 有一次　yǒu yícì　on one occasion, once

15. 又…又　yòu…yòu…　both…and…

16. 又因為　yòu yīnwei　for the further reason that

17. 一來…二來…　yìlai…èrlái…　in the first place…in the second place…,
　　　　first…second… (purpose or reason is implied or expressed)

18. 明白　　míngbai　　(1) understand, clearly, be clear about something ;
　　　　　　　　　　　(2) clear, clearly understandable

19. 明說　　míng shuō　state clearly, state frankly, state explicitly

20. 文明　　wénmíng　　(1) civilization, culture ; (2) civilized, cultured

21. 人民　　rénmín　　the people, the masses

22. 說明　　shuōmíng　　(1) explain, make clear ; (2) explanation

Who's Who and What's What

1. 中華民國　Zhōnghuá Mínguó　Republic of China (established 1912)

2. 民國　Mínguó　　　　　(abbreviation for Republic of China)

3. 三民　Sānmín　　　Three People's (abbreviation for <u>Sānmín Zhǔyì</u> 'Three People's Principles,' a book by Sun Yatsen. <u>Sānmín</u> is widely used in institutional names.)

4. 人民日報　<u>Rénmín Rìbào</u>　　<u>People's Daily</u> (published in Peking as the chief government organ of the People's Republic of China)

Note on Chinese Chronology

The Western system of chronology has been used in the People's Republic of China since 1949. Dates are written according to the following basic formula:

A 年　　B 月　　C 日　　　　　'A year　B month　C day'

After the establishmant of the Republic of China in 1912, a system of chronology was adopted (and still continues in use in Taiwan) in which the year is expressed as 'such-and-such year of the Republic of China' (counting 1912 as the first year):

中華民國　　A 年　　B 月　　C 日

　　　　　　　　　　'Republic of China　A year　B month　C day'

To turn a Western year into a year of the Republic, subtract 1911 (e.g. 1945 is 1945 minus 1911 or the 34th year). To turn a year of the Republic into a Western year, add 1911 (e.g. 34 plus 1911 equals 1945).

In both systems of chronology the spoken form 號 is replaced by 日 in the written style. One or the other is always used if the preceding number is ten or less; their use is optional with numbers over ten:

三月十號　　March 10

三月十四　　March 14

Dates are often abbreviated. Thus 中華民國 'Republic of China' is abbreviated to 民國 and even to 民. In correspondence, on library cards, and elsewhere even more condensed forms occur, some of which use only the numerals for year, month, and day separated by periods.

Study carefully the following ways of expressing Aug. 6, 1945 (starred items are written forms):

1. 一九四五年八月六號

2.*一九四五年八月六日

3. 中華民國三十四年八月六號

4.*中華民國三十四年八月六日

5. 民'國三十四年八月六號

6.*民國三十四年八月六日.

7. 民三十四年八月六號.

8.*民三十四年八月六日.

9. 三十四年八月六號.

10.*三十四年八月六日.

11.*一九四五. 八. 六.

12.*民三十四. 八. 六.

13.*三十四. 八. 六.

14.*1945年 8 月 6 日.

15.*民 34年 8 月 6 日.

16.*34年 8 月 6 日.

17.*1945. 8. 6.

18.*民 34. 8. 6.

19.*   34. 8. 6.

Exercise 1. Buildups

他去

他三號去

他四月三號去

他三十年四月三號去

他民國三十年四月三號去

他中華民國三十年四月三號去

他中華民國三十年四月三號去的

他是中華民國三十年四月三號去的

1. 他不是中華民國三十年四月三號去的

年月日

寫年月日

書上寫年月日

在書上寫年月日

他在書上寫年月日

2. 他在書上寫買書年月日

是一九五六年

他到中國來是一九五六年

3. 他頭次到中國來是一九五六年

Exercise 2. Pitfalls

1. 他要今天去.
   他要你們去.

2. 我想他到那兒去.
   我想到他那兒去.

3. 他是第一小學的校長.
   他是第一次到中國來.

4. 有一個家長要見校長.
   又一個家長要見校長.

Exercise 3. Practice on Dates

Read the following aloud and translate into Western chronology.
(Asterisked items are written forms.)

1.*一九四一年十一月七日.

2. 中華民國四十四年八月十七.

3.*1964年 7 月 29 日.

4. 從1956年到1961年.

5. 民國十年九月七號.

6.*1956.　2 ．　3 .

7. 從一八六一年到一八六五年.

8.*民24.　6 ．　9 .

9. 中華民國八年三月九號.

10.*一七七六年七月四日.

11. 從六月五號到九月五號.

12.*明年三月二十八日.

13.*從一九三一年九月十八日到一九三七年七月七日.

14.* 1947年 8 月10日.

15. 從民國三年到五十二年.

Exercise 4. Illustrative Sentences (Chinese)

1. 今天幾號？是四月三十號還是五月一號？

2. 因為他是第一次到外國去，所以他很想家.

3. 這是我第一次到中國來.

4. 我上次來他不在家. 我這次來他又不在家.

5. 又一個家長要見校長.

6. 中華民國五十年是一九幾幾年？

7. 他頭次到美國來是民國三十七年.

8. 我家在這條路北頭，三十號.

9. 在地圖上可以看到上海離南海很遠,
   離東海很近.

10. 下次我們兩個人一塊兒去比我一個
    人去好的多.

11. 他生在中華民國二十六年五月八日.

12. 我今年還沒看見他. 我還是去年看
    見他的.

13. 他說來說去還是沒說明那條路好走
    不好走.

14. 他在三民中學念書. 今年是第一年.

15. 他看書看的是很多.

16. 他明天不來, 因為甚麼他沒明說.

17. 張太太是第三十六小學的手工先生.

18. 他一天能會二十多個字.

19. 他是很好的學生. 在大學念書年年
    第一.

20. 從學校到書店，三號、四號車都可
    以坐．

21. 我不明白你為甚麼白天不念書．

22. 我是去年來到中國．我想明年走．

23. 你天天看<u>人民日報</u>嗎？

24. 從民國三十年到三十二年他在華西
    大學念書．

25. 有一天我是在文明書店看見他的．

26. 先生，我們念書嗎?… 不，寫字．
    先寫年月日．

27. 上海又是大城，又是大海口．

28. 有一次我到華北去，一來是看我姐
    姐，二來是看看長城．

29. 我到南華書店買書，是因為南華的

書很多, 又因為離學校很近.

30. 那條在海邊的小木船就能坐四個人.

Exercise 5. Dialogues

1. 年: 你是今年來的嗎?

   邊: 是的, 我是今年來的. 你也是
       今年來的嗎?

   年: 不是的, 我是去年來的.

 5 邊: 你念大學嗎?

   年: 我念大學.

   邊: 你念那個大學?

   年: 我念遠東大學.

2. 華: 這兒離三民中學有多遠?

   路: 不很遠, 就在這條馬路東口兒
       上. 你要到三民中學去嗎?

   華: 是的, 我要看看馬校長去.

 5 路: 馬校長今天可能不在學校. 他
       說今天他要到大華中學去.

3. 白: 毛大中, 你今天白天在家嗎?

毛：在家.

白：你的書很多. 我想到你那兒去
　　看書.

毛：你要看甚麼書？

5 白：我要看文言書.

毛：你為甚麼要看文言書呢？

白：我們學校馬先生説我們白話文
　　都會了. 他又要我們學文言文,
　　所以我要看文言書.

4. 學生：先生好？

　先生：你們好？坐下. 今天我們學
　　　　中文是第幾天了？

　學生：第二天.

5 先生：上次那五個字你們都會了嗎？

　學生：會了.

　先生：好. 今天我們還是學五個字,
　　　　下次都要會.

　學生：好的.

5. 路：你看見華小姐了嗎？

文：我今年看見他兩次. 頭一次是
　　在西東大學，還有一次是在毛
　　太太家裏頭. 你没看見他嗎？

路：没有. 我還是去年二月看見他
5　　的. 華小姐説甚麼了？

文：他説明年不在這兒念書了. 他
　　可能到日本去，要不然他就到
　　中國去.

6. 毛：你看人民日報嗎？

張：我不看人民日報. 我看華美日
　　報.

毛：人民日報上有小説嗎？

5張：没有小説.

毛：華美日報呢？

張：有. 我看報為的是看小説，所
　　以我看華美日報.

毛：華美日報是白話的嗎？

10張：華美日報上又有文言又有白話.

7. 田：高一民説他明年不念書了.

毛：是嗎？他書念的很好，家裏又
　　有錢．我不明白他為甚麼不想
　　念書了呢．

田：他没明説，我也不明白．

8. 華：邊書城的家在那兒？

文：他家就在中山路北口兒，五十
　　六號．

華：路東，路西？

5 文：路西．你想看邊書城去嗎？

華：是的．他説他要到日本去了，
　　所以我去看看他．

文：他又要上日本了．他為甚麼年
　　年到日本去？

10 華：他一來是因為在日本有買賣，
　　二來又因為他姐姐在那兒，所
　　以他年年都去日本．

9. 馬：那張人口圖上有没有説明？

路：没有説明．就有年月日．

馬：是那年，那月？

路：是一九一八年二月二十八日．

馬：是中華民國幾年？

路：是民國七年．

10. 華：有一天我在路上看見錢先生了．

毛：我還是去年看見他的．他家在
　　那兒？我們去看看他好不好？

華：他家就在城裏頭，南華路東口
　　兒，十八號．離這兒不到三里
　　路．你要今天去嗎？

毛：是．馬上去可以嗎？

華：可以，可以．

毛：要不要坐車？

華：不要坐車．我們走路去．

11. 先生：你們先看地圖．中國在那兒？

學生：中國在遠東．

先生：中國是個大國是個小國？

學生：中國是一個大國．

先生：是，中國是個大國，人口很
　　　多，在遠東是第一個大國，

　　是一個文明國家.

12. 華：今天你在家不在家？

　　錢：不在家.

　　華：你為甚麼天天不在家呢？是不
　　　　是又是看<u>文</u>小姐去？

　5 錢：是看小姐，可不是<u>文</u>小姐，是
　　　　又一個小姐了. 你想我看那個
　　　　小姐？

　　華：你看<u>白</u>小姐？

　　錢：我去看我的中文先生<u>高</u>小姐.

Exercise 6. Narratives

1. 有一次一個文學家、一個小說家兩
　個人在一條船上，都去日本. 船上
　的人很多. 有的在船裏頭看書，有
　的在船邊上看海. 那個文學家本來
　5 看海呢. 那個小說家說："我們兩
　個人在一塊兒，一邊看海，一邊說
　話."他們說來說去說到小說了. 文

學家說:"有一天,我在<u>白話報</u>上看
見了一個小說「海」,寫的很好. 今
天我在這裏看見海. 我又想看那個
小說了."小說家說: "那個小說我
₅也看了,寫的是很好."

2. 國文先生說: "要是有國家就有人
民. 人民是國家的,國家就是人民
的. 你們都明白嗎?"

3. 去年的今天,我在家中.
今年的今天,我在海外.
明年的今天,我又在那裏?
今天、今天,年年有今天.

4. 東華小學在一個小城裏頭. 那個小
城離上海很近,不到十里路. 有一
次學生念到「遠、近」兩個字. 先
生說: "你們說上海離我們近呢,
₅還是天離我們近?" 一個學生說:
"上海近,天遠."又一個學生說:

"不是. 我説天離我們近, 上海離
我們遠, 因為我們能看見天, 不能
看見上海."

5. 有一天高文英在人民書店買了一張
人民日報. 大家都要看. 高文英説:
"你們看報, 都是想看報上的小説.
你們心目中就有小説. 人民日報上
没有小説. 你們不要看了. 下次我
買小説月報, 你們可以看看."

6. 我今天在地下車上看見田小英. 他
説他們學校馬校長走了, 國文先生
也走了, 學校裏好先生都走了, 很
多學生都不想在那裏念書了.

7. 我坐船在日本海上. 有一天白天我
看見了一條魚很大. 有人説: "這
裏的魚不大. 東海的魚又大又多.
我上次在東海的一個海口看見很多

大魚."

8. 我頭次到中國是民國二十三年五月
十八號. 第二天我就在山東大學念
中文. 我是第一次到中國來念書.
因為我中國話說的不很好, 所以又
5 學說話, 又學白話文. 在大學的南
邊有一個第一小學, 還有一個三民
中學, 都是中國學生. 我看見他們
就說中國話. 他們說我中國話說的
好.

9. 這裏的圖書都是學校的, 可是這張
地圖在外. 是學生的.

10. 有很多中國人在海外. 有的是華東
人, 有的是華南人, 有的是華北人,
可是華西、華中的人就很少了.

11. 毛文華買了一本字典. 他在字典角
兒上寫「中華民國三十五年五月十

六日在文明書店買」.他説他所有的
書他買了就在書上寫年月日.

12. 張大中有一張中國人口圖. 在圖上
可以看到華東、華南人口多, 華北、
華中也不少. 就是華西少.

13. 白明中很會説話.人家説:"我們大
家一塊兒上山.你去不去?"他不明
説不去. 他説:"我想在家看書."

14. 馬小姐是馬先生的姐姐, 他們兩個
人都在外國念書. 馬先生很想家.
馬小姐説: "這裏有我們兩個人在
一塊兒, 比你一個人在這裏好的多
了. 你為甚麽還想家呢?"

15. 這個十字路口是這個城的中心. 白
天人很多. 有的從這裏走, 去上學.
有的從這裏走, 去買東西. 我天天
上學也是走這個十字路口.

16. 路大為、張東華都是本地人．他們
兩個人有很多水田．有二十多條水
牛，小牛在外．他們還有馬車、人
力車，在城裏還有很多買賣．那裏
5 的人都說他們兩個人錢很多，可是
他們兩個人本人都說没有錢．

17. 城外頭有一個大山．很多學生說明
天大家一塊兒上山．毛小姐說他不
去．他說一來山太高，二來路不好
走．

18. 高文英說："我念中文一天能念八九
十個字．"有人說："我看你没有那個
能力．你是說大話呢．"他說："我不
是說大話．你看我就寫：這是「八」，
5 這是「九」，這是「十」，還有這是「個」．
「八、九、十、個」這四個字我不是都
會了嗎？"

19. 「民國」就是「中華民國」，也就是「中國」.土地大，人口多，在遠東是一個大國.

20. 今天的書今天念，不要說「明天」.一天一天又一天，天天有明天.

21. 今年二月十六號我坐船從英國到中國來. 這是我頭一次坐船，也是我第一次來中國. 我是三月一號到中國的. 下了船，就坐火車到了山東，在山東大學學中文. 明年我要到西北大學，因為我想看看中國的西北.

22. 張先生在路上買了一張華美日報.他一邊走，一邊看. 我說："馬路上人多，車也多. 走路要小心，不要看報."張先生說："我買這張報為的是馬上要看. 要不然，我還不買這張報呢."

23. 國文先生說:"看書要看上下文. 不
    然, 就不明白."學生說:"看報是不
    是也要看上下文呢?"先生說:"看報
    也要看上下文."

24. 一個英國人坐了本國的船到遠東去.
    船走到地中海,他看見有很多大船,
    都是英國的. 他說: "我上次在這
    裏也看到很多英國船."

25. 有一個外國人到了中國想去看長城.
    有一個中國人說:"張家口離長城很
    近. 在張家口可以看見長城."那個
    外國人說:"張家口在那兒呢?"這個
    5 中國人說:"張家口在河北."

26. 我們學校離大華書店太遠了, 有七
    八華里. 我們學校在中華路. 書店
    在中山路、東華路的十字路口上.

27. 我是一個美國學生. 我雖然能說中

國話，可是還沒有能力看中文書.
今天買了一本中文書. 書上有英文
説明. 要是不明白就看看英文.

28. 高先生近來買了很多英文圖書，還
有英文學報甚麼的. 我想高先生不
會英文，為甚麼買很多英文書報呢？
有人説高先生的兒子英文很好，是
5 他兒子要看英文書.

29. 有一個外國人學中文. 他一天能會
十個字. 有人説他念的很好. 他説：
"有人一天能會二十多個字. 可見
人家比我還好呢."

30. 高先生、田先生都是本地人，都在
本地的中學念書. 高先生説："我們
明年就要念大學了. 我想到外國去
念大學. 你呢？" 田先生説："我想
5 在本國念大學."

Exercise 7. Illustrative Sentences (English)

1. What day of the month is it today? Is it April 30th or May first?

2. Because this is his first trip abroad, he's very homesick.

3. This is my first trip to China.

4. When I came last time, he wasn't at home. When I came this time, he still wasn't home.

5. Still another parent wants to see the principal.

6. The fiftieth year of the Republic is nineteen hundred and what?

7. The first time he came to America was in 1948.

8. My home is at the northern entrance to this street, No. 30.

9. On the map one can see that Shanghai is quite far from the South China Sea (but) quite close to the East China Sea.

10. Next time it would be a lot better for both of us to go together than for me to go alone.

11. He was born on May 8th in the 26th year of the Republic of China [i.e. 1937].

12. I haven't seen him yet this year. It was (as long ago as) last year that I saw him.

13. He's talked and talked but still hasn't explained whether that road is passable or not.

14. I'm studying at Sanmin Middle School. This [year] is (my) first year.

15. He does read a lot of books.

16. He's not coming tomorrow; he didn't state clearly why.

17. Mrs. Zhang is the handicrafts teacher at Elementary School No. 36.

18. He can learn over twenty characters a day.

19. He's an excellent student. [Studying] in college he's first year after year.

20. From the school to the bookstore you can take either the No. 3 or the No. 4 bus.

21. I don't understand why you don't study in the daytime.

22. I came to China last year. I plan to leave next year.

23. Do you read People's Daily every day?

24. From 1941 to 1943 he studied at West China Union University.

25. I saw him one day at the Wenming Bookstore.

26. Teacher, shall we read ? ···No, let's write characters. First write the date.

27. Shanghai is both a big city and a great seaport.

28. Once I went to North China, first of all to see my sister and second to see the Great Wall.

29. I'm going to the South China Bookstore to buy some books because it has a lot of books and also because it's close to school.

30. That little wooden boat on the beach can seat only four people.

Lesson 18

Exercise 1. Review of Single Characters

1. 遠	9. 了	17. 來	25. 船	33. 東	41. 兒	49. 因
2. 邊	10. 次	18. 雖	26. 湖	34. 坐	42. 明	50. 北
3. 華	11. 上	19. 第	27. 號	35. 離	43. 裏	
4. 為	12. 今	20. 家	28. 南	36. 所	44. 里	
5. 走	13. 西	21. 去	29. 可	37. 條	45. 報	
6. 在	14. 以	22. 下	30. 民	38. 校	46. 近	
7. 天	15. 從	23. 年	31. 頭	39. 到	47. 城	
8. 店	16. 海	24. 河	32. 路	40. 然	48. 又	

Exercise 2. Distinguishing Partially Similar Combinations

A. Same Character in Initial Position

1	2	3	4	5	6
上船	中東	大家	海口	可是	本來
上次	中美	大中	海外	可以	本地
上海	中華	大刀	海邊	可能	本國
上下	中山	大學	海裏	可見	本子
上學	中心	大門			

7	8	9	10	11	12
明天	太湖	三次	手邊	文言	華北
明白	太太	三民	手工	文人	華中
明年	太大	三角	手上	文明	華美
明說					

164

13	14	15	16	17	18
東海	河南	華西	是的	山東	兒子
東北	河北	華南	是麽	山水	兒女
東西	河邊	華里	是嗎		

19	20	21	22	23	24
所以	看見	近東	南美	馬路	坐船
所有	看書	近來	南海	馬上	坐下

25	26	27	28	29	30
小姐	頭次	土地	能説	女人	不到
小心	頭兒	土人	能力	女兒	不然

31	32	33	34	35	36
日本	路口	美國	英里	中日	念文學
日報	路西	美女	英美	中英	念中學

B. Same Character in Final Position

1	2	3	4	5	6
門口	上次	海邊	大家	本來	人力
人口	這次	手邊	人家	一來	馬力
海口	下次	四邊	國家	二來	能力
山口	頭次	一邊	想家	近來	水力
水口	三次	這邊			

7	8	9	10	11	12
明天	學報	家裏	去年	兒子	女兒
白天	月報	那裏	明年	本子	這兒
今天	看報	海裏	年年	刀子	那兒
天天	日報	這裏	今年		

13	14	15	16	17	18
車上	家長	東海	河北	近東	東華
馬上	很長	上海	湖北	中東	大華
手上	校長	南海	東北	遠東	南華

19	20	21	22	23	24
還有	外頭	北美	文人	大中	國外
沒有	西頭	南美	工人	地中	在外
所有	上頭	華美	本人	華中	海外

25	26	27	28	29	30
白話文	民國	華東	地下	馬路	不然
上下文	中國	山東	上下	走路	雖然
文言文					

31	32	33	34	35	36	37
人民	馬車	小心	看書	因為	所以	西山
三民	火車	中心	圖書	以為	可以	火山

C. Same Character in Different Positions

1	2	3	4	5	6
學校	買書	西湖	中心	地下	東西
校長	書店	湖南	心裏	下次	西北

7	8	9	10	11	12
中學	校長	中日	中文	地圖	文明
學報	長城	日報	文人	圖書	明天

13	14	15	16	17	18
國家	人民	可以	馬路	工人	日本
家長	民國	以為	路南	人口	本來

D. Reversibles

1	2	3	4	5	6
兒女	外國	海上	土地	湖南	中華
女兒	國外	上海	地土	南湖	華中

7	8	9	10	11
山西	南華	華東	説明	九十
西山	華南	東華	明説	十九

Exercise 3. Review of Special Combinations

The following list includes all combinations presented in this unit other than those already reviewed in the preceding exercise.

1. 小説家　　6. 有一次　　11. 説大話
2. 要不然　　7. 年月日　　12. 一塊兒
3. 有一天　　8. 地中海　　13. 日本海
4. 為甚麽　　9. 上下文　　14. 中山路
5. 文學家　　10. 為的是　　15. 又因為

16. 所有的　21. 地下車　26. 華西大學　31. 可不是嗎
17. 又…又　22. 十字路口　27. 人民日報　32. 西東大學
18. 張家口　23. 東海大學　28. 西北大學　33. 一邊…一邊
19. 心目中　24. 遠東大學　29. 在心目中　34. 一來…二來
20. 不見了　25. 中華民國　30. 山東大學　35. 可不是麽

Exercise 4. Excerpts from Actual Publications

The characters we have studied so far are too few to enable us to do any extensive reading of actual Chinese publications. However, it is possible to find short passages limited to the characters already studied. Fifteen such passages are presented below. They are taken from the hit play Thunderstorm, by Cáo Yú (Tsao Yü), China's foremost dramatist.

1. 姐姐，你看，你看！

2. 不，女的——一個有錢的太太.

3. 你不要去.

4. 我在這兒.

5. 我們明天就走.

6. 我不明白你的話.

7. 我想你很明白.

8. 我們都是人.

9. 甚麼，還有一個女人？

10. 不，不，你不要見他.

11. 你不是我的，你不是我的兒子.

12. 他們就在門口.

13. 你…你…你走！

14. 你們在這兒說甚麼？

15. 好，我也去.

Exercise 5. Narratives

1. 張明海天天賣魚. 他有一條小船，他家就在小船上. 他没有太太，就有一個女兒. 白天張明海去賣魚，他女兒一個人在家，也就一個人在
5 船上. 有一天他的女兒不見了. 他在船的四邊都看了，都没有. 有人說："那河邊上不是你的女兒嗎？"

他馬上去看. 他女兒坐在河邊上, 手上還有一條魚呢. 他說:"你一個人在家要小心. 下次不可下船了."

2. 一個人的人力很小. 你看人力車就能坐一兩個人. 馬力比人力大, 馬車可以坐三四個人. 水力比馬力又大的多了. 你看, 這是河水的水口, ⁵水力很大, 比八九十個馬力還大呢.

3. 張文華是個水手. 他家在日本. 他去年上船去英國. 他在船上很想家. 今年這條船從英國走地中海, 又到了日本. 他心裏想今天可以到家了. ⁵船到日本, 他馬上就要下船. 有人說:"船上很多東西不見了, 船上所有的人今天都不能下船."那個水手心裏想:"我今天還是不能看見我家裏人."

4. 我是山東人. 因為東北土地很好,
人口不多, 所以我在中華民國十九
年五月四號就到東北去了. 我到了
東北沒念書, 就在一個書店裏學買
5 賣. 我第一天到書店去, 書店的張
先生要我寫家在那兒, 家裏有多少
人, 還要我寫那天的年月日.

5. 國文先生說:"念中文要看上下文,
不要就看兩三個字.不然,就不能明
白."學生說:"上下文都要看嗎?"
先生說:"有的看上文,有的看下文,
5 也有的上下文都要看."

6. 有一個人就會說大話. 有一次他說
他們家裏很有錢,這裏所有的大山、
水田都是他的. 有人說:"那個山是
國家的. 水田有的是張先生的, 有
5 的是馬先生的, 你為甚麼說是你的
呢?" 他說:"他們為甚麼說是他們
的呢?"

7. 那個十字路口的東邊有一個小書店，
在小書店的東邊不遠還有一個大書
店，那是文明書店．文明書店圖書
雖然很多，可是我到那兒買中國人
5 口圖，他們沒有．他們說離這裏不
遠還有一個大書店，他們有中國人
口圖．

8. 他上次寫書寫的很好，這次寫書又
寫的很好，可見他很有能力．有人
說他下次不想寫了，因為甚麼他沒
明說．

9. 馬小姐是第一小學的手工先生．學
生都說他的手工很好．

10. 我是一個女學生，在第一中學念書．
我還有一個姐姐，他在遠東大學念
書．因為我們不是在一個學校，所
以我們兩個人一年就能在一塊兒一
5 次．去年我到遠東大學去看我姐姐，
今年我姐姐要到這兒來看我．

11. 一個英國人在中國學中文. 不到一
年就能看報, 也能寫很多字. 有一
天他看見湖邊有水田、小船, 還有
山在東邊, 月在天上, 他就寫:

5　　『南北湖邊水田,來去兩三小船,
　　　遠近人家兒女, 都看月上東山.』
大家看了, 都說他寫的很好. 有人
說他本來是英國一個文學家.

12. 馬先生是大中中學校長. 他太太也
在大中中學, 是國文先生. 他們没
有兒子, 就有兩個女兒, 都在這個
中學念書.他們家離這個中學很近,

5　不到二里路, 是在一個山上. 山下
邊有一條河, 河邊有一條小路. 他
們家四口人天天從這條小路上學校.
他們在路上一邊走一邊說話. 有一
天白天,他們在路上走,小女兒說:

10　 "我說天上有一個字, 你們能說是甚麼字嗎？"他姐姐説："天上没有字."馬太太説："我也没看見."馬先生看看天上説："我明白了可是我不説."小女兒説："你不要説. 我先説

5 你們看，「日」「月」都在天上.「日、月」在一塊兒,那不是個「明」字嗎？"馬太太説："我小女兒想的很好."

13. 我上次坐英國船到日本去. 那是我頭次坐英國船. 那條船又大又好. 我可能年年到日本. 要是明年又到日本去，我還是坐那條英國船.

14. 高先生是美國人，在中國念大學.他有一個姐姐，在日本念書. 高先生説他明天要走了，要到日本去.可是他没説為甚麼要到日本去. 有

5 人説高先生到日本去，一來是看他姐姐，二來是他想在日本念大學.

15. 我的小説很多. 今天我又要去買小
    説. 姐姐説:"你又買小説. 你的小
    説太多了. 為甚麼還要買呢?" 我
    説:"因為三民書店近來又有一本很
  5 好的小説, 又因為這本小説學校裏
    所有的學生都有一本, 所以我也要
    買一本."

16. 我在大華書店看見一張很好的地圖.
    上頭有中文説明, 也有英文説明.

UNIT IV

Lesson 19

1	2	3	4	5
用	給	對	過	最

6	7	8	9	10
前	後	時	候	初

1. 用　yòng　　　　use (N/V)

2. 給　gěi　　　　(1) give ; (2) for, to (coverb and postverb)

3. 對　duì　　　　(1) be correct ; (2) to, toward ; (3) opposite, facing

4. 過　guò　　　　(1) pass, pass through, pass by ; (2) celebrate (birth-
　　　　　　　　　days, holidays, etc.) ; (3) after (followed by a time-word)

　　　guo　　　　(verb suffix)

5. 最　zuì　　　　most

6. 前　qián *　　　front, before

7. 後　hòu *　　　after, afterwards

8. 時　shí *　　　time

9. 候　hòu *　　　time

10. 初　chū *　　　(at the) beginning, (at) first

11. 的　dì *　　　an aim

12. 會　huǐ *　　　a moment

13. 了　liǎo　　　　(used in resultative verb compounds)

14. 生　shēng *　　(1) unfamiliar, strange, new ; (2) raw, uncooked

Special Combinations

1. 不過　bú guò　　(1) not pass by (somewhere) (TV) ; (2) not exceed,
   not surpass (also used as RV ending); (3) however

2. 不用　bú yòng　　(1) not use ; (2) not need (to do something)

3. 初次　chūcì　　first time

4. 初小　chūxiǎo　　lower elementary school, primary school

5. 初中　chūzhōng　　lower middle school, junior high school

6. 從來　cónglái　　hitherto, always (See Supplementary Notes)

7. 從前　cóngqián　　previously, formerly

8. 對門(兒)　duìmén(r)　　(1) the house across the street, the opposite
   building ; (2) be opposite

9. 高小　gāoxiǎo　　upper elementary school

10. 高中　gāozhōng　　upper middle school, senior high

11. 工錢　gōngqián　　wages

12. 過路　guò lù　　(1) cross a road, cross a street ; (2) pass by

13. 過年　guò nián　　(1) pass into the new year, celebrate the new year ;
    (2) period of the new year, New Year's

14. 過日子　guò rìzi　　(1) pass the days ; (2) live

15. 過生日　guò shēngri　　celebrate a birthday

16. 後來　hòulái　　afterwards, later on

17. 後年　hòunián　　year after next

18. 後天　hòutiān　　day after next

19. 路過　lùguò　　pass on the way

20. 賣給　màigěi　　sell to

21. 明後　míng-hòu　　next or the one after (as in míng-hòunián 'next year
    or the year after')

22. 目的　mùdì　　aim, objective

23. 前年　qiánnián　　year before last

24. 前天　qiántiān　　day before yesterday

25. 然後　ránhòu　　afterwards

26. 日用　rìyòng　　daily expenses, daily needs

27. 日子　rìzi　　　day

28. 生日　shēngri　　birthday

29. 生字　shēngzì　　unfamiliar character, new character

30. 時候　shíhou　　time

31. 要不是　yàobúshi　if it were not that, but for

32. 一會（兒）　yìhuǐ(r)　a moment

33. 以後　yǐhòu　　after, afterwards

34. 以前　yǐqián　　before, previously

35. 用人　yòng rén　employ people, make use of people

　　　　 yòngren　　servant

36. 用心　yòngxīn　(1) use one's brains, do mental work; (2) diligent
　　　　　　　　　　(in mental work)

37. 有用　yǒuyòng　useful

38. 最初　zuìchū　　at first

39. 最好　zuìhǎo　　(1) be best; (2) it would be best

40. 最近　zuìjìn　　(1) be closest; (2) most recent; (3) very recently,
　　　　　　　　　　very soon

41. 最後　zuìhòu　　last. final, ultimate

Note on the Chinese School System

The Chinese school system is divided into six years of elementary school
(小學 xiǎoxué), six years of middle school (中學 zhōngxué), and four years
of college (大學 dàxué). Elementary school is further subdivided into four
years of primary or beginning elementary (初小 chūxiǎo) and two years of
higher elementary (高小 gāoxiǎo). Middle school is divided into three years
of lower or beginning middle (初中 chūzhōng) and three years of higher
middle (高中 gāozhōng). The year of school is expressed by 一年 yìnián
'one year' or 'first year,' 二年 èrnián 'two years' or 'second year,' and

so on. There are several alternate forms. A full listing is given in exercise
3 below. Here are a few examples :

初小一年 or 初小一 'first year of primary school'
高小二年 or 高小二 'second year of higher elementary school'
初中三年 or 初中三 or 初三 'third year of lower middle school'
大學四年 or 大四 'fourth year of college' or 'senior year'

Note on Relative Clauses

Since relative clauses are used more often and in a more complicated form
in written Chinese than in spoken Chinese, they need to be studied with special
care. Such clauses are sentences from which a noun has been extracted and
everything else (except for occasional deletions) has been placed in front of
the noun with an intervening subordinating particle de. For example:

先生看報 'The gentleman is reading the newspaper.'

先生看的報是上海時報 'The newspaper which the gentleman is reading
is the Shanghai Times.'

看報的先生是毛先生 'The gentleman who is reading the newspaper is
Mr. Mao.'

Often the noun which would normally come after de is not expressed :

看報的是毛先生 'The one who is reading the newspaper is Mr. Mao.'

Often some changes occur in the transition from full sentence to relative
clause :

他去年買了一條船 'He bought a boat last year.'

他去年買的那條船很小 'The boat which he bought last year is very
small.'

Occasionally, especially in phrases which would be translated into English
as 'at which,' 'in which,' 'by which,' etc., some elements are deleted from the
sentence :

他在那個學校念中文 'He is studying Chinese in that school.'

他念中文的那個學校很好 'That school at which he is studying
Chinese is very good.'

Study carefully the pairs of sentences in exercise 4, noting the relation between the first sentence and the relative clause in the second sentence.

Exercise 1. Buildups

書在這兒

那本書在這兒

我買的那本書在這兒

我前天買的那本書在這兒

我前天在書店買的那本書在這兒

1. 我前天在大華書店買的那本書在這兒

我有字典

我有好的字典

2. 我有比這個好的字典

他買書

他去買書

他到書店去買書

他到書店去買書的時候

3. 他到書店去買書的時候我也去

Exercise 2. Pitfalls

1. 我今天買了一本書，很好.
   我今天買的一本書很好.

2. 那本書我給他賣了.
   那本書我賣給他了.

3. 你給他們甚麼東西？
   你給他買甚麼東西？

4. 他在書店看過的那四本字典很好.
   他在書店看過的是日本字典不是？

Exercise 3. Learning the Designations for School Years

The following outline summarizes the designations for the sixteen years of school from first grade through the fourth year of college. Note especially

the alternative abbreviated designations. Study the table and translate the
terms.

Ⅰ. 小學

  A. 初小

    1. 初小一年　　初小一

    2. 初小二年　　初小二

    3. 初小三年　　初小三

    4. 初小四年　　初小四

  B. 高小

    5. 高小一年　　高小一

    6. 高小二年　　高小二

Ⅱ. 中學

  A. 初中

    7. 初中一年　　初中一　　初一

    8. 初中二年　　初中二　　初二

    9. 初中三年　　初中三　　初三

  B. 高中

    10. 高中一年　　高中一　　高一

    11. 高中二年　　高中二　　高二

    12. 高中三年　　高中三　　高三

Ⅲ. 大學

    13. 大學一年　　大一

    14. 大學二年　　大二

    15. 大學三年　　大三

    16. 大學四年　　大四

Exercise 4. Practice on Relative Clauses

1. 我今天買了一本字典.
   我今天買的那本字典在那兒？

2. 學校離書店不遠.
   離書店不遠的那個學校是小學.

3. 他給我書.
   他給我的書都是中文書.

4. 所有的人都在家裏.
   所有的在家裏的人都是女人.

5. 那本字典比這個好.
   我們没有比這本好的字典.

6. 先生在那兒看報.
   在那兒看報的先生是張校長.

7. 那條船從英國到中國去.
   從英國到中國去的船都很大.

8. 外國人到這兒來念書.
   到這兒來念書的外國人很少.

9. 那個外國人從民國二十三年到二十五年在遠東大學念過書.
   從民國二十三年到二十五年在遠東大學念過書的那個外國人
   又要到中國來了.

10. 他今天在大中書店買了一本中英字典.
    我可以不可以看看他今天在大中書店買的那本字典?

11. 那個小姐看大中月報.
    看大中月報的那個小姐是外國人.

12. 校長對我說話.
    我明白了校長對我說的話.

13. 那個車從中山路到山上去.
    從中山路到山上去的車天天有嗎?

14. 學生到這兒來念書.
    到這兒來念書的不都是外國學生.

15. 你買甚麼東西?
    你買的是書還是地圖?

Exercise 5. Illustrative Sentences(Chinese)

1. 你後天不上學你對先生說過了嗎？

2. 我在書店看過的是日英字典，不是中英字典．

3. 最近張先生給我兩本他寫的書．

4. 你念中文的時候這本中英大字典對你很有用．你不用買．我給你．

5. 我初次看見他是我沒念中學以前．

6. 他念英文最後目的是能在美國的大學念書．

7. 他過馬路的時候從來也不看人，也不看車．

8. 他不會用人．他給用人的工錢太少了，所以人家要走了．

9. 我們對門兒南家的人口多，一個月過日子要用很多錢．

10. 我一天日用不過五塊錢.

11. 他賣給我的那本書對我沒有用.

12. 我想他念不過你.

13. 他是高三的學生！我以為他念初中呢.

14. 後天是邊小姐生日. 你說我給他買甚麼好呢？

15. 今天我們學過的生字, 先生要我們後天都會.

16. 我先到學生中心, 後到學校去. 我不路過書店.

17. 這本小說就是美日書店有. 最好你到那兒去買.

18. 我很多時候沒看見他了. 還是去年過年的時候看見他的.

19. 從我家到學校車錢很多。要不是我
    的書太多，我就走路了。

20. 高小、初中所有的學生，那個對文
    言文會的最多？

21. 你不用到他那兒去。他一會兒就到
    這兒來。

22. 我從來沒看見過長城。

23. 他今年在南美。明後年他就要到北
    美去。

24. 我是前年在西山過的生日。

25. 我想他念的了高中，念不了大學。

26. 校長說：“我們初小的學生也很用心
    念書。”

27. 我先到華北去，然後到華中去，最
    後到華南去。

28. 張長木從前在山東大學念書，後來在西北大學．不到一年又到華西大學去了．

29. 從河北到湖南也可以坐船，可是要用很多日子．

30. 我想後年到遠東去念書．

31. 我到中國去以前想在西東大學念中文．

32. 我最初在東海大學念書，以後又到遠東大學去了．

33. 他是前天坐船到近東去的．

34. 田小姐很好看．大家都説他是一個美女．

35. 太湖比西湖大，可是西湖的山水比太湖好看．

Exercise 6. Dialogues

1. 邊：你是從湖南來的嗎？

文：是的．我來的時候先從湖南到
　　上海，然後我又從上海到這兒
　　來．

邊：你來的時候看見華先生他們了
5　　嗎？

文：我來以前看見他們了．華先生
　　說他們最近可能到華北去．

2. 錢：你到張先生家走中山路嗎？你
　　要是路過大華書店給我買一本
　　初中國文好不好？

馬：我走不到那條路．張先生家在
5　　大華路後頭一條小路上．

錢：要是你不走那條路就不要買了．

馬：你今天用不用？

錢：今天不用．明後天用．

馬：我後天到中山路．後天給你買
10　　可以嗎？

錢：可以，可以．

3. 文：明天是田先生生日．他説要我
　　　們四個人明天到他家去．

　白：對了．明天是田先生過生日．
　　　我以為是後天呢．去！我們都
5　　　去．他説要我們明天甚麼時候
　　　去呢？

　文：他没説，他對我説一會兒到我
　　　們這兒來．

　白：我們給他買甚麼東西呢？

10 文：最好我們四個人到華美書店給
　　　他買一本中英大字典，因為前
　　　天我們一塊兒到書店去，他很
　　　想買那本中英字典，他對我説
　　　那本字典對他很有用．

4. 毛：張先生的兒女都在那個學校念
　　　書？

　馬：大兒子、大女兒都在遠東大學
　　　念書，二兒子在中華中學高中
5　　　一，小兒子、小女兒都在中心

小學念初小.

　毛：學校離他們家很遠. 我想他們
　　　天天車錢也不少.

　馬：可不是嗎！不過有的時候他們
5　　　不坐車.

5. 錢：張太太！上那兒去？

　張：我去買東西.

　錢：為甚麼用人不去買呢？

　張：我們那個用人走了. 没有用人
5　　　了.

　錢：要過年了. 為甚麼他走了呢？

　張：我想是因為我給他的工錢少.

　錢：這兒工人的工錢很高,是不是？

　張：可不是嗎！要不是我兒女多,
10　　我就不用人了.

6. 張：從這兒到毛先生家要是坐火車
　　　要多少時候？

　田：一會兒就到. 你想到毛先生家

去嗎？

張：是的，我們兩個人很多時候不
　　見了.我還是前年看見他的.後
　　來就沒看見他.我想看看他去.

7. 一山：姐姐，為甚麼我們門口兒有
　　　　很多人？

　　美英：是嗎？我去看看.

　　一山：是不是到我們這兒來的？

5　美英：不是的，是過路的.

　　一山：我們這兒是條小路. 為甚麼
　　　　今天很多人從我們這兒過路
　　　　呢？

　　美英：可能都是上西山去，要不然
10　　　　走不到我們這條路.

8. 毛：你念中文的目的是甚麼？

　　白：我念中文目的是要看中文小說.

　　毛：你最初學中文是先寫字呢，還

是先念書呢?

白: 我是先念書後學寫字.

9. 錢: 前天學的字你都會寫了嗎?

文: 不會呢. 你呢?

錢: 我也不會呢. 高文說他都會了.

文: 他是好學生. 他寫字念書都很
　　用心.

錢: 以後我們兩個人也要用心念書
　　了,要不然我們書也念的不好,
　　字也寫的不好.

文: 人家說高文以前也不很用心.

錢: 不. 他從來就用心念書.

10. 邊: 張太太有五六個兒女,是不是?

南: 是的,他有四個女兒、兩個兒子.

邊: 他們兒女又多又都念書. 一個
　　月過日子要用很多錢了.

南: 張太太對我說他們一天日用最

少要三十塊錢.

邊：是不是張先生明後年就要到日
本去了？他們家裏人都去嗎？

南：他後年去．路又遠人又多．我
5　想他們家裏人去不了．

11. 毛：你買甚麼？

白：我要一本高中國文．多少錢？

毛：兩塊二．我們有刀子、本子.
你要不要？

5白：我要五個本子．

毛：好．你念高中了嗎？

白：是的．

毛：你在學校裏都學甚麼？

白：我學中文、英文、還有三角兒．

10毛：三角學高小有没有？

白：没有．

毛：你從前没到這兒買過書，是不
是？

白：我這次是初次. 我從來没到這
　　兒買過書. 我都是在中華書店
　　買.

毛：以後你要是買書、本子、甚麼
　　的不用到中華書店買. 就到這
　　兒來買.

白：好. 我以後要是買書就到你們
　　這兒買.

12. 馬：你最近看見<u>張一文</u>了嗎？
　　毛：我没看見他. 你呢？
　　馬：我最後一次看見他是在去年.
　　　　他可能不在本地了.

13. 邊：山前頭那塊地, 他們賣了没有？
　　文：<u>華</u>先生説最近賣了. 他説賣給
　　　　他們對門兒<u>張</u>家了.

Exercise 7. Narratives

1. 從前我過生日的時候, 我姐姐都給

我買最好的東西．後天又是我的生
日，所以我姐姐前天對我說："這次
你過生日,我給你買最有用的東西."
我說:"是不是也是最好的東西?"我
5 姐姐說:"最有用的東西就是最好的
東西."

2. 張中華有三個兒子.大兒子念高中，
二兒子念初中，小兒子念初小．大
兒子、二兒子念書都很用心，就是
小兒子不用心．他說他念高小、中
5 學、大學的時候就要用心了.

3. 張小姐家在中華路．我家也在中華
路．我們兩家是對門兒．我們天天
上學都是一塊兒坐車去．我天天到
他家門口，然後我們就坐車到學校
5 去．有一天，張小姐說:"今天我們
不用坐車了，我們走路去."我說:
"好."我們走了一會兒,路過一個十

字路口. 過路的車也多人也多, 很
不好走. 張小姐説:"這個十字路口
太不好走了. 我們要小心." 我説:
"對了, 我們要小心."

4. 一個美國學生在本國大學念中文.
他説他想明後年到中國去. 他去的
目的是要學中國話, 念中文. 有人
説:"他還有一個目的, 是想要一個
5 中國太太."

5. 先生、小學生在一條船上. 先生説:
"河裏有一條大魚. 你看見了嗎?"
小學生説:"我没看見."先生説:"你到
這裏來, 就看見了." 小學生走到先
5 生那裏看看説:"我還是看不見." 先
生又看看説:"為甚麼那條大魚不見
了?"小學生説:"先生, 你看, 在這
裏呢. 這不是一條大魚嗎?"

6. 毛先生的車賣給張先生了. 在賣車

的時候毛先生說過了要在過年以前
給他錢. 明天就是今年最後一天了.
張先生沒有錢, 給不了. 張先生想
在過年以後給錢. 毛先生對張先生
5 說:"在賣車的時候我就對你說了,
要在過年以前給錢, 因為我過年的
時候要用錢,要不然我也不賣車了."

7. 有一個外國人寫中國字, 本來寫的
不好, 可是人家看見了都說是寫的
很好. 前天張先生也對我說那個外
國人是寫的很好. 我說, 我要去看
5 看. 有一天我們兩個人一塊兒去看
那個外國人, 我是要看看他寫的字
好不好. 我們看見了那個外國人,
我對他說:"你寫的字可以給我看看
嗎?"他說:"我寫的字都不在我手上,
10 可是我可以馬上就給你寫."他一邊
說一邊寫. 寫了以後, 就給我看,

張先生也在我後邊看. 看了一會兒,
張先生說: "是不是寫的很好?" 我
說: "是「寫的很好」." 本來這個外國
人寫的是四個字, 第一個字是「寫」,
5 第二個字是「的」, 第三、第四個字寫
的是「很」、「好」. 所以人家看見那個
外國人寫的字都說是「寫的很好」.

8. 中國人家裏, 有用人的很多, 外國
人家裏, 有用人的很少. 有人說有
用人好, 有人說沒有用人好. 我想
最好不用用人, 因為有了用人就要
5 給用人工錢, 家裏日用的錢就要多
了. 不過要是兒女太小, 還是有用
人好.

9. 高大生是工人, 家裏的人很多, 一
個月要用很多錢. 他說: "天天過日
子要用錢. 兒子是大學生, 女兒是
中學生, 念書都要用錢. 要不是我

的工錢多, 我兒女就不能念書了."

10. <u>馬大為</u>是美國人. 前年初次來中國. 最初他沒想學中文. 後來因為天天要用中文, 他就在中大學中文. 有人說他的中文比中國的中學生還好

5 呢.

11. <u>毛一文</u>念書從來就不用心. 他念了不少的英文, 可是也不會說也不會寫. 有一次英文先生說:"你們寫寫你們學過的生字, 看那個人會的最

5 多." 人人都寫了, 就是<u>毛一文</u>一個人沒寫.

12. 我、我姐姐都在美國念書. 我們兩個人都在一個學校念書, 所以天天在一塊兒也不想家. 可是最近我姐姐很想家. 明天是我姐姐生日了.

5 我給他買甚麼好呢? 我想還是不買東西, 我們一塊兒到小湖坐小船去.

13. 我們學校近來來了兩個中東學生.
他們到這裏來, 目的是要學中國話.
他們先到中國的東北, 又從東北坐
船到山東. 他們説東北的土地很好,
₅山東有很高的大山. 他們也想去河
南、 湖北. 去過河南、 湖北以後,
還要去華西、 華東看看.

14. 我要買文學月報. 先到大中路東華
書店, 書店的人説没有. 又到大華
路南華書店, 也買不到. 後來在文
人書店買到了. 有人説:"本地的書
₅店圖書都很少. 就是文人書店的書、
報多."

15. 我今天要到書店去, 目的是買三角
學. 走在路上看見毛大文了. 我們
兩個人一邊走路一邊説話, 没到書
店去, 所以三角學也没買.

16. 有一個學校離城裏有三華里. 有一

天，初中三的學生要到城裏頭去.
先生對學生說:"到城裏可以坐車,
也可以走路.你們有幾個人要坐車,
幾個人想走路?"學生說:"坐車要多
5 少錢?"先生說:"要是坐車一個人要
五毛錢."學生說:"我們都走路去.
我們甚麼時候走?"先生說:"我們一
會兒就走."學生說:"我們一會兒走
的了嗎?"先生說:"為甚麼走不了?
10 我們馬上就走."

Exercise 8. Illustrative Sentences (English)

1. Did you tell the teacher that you're not coming to school day after tomorrow?

2. What I saw in the bookstore was a Japanese-English dictionary, not a Chinese-English dictionary.

3. Very recently Mr. Zhang gave me two books that he had written.

4. When you study Chinese, this big Chinese-English dictionary will be very useful [to you]. You don't need to buy it. I'll give it to you.

5. The first time I saw him was before I attended middle school. [Note the use of the negative in this sentence. It gives the effect of 'Before, when I had not yet attended middle school.')

6. His ultimate objective in studying English is to be able to study at an American university.

7. When crossing the street, he never looks out for people or cars.

8. He doesn't know how to employ people. He gives his servants too little wages, so they want to leave.

9. There are a lot of people in the Nan family (who live) opposite us. Each month they have to spend [lit. use] a lot of money to live.

10. My daily expenses [for one day] do not exceed $5.

11. That book he sold me is of no use to me.

12. I don't think he's capable of surpassing you in studying.

13. He's a senior in upper middle school. I thought he was studying in lower middle school.

14. Day after tomorrow is Miss Bian's birthday. What do you think I should buy for her?

15. The teacher wants us to learn by day after tomorrow all the new characters that we studied today.

16. I'm going to the student center first and then to school. I won't be passing the bookstore on the way.

17. Only the American-Japanese Bookstore has this novel. It would be best for you to go there to buy it.

18. I haven't seen him for a long time. It was last year at New Year's that I saw him.

19. The fare from my home to school is expensive. If it weren't that I have too many books, I'd go on foot.

20. Of all the students in upper elementary school and lower middle school, which one knows the most literary Chinese?

21. You don't need to go to his place. He'll come here in a few moments.

22. I've never seen the Great Wall.

23. This year he's in South America. Next year or the year after he'll go to North America.

24. I celebrated my birthday in the Western Hills year before last.

25. I think he'll be able to cope with [lit. study] upper middle school but not college.

26. The principal said: "Our pupils in lower elementary school also study hard".

27. I'm going first to North China, then to Central China, and last of all to South China.

28. Zhang Changmu formerly studied at Shantung University. Later he was at Northwest University. In less than a year he [again] went to West China Union University.

29. It is also possible to go from Hopeh to Hunan by boat, but it takes quite a few days.

30. I plan to go to the Far East to study year after next.

31. Before going to China, I plan to study Chinese at Seton Hall University.

32. First of all I studied at Tunghai University. Later I [also] went to Far Eastern University.

33. He left by boat for the Near East day before yesterday.

34. Miss Tian is very pretty. Everyone says she's a beauty.

35. Tai Lake is larger than West Lake, but the scenery at West Lake is more beautiful [than that at Tai Lake].

Supplementary Notes

從來 "hitherto, always" has a past reference in time. It is often followed by 就, less often by 都. With a negative verb it is often followed by 就, 都, and 也 and is most conveniently translated as "never": 他從來就用心 "He's always been diligent". 他從來都不用心 "He's never been diligent". 我從來也没看見過他 "I've never seen him".

Question words are often used with 好(呢). For example: 到那兒去好呢? "Where would it be best to go?" 給幾本書好? "How many books would it be best to give?" 買甚麽好呢? "What would it be best to buy?" 你說給多少錢好呢? "Tell (me), how much money would it be best to give?"

Lesson 20

1	2	3	4	5
方	法	研	究	語

6	7	8	9	10
百	千	萬	開	主

1. 方　fāng*　　(1) region, place; (2) method, way; (3) (a surname)

2. 法　fǎ, fá*　　method, way
　　　Fǎ, Fà*　　France, French

3. 研　yán*　　study, research

4. 究　jiū*　　investigate

5. 語　yǔ*　　speech, language

6. 百　bǎi　　hundred

7. 千　qiān　　thousand

8. 萬　wàn　　(1) 10,000; (2) (a surname)

9. 開　kāi　　(1) open; (2) start, get under way (ships, vehicles, etc.); (3) put in operation, operate (vehicles); (4) away (as a pòstverb)

10. 主　zhǔ*　　chief, master

11. 會　huì　　(1) meeting; (2) organization, society

12. 所　suǒ*　　office, bureau, institute

13. 上　shàng　　last (e.g. before yuè 'month')

14. 下　xià　　next (e.g. before yuè 'month')

204

Special Combinations

1. 比方　　bǐfang　　　　(1) (for) example ; (2) if (for instance)

2. 比方説　bǐfang shuō　(1) for example ; (2) if (for instance)

3. 地方　　dìfang　　　　(1) place, locality, space ; (2) local

4. 地主　　dìzhǔ　　　　landowner, landlord

5. 東方　　Dōngfāng　　the East, the Orient

6. 法國　　Fǎguo, Fàguo　France

7. 法文　　Fǎwén, Fàwén　French (language and literature)

8. 法子　　fázi　　　　　method, plan, way (of doing something)

9. 方法　　fāngfǎ　　　method, plan, way (of doing something)

10. 方言　　fāngyán　　　regional speech, dialect

11. 國語　　Guóyǔ　　　National Language (replaced by pǔtōnghuà ‘Com-
　　　　　　　　　　　　mon speech’ in the PRC, but still used in
　　　　　　　　　　　　Taiwan)

12. 會長　　huìzhǎng　　head (of an organization with huì as part of its
　　　　　　　　　　　　name)

13. 開車　　kāi chē　　　drive a car (or other vehicle)

14. 開會　　kāi huì　　　hold a meeting, attend a meeting

15. 開學　　kāixué　　　start school

16. 看法　　kànfǎ　　　way of looking at something, viewpoint, opinion

17. 離開　　líkai　　　　leave (a place) (RV)

18. 没法子　méi fázi　　(1) lack a way of doing something ; (2) it can’t
　　　　　　　　　　　　be done ; (3) there’s no help for it.

19. 民主　　mínzhǔ　　　(1) democracy ; (2) democratic

20. 上(個)月　shàng(ge) yuè　last month

21. 所長　　suǒzhǎng　　head (of an organization with suǒ as part of
　　　　　　　　　　　　its name)

22. 外來語　wàiláiyǔ　　word adopted by one language from another, loan
　　　　　　　　　　　　word

23. 文法　　wénfǎ　　　grammar

24. 西方　　Xīfāng　　　the West, the Occident

25. 下(個)月　xià(ge) yuè　next month

26. 學會   xuéhuì   (1) to master by studying (RV); (2) scholarly
                                organization

27. 研究   yánjiu   (1) investigate, study, do research on;
                                (2) investigation, study

28. 研究生   yánjiushēng graduate student, student in a graduate or re-
                                search institute

29. 研究所   yánjiusuǒ   (1) research institute; (2) school

30. 以來   yǐlái   since, during the past (occurs at the end of a
                                phrase; often paired with cóng 'from' at
                                the beginning of a phrase)

31. 語法   yǔfǎ   grammar

32. 語文   yǔwén   language (and literature)

33. 語言   yǔyán   (1) language; (2) philology

34. 語言學   yǔyánxué   linguistics

35. 語言學家   yuyánxuéjiā linguistic scientist, linguist

36. 主人   zhǔrén   (1) master; (2) host

37. 主因   zhǔyīn   chief reason

Who's Who and What's What

1. 千字文   Qiān Zi Wén   Thousand Character Classic(a book of 1,000
                                different characters, each occurring only once, used as one
                                of the basic beginning textbooks in pre-modern Chinese
                                schools

2. 遠東學會   Yuǎndōng Xuéhuì Far Eastern Association (predecessor
                                of the Association for Asian Studies, the leading organ-
                                ization in the United States of scholars interested in
                                Asia)

3. 中國語文   Zhōngguo Yǔwén   Chinese Language (leading linguistic jour-
                                nal published in the People's Republic of China; a journal
                                with this title is also published in Taiwan)

Exercise 1. Buildups

人不少

外國人不少

研究語言的外國人不少

到東方來研究語言的外國人不少

1. 最近到東方來研究語言的外國人不少

所長

研究所的所長

語言研究所的所長

語言研究所的所長說話

語言研究所的所長對我說話

2. 語言研究所的所長對我說的話我明白

那天是我的生日

那天就是我的生日

我坐船的那天就是我的生日

3. 我坐船走到地中海的那天就是我的生日

Exercise 2. Pitfalls

1. 你們學會是語文學會嗎？
   你們學會了中國語文嗎？

2. 他上個月去。
   他上那兒去。

3. 學說話的時候你最好不要念書。
   學說話的時候多，念書的時候少。

4. 美國的大學最近研究東方語文的人很多。
   美國的大學最近研究東方語文的也很多。

Exercise 3. Illustrative Sentences (Chinese)

1. 他是語言研究所的研究生.

2. 他學不會中文的主因是因為他不用心念書.

3. 從一九六二年以來他對中國語言裏頭的外來語很有研究.

4. 車沒法子開了因為車門開不開了.

5. 西方語言學家最近到東方來研究語言的不少.

6. 我本來不想念文言, 可是沒法子.

7. 他說他下月走. 我看他下月走不了.

8. 第一年學中文學說話的時候多, 念書的時候少.

9. 中國語文研究所的所長對外國研究生太好了.

10. 中英字典裏頭沒有比這本好的了.

11. 研究中國方言的，最好的我想是張
會長了.

12. 萬先生是大地主. 這個地方的水田、
山地都是他的.

13. 我的看法，書念的最好的是張一文
了. 比方說，說話、寫字、念書、
甚麼的年年都是他第一.

14. 你是研究甚麼的？

15. 在那個學校開會甚麼的，他們用中
文的時候多.

16. 民國三十八年遠東學會的會長是中
國人還是外國人？

17. 他到美國念書以來就不說中國話了.

18. 他說没法子買人民民主國家人口研
究那本書.

19. 要念大學的學生在中學的時候要念
第二外國語.

20. 你去年在那兒過的生日？

21. 他是前天離開法國到東方去的.

22. <u>千字文</u>是文言的，<u>中國語文</u>是白話的.

23. <u>法文文法</u>那本書不過三塊錢.

24. 湖南有很多人不說國語，還是說湖南方言.

25. 你學寫中國字學的會學不會？

26. 語言學家用甚麼方法研究語言學？

27. 上月語言研究所買了一千五百塊錢的書.

28. 小學、中學都是九月四號開學.

29. 你說先學語法後學說話好，還是先學說話後學語法好？

30. 我手邊没有書. 我的書都在家裏呢.

31. 他没有能力寫小說，所以他寫的小說都不好.

32. 這裏的地土很不好，四邊都是山，
所以<u>張</u>先生那塊地没有人買.

33. 他就念過中學. 他説他念過大學.
可見他是説大話呢.

34. <u>高</u>先生要用一個用人. <u>高</u>太太説不
用.

35. 上次我在火車上看見他. 那是頭次.

Exercise 4. Dialogues

1. 方: 你是學甚麽的？
萬: 我研究中國文學還有中國語言.
方: 研究中國語言就是學説中國話
嗎？
5 萬: 不是. 我是研究中國語言的語
法.
方: 語法就是文法嗎？
萬: 語法就是文法.
方: 你研究方言還是研究國語？

萬：我研究國語.

方：近來是不是有很多語言學家在
　　這兒研究語言學？

萬：也不太多.

2. 南：你們開學了嗎？

錢：沒有呢. 你們呢？

南：我們上個月就開學了.

錢：你還是念文學嗎？

5 南：是的，我近來又念法文了.

錢：法文先生是法國人嗎？

南：是法國人. 他是研究中國語言
　　的.

3. 方：我最近要到法國去.

文：你甚麼時候走？

方：我下月就離開這兒. 我想先到
　　英國去看看，然後到法國去.

5 文：你到法國學甚麼？

方：學法國文學.

4. 路：<u>邊有民</u>，你為甚麼要念法文呢？

邊：因為我們學校高中二的學生都要念第二外國語，所以我不能不念法文．我本來不想念．没法子．

5

路：你會説法國話了嗎？

邊：我還没學會呢．

5. 萬：你念過<u>千字文</u>嗎？

高：念過．我小的時候念過．

6. 馬：<u>文</u>小姐會開車了．

南：是嗎？你在甚麼地方看見他開車了？

馬：有一天我路過民國路，在民國路看見他開車過去了．

5

7. 萬：你們學中國話是用甚麼方法？

華：我們學中國話的法子是先學文法然後學對話．

8. 田： 西方國家是不是都用英文？

高： 雖然不是都用英文，可是英文
很有用．在西方國家開會甚麼
的，他們用英文的時候多．

5 田： 所以東方、西方國家的學校有
很多從小學就有英文．

9. 白： 萬先生為甚麼離開語言研究所
了？

張： 因為近來所長對他不太好，所
以萬先生不在這兒了．

5 白： 萬先生在那兒呢？

張： 他最近在語言學會呢．

白： 萬先生對方言很有研究．

張： 我說萬先生是最好的語言學家．

白： 萬先生走了以後研究所裏沒有
10   比他好的了．

10. 華： 馬大能是地主嗎？

路： 是，他是個大地主．這兒所有

的水田都是他的. 他還有三百
多條水牛.

華: 人家説他很有錢. 他有五十萬
是不是 ?

5 路: 可能.

華: 他們家有很多工人、用人是不
是 ?

路: 是. 他們用錢用的很多. 一個
月過日子要用三千多塊錢呢.

11. 毛: <u>張</u>先生， 你説你今天到學校來
是最後一次了. 你為甚麼以後
不到學校來了呢 ?

張: 我不到學校來，主因是因為我
5 這兩三年以來天天給學校寫書.
我寫的太多了. 我以後不想寫
了.

12. 方: 你到遠東大學去研究甚麼 ?

錢: 我想研究中文裏的外來語.

方： 為甚麼你要研究外來語呢？

錢： 因為研究外來語的研究生不
多,所以我要研究研究.

13. 高： 這次的會比方說人少也開嗎？

白： 要是人太少了就不開了.

高： 會長說過了嗎？

白： 他沒明說. 我的看法，人少不
會開.

14. 方： 從前遠東學會年年開會嗎？

南： 是的. 他們一年開一次會.

15. 錢： 張大生，你是甚麼時候到毛會
長這兒來的？

張： 我是前年來的.

錢： 毛會長、毛太太對你都很好是
不是？

張： 是的. 我的主人對我們用人太
好了.

16. 文： 我姐姐說明天上西山去，可是
　　 我不想去．

　　萬： 你不想去為甚麼還要去？

　　文： 因為我姐姐要去．

5 萬： 我們家很民主．比方要上山，
　　 我們家所有的人都在一塊兒開
　　 會．大家都想上山，我們就去．
　　 要是有人不想去，我們就不去．

Exercise 5. Narratives

1. 我是美國人．在中國念書．我是中
國語文研究所的研究生．這個研究
所的研究生很多．有的研究中國文
學，有的研究中國語言．中國語言
5 裏有研究國語的，也有研究中國方
言的．我是研究國語．有人說研究
語言的方法最好是先研究語法，所
以我很用心研究語法．我是前年到
中國來的，今年過年以前我要離開

中國了. 離開以後我要去日本, 研
究日本語文.

2. 美國的大學最近研究東方語文的很
多. 有研究中國語文的, 有研究日
本語文的. 研究的方法, 有的是先
學說話, 然後念書. 有的是一邊學
⁵說話, 一邊念書. 我想還是一邊學
說話一邊念書是最好的方法.

3. 一個中國人從小的時候就在外國,
從來沒到過中國. 他到過英國、法
國、美國、日本. 他會說英國話,
也會說法國話, 就是不會說中國話.
⁵他很想說中國話, 所以最近天天學
國語. 他說他下個月要上國語學會
學國語呢.

4. 我們學校今天開學了. 我本來想開
車去上學, 可是我的車門開不開了.

我没法子開車，所以我就走路到學校.

5. 高先生是東方語言研究所所長. 他是語言學家，對語言學很有研究. 他最近研究中國語言. 他寫的書很多. 有中國語法、國語裏的外來語、山西方言、甚麽的. 看過的人都説他書寫的好.

6. 在民主國家裏,人民是國家的主人. 美國、英國、法國都是西方的民主國家. 東方也有民主國家，可是很少.

7. 方先生是大地主. 這個地方的水田都是他的. 萬先生也是地主. 在這個地方有很多山地. 有一次方先生對萬先生説:"我的水田可以用河水, 你的山地没有法子用河水，所以我的看法，水田比山地好."萬先生説:

"是的, 你的看法很對. 不過, 比方
說有一天河水太大了, 所有的水田
都是大河了, 那個時候山地就比水
田好了."

8. 文明書店在大學的對門. 書店的主
人是中國人. 從前他去過法國、英
國. 他會法文、英文. 他開書店的
主因, 為的是能看書, 又因為他要
研究中國語文. 大學裏有不少外國
學生, 都是研究中國語文的. 他們
天天到書店來, 一來是看書, 二來
是他們有一個「六一學會」.會長就
是書店的主人, 所以他們就用書店
的地方開會.「六一學會」是研究中
文的. 因為第一次開會的年月日是
中華民國三十二年六月一日, 所以
他們說這個會是「六一學會」.有的
時候他們要到書店去, 他們不說要

到書店去，他們説到「六一」去.
「六一」裏頭有很多中文報. <u>人民日</u>
<u>報</u>、<u>中華日報</u>、<u>華美日報</u>都有. 還
有<u>中文學報</u>、<u>三民月報</u>、<u>人民文學</u>、
5 甚麼的. 這個學會的目的是研究中
國語文.

9. 我現在是高中學生. 我念初小的時
候天天用心念生字. 最初一天念五
個生字,以後一天念七八個,到了高
小我會兩千五百多個字了. 從念初
5 中以來就學文法了，没法子天天念
生字了，可是書裏頭的生字也不多
了.

10. 我是美國人,來中國研究中國語文.
我是上個月來的. 我想後年離開中
國. 離開中國以前，我要學會中文,
因為中文很有用.

11. 我姐姐説:"一會兒<u>毛文美</u>小姐到我
    們家來看我." 我姐姐還説<u>毛文美</u>來
    了以後我們大家一塊兒到海邊去.

12. 我家就在中山路. 因為中山路是一
    條大路, 所以天天過路的人很多.
    有學生、工人, 也有買賣人, 也有
    坐車的, 也有走路的.

13. <u>國家</u>   <u>人口</u>
    中國   七萬萬一千六百萬
                        (一九六一年)
    美國   一萬萬八千七百萬
5   (一九六二年)
    日本   九千四百萬
                        (一九六一年)
    法國   四千七百萬
                        (一九六二年)
10 英國   四千三百萬
                        (一九六一年)

14. 我到學校念書以前，我在家裏念過千字文，所以我在學校裏國文第一.

15. 西方國家没有人力車. 東方國家現在有人力車的也很少了.

16. 東海書店在中山路一百二十五號，離我家不遠. 有時候我到那裏去買中國小説. 有一天白天我路過東海書店，書店裏有一個人對我説:"書店裏來了很多小説，都是文言的." 我説:"文言的小説我看不了. 我就能看白話的." 書店人説，有一本南海是白話的. 我説:"好,我買一本."

17. 有人對馬先生説:"你為甚麼不買車呢?"馬先生説:"我很想買，可是我的工錢都用在過日子了.我買不了."

18. 上月我過生日，田先生給我買了一本字典. 明天是二月五號，是田先生生日. 我想給他買兩本小説.

19. 我下月要買車. 這是我初次買車,
所以我要研究研究買甚麼車好呢.

20. 學校開學了.學生都在學校裏買書.
今天、明天、後天都可以買. 後天
是最後一天. 今天我没有錢, 不能
買, 所以我明後天要買書. 要不然
就買不到了.

21. 我在馬路上看見張小姐. 他説他下
月就要到中國去. 他為甚麼到中國
去, 雖然他没明説, 可是我心裏明
白, 他是到遠東大學看文先生去.

22. 從美國坐船到英國, 最多是六七天
就到了. 上月有一條船走了很多日
子還没到英國.這條船是先到日本,
後來又到中國, 然後到英國.

23. 有人説張先生買的刀是日本刀. 張

先生本人説不是. 張先生説:"刀上
有年月日, 是中國的年月日. 可見
是中國刀, 不是日本刀."

24. 去年我買了一條水牛. 這條水牛本
來是高先生的. 高先生因為日用没
有錢, 所以賣水牛. 我買了這條水
牛以後又買了一塊水田. 我又有水
₅牛, 又有水田.

25. 那張中國地圖很好, 可是地圖上的
説明就有中文, 没有英文, 所以外
國學生没法子看.

Exercise 6. Illustrative Sentences (English)

1. He's a graduate student at the Linguistics Research Institute.

2. The main reason (why) he can't master Chinese is that he doesn't apply himself to his studies.

3. Since 1962 he's done a lot of research on loan words in Chinese.

4. There's no way of driving the car because the car door can't be opened.

5. Quite a few Western linguists have gone to the Orient recently to do research on languages.

6. I hadn't originally planned to study literary Chinese, but there was no way out of it.

7. He said he's leaving next month. I don't think he'll be able to leave next month.

8. In the first year of studying Chinese, more time is spent on learning to speak than on learning to read.

9. The head of the Chinese Language Research Institute is very nice to foreign graduate students.

10. Among Chinese-English dictionaries there is none better than this one.

11. Of those who do research on Chinese dialects, the best is, I think, Association President Zhang.

12. Mr. Wan is a big landlord. All the irrigated fields and hilly land in this region are his.

13. In my opinion the one who is the best in his studies is Zhang Yiwen. For example, in speaking, writing, reading, and so on, he is always first year after year.

14. What are you doing research on?

15. In holding assemblies, and so on, they use Chinese most of the time [lit. the time of their using Chinese is more] at that school.

16. Was the president of the Far Eastern Association in 1949 a Chinese or a foreigner?

17. Since coming to the United States to study, he has stopped speaking Chinese.

18. He says there's no way of buying Population Studies of the Peoples' Democracies.

19. Students who want to attend college must study a second foreign language when (they are) in middle school.

20. Where did you celebrate your birthday last year?

21. He left France for the Orient day before yesterday.

22. The Thousand Character Classic is in the literary style, Chinese Language in the vernacular style.

23. [The book] Grammar of French is only $3.

24. In Hunan there are a lot of people who do not speak the National Language but still speak the Hunan dialect.

25. Can you learn to write Chinese characters?

26. What techniques do linguists use to do research in linguistics?

27. Last month the Linguistic Research Institute bought $1,500 worth of books.

28. Elementary and middle schools both start [school] on September 4th.

29. Do you think it would be better to study grammar first and then learn to speak or to learn to speak first and then study grammar?

30. I don't have any books here [at hand]. My books are all at home.

31. He doesn't have the ability to write novels, so none of the novels he's written are any good.

32. The land here is very poor. It's hilly all around, so no one wants to buy that plot [of land] belonging to Mr. Zhang.

33. He's attended only middle school. He says he attended college. Obviously he exaggerates.

34. Mr. Gao wants to hire a servant. Mrs. Gao says there's no need to.

35. I saw him previously on the train. That was the first time.

Lesson 21

1	2	3	4	5
懂	畫	活	叫	請

6	7	8	9	10
問	誰	現	名	古

1. 懂 dǒng — understand

2. 畫 huà — (1) draw, paint ; (2) drawing, painting

3. 活 huó — (1) live ; (2) be alive

4. 叫 jiào — (1) call, cry, shout ; (2) call (someone by such-and-such name); (3) summon, let, cause to, ask (someone) to do something ; (4) be called

5. 請 qǐng — (1) ask, invite ; (2) please (do something)

6. 問 wèn — ask, inquire (refers specifically to questions)

7. 誰? shéi, shuí? who?

8. 現 xiàn* — (1) appear, be revealed ; (2) now, the present

9. 名 míng* — (1) a name ; (2) famous (before a noun)

10. 古 gǔ — (1) ancient ; (2) (a surname)

11. 號 hào — (1) courtesy name ; (2) have the courtesy name of …

12. 字 zì — (1) courtesy name ; (2) have the courtesy name of …

Special Combinations

1. 大水 dàshuǐ a flood

2.	地名(兒)	dìmíng(r)	(1) place-name; (2) address
3.	對話	duìhuà	dialogue, conversation
4.	古典	gǔdiǎn	classical
5.	古今	gǔ-jīn*	ancient and modern
6.	畫兒	huàr	painting, drawing
7.	畫報	huàbào	illustrated periodical, pictorial (magazine)
8.	畫畫(兒)	huà huà(r)	paint pictures, draw pictures, make illustrations
9.	畫家	huàjiā	painter (an artist)
10.	畫圖	huà tú	make a chart (map, plan, etc.)
11.	會話	huìhuà	conversation, dialogue
12.	會所	huìsuǒ	office (of an organization)
13.	叫車	jiào chē	summon a car
14.	叫門	jiào mén	knock on the door
15.	看懂	kàndǒng	(read and) understand (RV)
16.	名人	míngrén	famous person, celebrity
17.	名子	míngzi	name (of a thing), given name (of a person)
18.	名字	míngzi	given name (of a person)
19.	山水畫(兒)	shānshuǐ huà(r)	landscape (painting)
20.	請問	qǐng wèn	may I ask? Excuse me, …
21.	人名(字)	rén míng(zi)	name of a person
22.	生活	shēnghuó	(1) life; (2) livelihood; (3) live
23.	圖畫	túhuà	(1) illustration, painting, chart; (2) art (as a school subject)
24.	外號(兒)	wàihào(r)	nickname
25.	問…好	wèn…hǎo	best regards to…, say hello to…, ask after…
26.	問路	wèn lù	inquire about the way
27.	現在	xiànzài	now, at present
28.	小名(兒)	xiǎomíng(r)	childhood name
29.	學問	xuéwen	learning, erudition, scholarship, knowledge

30. 學名(兒)   xuémíng(r)   school name, name given after starting to
study

31. 以外   yǐwài   beyond, apart from, besides, except for
(used after a phrase)

32. 有名   yǒumíng   famous

33. 字畫(兒)   zìhuà(r)   character-scroll

Who's Who and What's What

1. 張大千   Zhāng Dàqiān   name of a well-known Chinese painter
2. 人民畫報 Rénmín Huàbào   China Pictorial [lit. People's Pictorial]
(a pictorial magazine published in Peking in Chinese, English, and other languages)
3. 生活畫報 Shēnghuó Huàbào   Life (pictorial magazine published in the
United States)
4. 四書   Sì Shū   The Four Books (a Chinese classic containing
the sayings of Confucius and other early philosophers)
5. 萬里長城 Wànlǐ Cháng Chéng   [Ten Thousand Mile] Great Wall
(see maps pp. 31 and 117)

Exercise 1. Buildups

這是馬小姐
這是馬小姐的畫兒
1. 這是馬小姐畫的畫兒

有用
這本書有用
這本書很有用
這本書對我很有用
2. 這本書對我是很有用的

有學問

他有學問

他很有學問

他是很有學問的人

3. 他是一個很有學問的人

Exercise 2. Pitfalls

1. 他問你去不去.
   他問你姐姐好.

2. 這是高校長的書.
   這是校長買的書.

3. 請你給我兩塊錢.
   請你給我買地圖.

Exercise 3. Illustrative Sentences (Chinese)

1. 這是高小姐畫的畫兒.

2. 校長給學生說念書的方法.

3. 他是用中文說的, 還是用英文說的?

4. 文言文我看的懂, 可是我寫不了.

5. 中國人懂國語的人多, 懂方言的人少.

6. 你的名字、地名請你給我寫下來.

7. 現在我到遠東大學去開會.

8. 人家給他一個外號叫「活字典」.

9. 生活畫報是英文的. 人民畫報有中文的, 也有英文的.

10. 古先生對那個學生的看法是那個學生是學校裏最好的學生了.

11. 這個東西叫甚麼名子？…那個東西叫人力車.

12. 他叫我買一本古典文學書.

13. 請你問古先生好.

14. 毛以文他雖然沒學過圖畫, 可是他很會畫圖、畫畫兒.

15. 張大文的學問很好. 雖然馬有為的學問也好, 不過還是張大文比他好.

16. 你去看看誰叫門？…是問路的.

17. 張大千是中國有名的畫家.

18. 馬先生小名叫「小牛」，學名「九城」，字「海山」，號「一民」，還有一個外號叫「萬能先生」.

19. 我今天買了兩張畫. 一張是馬先生畫的山水畫，一張是他寫的字畫.

20. 你看上下文. 在這兒「東海」是人名，不是地名.

21. 張家口離萬里長城很近.

22. 請問，語言研究會的會所在那裏？

23. 對話以外那本書裏還有甚麼？

24. 我在生活書店買了一本古今名人山水畫、三本中國畫報、還有一本四書.

25. 這個會話的語法你都懂嗎？

26. 今年的大水比去年的還大.

27. 我要走了. 請你給我叫個車，好不好？

28. 他寫的那本中文文法我看不懂.

29. 你們大學有多少研究生研究語言學？

30. 比方説我有車，我就天天坐車上學.

31. 我下個月要離開法文學會.

32. 那個地方我不想去. 比方你是我，你也不想去.

33. 那本書裏有兩百多張圖畫.

34. 要是你們還説話，我就没法子念書了.

35. 那個大學的研究生有三百多人.

Exercise 4. Dialogues

1. 萬：張大千是有名的畫家. 他的畫兒你看見過嗎？

方：看見過. 我有他的畫兒，我有三張他畫的山水畫. 山水畫以外還有一張他寫的字畫.

5

2. 張：請問，你是<u>馬大文</u>先生嗎？

馬：是，我就是<u>馬大文</u>．你是…?

張：我是<u>張有方</u>．

馬：<u>張</u>先生，你好？

5 張：好．甚麼時候離開美國的？

馬：我是上月八號離開美國的．

張：離開美國就到中國來了嗎？

馬：沒有．我是先到日本然後到中
國來的．

10 張：<u>萬</u>先生說你的中國學問很好．
中國古典文學你學過了嗎？

馬：學過．不過學的很少．

張：你能用文言文寫東西嗎？

馬：不能．我看的懂，可是我寫不了．

3. 錢：你學甚麼？

張：我學語言學．

錢：語言學就是學語言是不是？

張：不是．語言學是研究語言，不
5 　　就是學語言．

錢：我明白了．現在有很多外國人
　　學中國語言是不是？

張：是的．很多人學國語．

錢：為甚麼都學國語呢？

5　張：因為中國人說國語的人多，所
　　以大家都學國語．

錢：你們學國語用甚麼方法？

張：我們先學對話然後學語法．

錢：對話是不是會話？

10　張：是．對話就是會話．

4. 田：我們國文先生外號叫「活字典」．

萬：為甚麼叫「活字典」呢？

田：要是我們問他字典上的字他不
　　用看字典，所以大家叫他「活
5　　字典」．

萬：是不是馬書城先生？

田：是的．他很有名．他對方言很
　　有研究．你見過他嗎？

萬： 見過. 在遠東學會開會的時候
我見過他一次. 要是你看見他,
就説我問他好.

田： 好的.

5. 錢： 請問你有<u>生活畫報</u>嗎?

邊： 有. 誰要看?

錢： 我想看.

邊： 你不會英文, 能看那本畫報嗎?

5 錢： 我雖然看不懂英文, 可是我要
看看那本畫報上的圖畫.

6. 錢： 語言學會開會, 你去不去?

邊： 甚麽時候?

錢： 下月五號.

邊： 好的. 我去.

5 錢： 我們請了一個名人來. 他給我
們説中國語言裏的外來語.

邊： 會所地名請你給我寫下來. 我
以前没去過. 遠不遠?

錢： 不很遠． 可是你是頭次去． 最
好還是叫個車去，要不然你要
問問路．

7. 田： 人名字都寫了嗎？

高： 寫了．

田： 請你給我看看⋯家長的名字你
也寫上了． 請你還要寫一次．
5   就寫學生的名字，不要寫家長
的名字．

8. 英： 門口兒有人叫門． 你去看看是
誰．

文： 是張天有． 他到我們門口兒來
問我遠東書店在那兒． 他現在
5   走了． 他叫我問你好．

英： 他是要買書嗎？

文： 不是買書． 他說遠東書店請他
去畫圖．

英： 他們近來生活好不好？

10 文： 我看比以前好的多了．

9. 古: 有一本很好的文法書你看了嗎?

   毛: 甚麼名子?

   古: 叫古今文法研究.

   毛: 你要買嗎?

   5 古: 我想買. 比方説你買我就不買了.

10. 張: 你兒子小名兒叫甚麼?

    文: 我兒子小名兒叫小毛兒.

    張: 學名兒呢?

    文: 叫大文.

11. 馬: 我在人民畫報上看見一張畫兒是萬里長城.

    毛: 萬里長城很長是不是?

    馬: 是.因為很長所以叫萬里長城.

12. 白: 你們那兒是不是有一條大河?

    文: 是. 我們那兒那條大河年年有大水.

Exercise 5. Narratives

1. 毛先生、白先生都是外國人. 都會
說中國話. 毛先生説的很好，白先
生説的不好. 有一天他們兩個人到
一個地方看畫. 那裏的畫很多. 有
5 古今名人的山水畫、字畫、甚麼的.
還有一個畫家在那裏畫畫兒. 毛先
生對那個畫家説:"你畫的很好. 我
想請你給我畫一張山水畫可以嗎?"
那個畫家説:"可以, 可以." 白先生
10 也對畫家説:"我看那張字畫也很好.
請你給我畫一張字畫." 畫家説:"我
們説'寫字畫,'不説'畫字畫.' 我給
你寫一張字畫."

2. 前天我到語文學會去開會. 我是開
車去的. 開到一條小路上，我的車
不能走了. 我就想叫車去, 可是這
條路上沒有車. 我沒法子. 就走路.
5 語文學會在東山路. 那個地方我沒

去過，我走一會兒就問路，走一會
兒就問路，問了很多次. 我到了語
文學會人家都來了，都開會了.

3. 中國人有很多名字. 先有一個小名.
念書的時候有學名. 這兩個名字以
外有一個「號」，還有「字」. 比方說張
先生小名叫「大牛」，學名叫「文田」，
5 號叫「一山」，字「文遠」. 要是叫他，
最好叫他「一山」、「文遠」都可以. 不
能叫他「大牛」，也不要叫他「文田」.

4. 古長木從小學到中學都很用心學圖
畫. 後來在大學就研究畫畫兒. 現
在他給生活畫報畫畫兒，也畫圖.
是一個有名的畫家.

5. 叫門，叫門，是誰叫門？
是我，是我，是我叫門.
為甚麼叫門？ 為甚麼叫門？
我來看看用心念書的人，
5 我來看看用心念書的人.

6. 田先生是一個很有學問的人．他現
在在中國文學研究所研究中國的古
典文學．他説他從研究古典文學以
來買了很多中國古書——有四書甚麼
的．有的看的懂，有的看不懂，因
為那都是古時候的語文，現在的人
没法子都懂．

7. 我想買一本中文書．最好書裏有語
言學家的人名，也有現在中國語文
的書名，也有中國地方的地名．要
是有這本書，對我是很有用的，因
為我現在研究中國方言．

8. 中國有一個名畫家，他的名字叫張
大千．他畫的畫兒有很多是山水畫．
他雖然不懂法文，可是他去過法國．
他去法國的主因是去看法國的一個
名畫家．法國的名畫家對張大千畫
兒的看法是張大千的畫兒在東方可
以説是第一了．

9. 中國語文學會的會所從前在一個大
學裏. 今年不在那兒了. 今年的會
所是在馬先生的書店裏, 因為馬先
生是書店的主人, 也是中文學會的
5會長.

10. 有人説, 因為要有學問所以念書.
也有人説, 因為要生活所以念書.
我説念書為的是要有學問. 有很多
人沒念過書, 他們也有法子生活.

11. 方先生是東方語文研究所的所長.
他説:"很多國家的語言裏都有外來
語." 他又説:"最好的對話就是最好
的文學."

12. 張有文是一個地主. 他有一個兒子
書念的不好, 天天畫畫兒, 可是畫
兒畫的也不好. 人家給他兒子一個
外號叫「大畫家」. 他的兒子在中學
5念書,從開學到現在也沒用心念書.

他的畫報不少. 中華畫報、生活畫
報他都有.

13. 有的國家本來不是民主國家，現在
是民主國家了. 有的國家本來是民
主國家，後來不是民主國家了.

14. 中國的萬里長城是很長的. 因為太
長了，所以名子叫萬里長城，可是
這個長城沒有一萬里.

15. 一個小學生説："我畫的圖畫是火山，
是活火山. 你看山上還有火呢. 這
張畫兒都是水. 你看，是大水."

16. 有一個法國畫家，上個月到東方來，
看見了中國畫、日本畫. 他説："東
方畫有東方畫的畫法，西方畫有西
方畫的畫法. 現在有不少西方人研
究東方畫，也有不少東方人研究西
方畫."

17. 高小姐給了我一本國語會話. 這本書上有兩個很小的字「小英」. 有人問:"是誰的名字? 是高小姐的名字嗎?" 我說不是. 後來又有人說那兩個很小的字是高小姐的小名. 前天我看見高小姐我就問他. 我說:"請問,小英是你的小名嗎?"他没說是, 也没說不是.

18. 你們誰看見馬校長了? 我很多天没看見馬校長了. 要是有人看見他就說我問他好.

Exercise 6. Illustrative Sentences (English)

1. This is a painting done by Miss Gao.
2. The principal told the students how to study [lit. ways of studying].
3. Did he speak in Chinese or English?
4. I can read but not write literature in the classical style.
5. There are more Chinese who understand the National Language than [there are those who] understand the dialects.
6. Please write down your given name and address for me.
7. I'm going to Far Eastern University now to attend a meeting.
8. People have given him the nickname "Living Dictionary."

9. <u>Life</u> is in English.   <u>China Pictorial</u> is in Chinese and English.

10. In Mr. Gu's opinion [regarding that student], that student is the best [student] in the school.

11. What's this thing called? ··· That [thing] is called a rickshaw.

12. He asked me to buy a book on classical literature.

13. Please give my best to Mr. Gu.

14. Although Mao Yiwen has never studied drawing, he's very good at making charts and illustrations.

15. Zhang Dawen is very learned. Ma Youwei is quite learned too, but Zhang Dawen is even more so.

16. Go see who's knocking at the door. ··· It's someone asking the way.

17. Zhang Daqian is a famous Chinese artist.

18. Mr. Ma's childhood name is Little Ox, his school name is Nine Cities, his <u>zì</u> is Seas and Mountains, and his <u>hào</u> is One People.   He also has a nickname "Mr. Can Do Anything."

19. I bought two paintings today.   One is a landscape by Mr. Ma, the other a character scroll by him.

20. Look at the context.   Here Eastern Sea is a personal name, not a place-name.

21. Kalgan is close to the Great Wall.

22. Excuse me, where is the office of the Linguistic Research Society?

23. What does that book have besides dialogue?

24. I bought a copy of <u>Landscape Paintings by Famous People of Past and Present</u>, three copies of <u>China Illustrated</u>, and a copy of the <u>Four Books</u> at Life Bookstore.

25. Do you understand all the grammar of this dialogue?

26. This year's flood is even greater than last year's.

27. I'd like to leave.   Would you please call a cab for me?

28. I can't understand his <u>Grammar of Chinese.</u>

29. How many graduate students at your university are studying linguistics?

30. If I had a car, I'd go to school by car every day.

31. I'm going to leave the French Language Association next month.

32. I don't want to go to that place.   If you were me, you wouldn't want to go either.

33. There are over two hundred illustrations in that book.

34. If you keep on talking, I won't be able to study.

35. There are over three hundred graduate students in that university.

Lesson 22

1	2	3	4	5
早	晚	難	容	易

6	7	8	9	10
再	知	道	原	省

1. 早 zǎo   (1) early;   (2) long ago, long since;   (3) morning (in compounds)

2. 晚 wǎn   (1) late; (2) evening (in compounds)

3. 難 nán   difficult, hard

4. 容 róng*   (1) contain, accommodate; (2) easy

5. 易 yì*   easy

6. 再 zài*   once more, again

7. 知 zhī*   know

8. 道 dào*   (1) road; (2) way, doctrine, principle

9. 原 yuán*   (1) source, origin; (2) a plain; (3) originally, actually

10. 省 shěng   province

11. 子 zǐ*   seed, kernel

Special Combinations

1. 不會的 búhuìde   (that's) not likely

247

2. 高原　　　gāoyuán　　　plateau

3. 難過　　　nánguò　　　(1) difficult to pass, hard to get through;
　　　　　　　　　　　　　(2) sad, distressed

4. 難看　　　nánkàn　　　(1) ugly; (2) hard to read

5. 難念　　　nánniàn　　　(1) ugly; (2) hard to read

6. 難説　　　nánshuō　　　difficult to say, hard to predict

7. 年會　　　niánhuì　　　annual meeting

8. 前後　　　qián-hòu　　　(1) before and after, before or after; (2) first
　　　　　　　　　　　　　and last, altogether; (3) about

9. 日語　　　Rìyǔ*　　　Japanese language

10. 日子難過　rìzi nánguò　(making a) living is hard

11. 容不下　　róngbuxià　　can't hold, can't accommodate

12. 容易　　　róngyi　　　easy

13. 省城　　　shěngchéng　provincial capital

14. 省長　　　shěngzhǎng　provincial governor (used before 1949)

15. 時報　　　Shíbào　　　Times (in names of newspapers)

16. 土話　　　tǔhuà　　　dialect, patois (more restricted in area than
　　　　　　　　　　　　　fāngyán)

17. 晚報　　　wǎnbào　　　evening newspaper

18. 晚會　　　wǎnhuì　　　evening meeting, evening party

19. 晚上　　　wǎnshang　　evening

20. 為了　　　wèile　　　for, because (of), in order to, for the sake of

21. 英語　　　Yīngyǔ*　　English language

22. 原來　　　yuánlái　　　(1) originally; (2) actually, indeed, as a matter
　　　　　　　　　　　　　of fact

23. 原因　　　yuányīn　　　reason

24. 原子　　　yuánzǐ　　　atom

25. 原子能　　yuánzǐnéng　atomic energy

26. 再不然　　zàiburán　　otherwise, in that case

27. 再見　　　zàijiàn　　　see again, goodbye

28. 早上   zǎoshang   morning, forenoon
29. 早晚   zǎo-wǎn   (1) morning and evening ; (2) sooner or later
30. 知道   zhīdao   know
31. 中西   Zhōng-Xī   China and the West, Sino-Western

Exercise 1. Buildups

到這兒來
他到這兒來
他能到這兒來
他不能到這兒來
他能不能到這兒來
他明天能不能到這兒來
他明天能不能到這兒來很難説

1. 他明天能不能到這兒來現在很難説

寫小説
用方言寫小説
用方言寫的小説
有用方言寫的小説
文學月報有用方言寫的小説

2. 文學月報有用方言寫的小説没有 ?

Exercise 2. Pitfalls

1. 寫這張字畫的學生是個外國人.
   寫這張字畫的原來是個外國人.

2. 我想這本書不好.
   我想太早了不好.

3. 他們是學生的家長.
他們是學原子能的.

4. 對話很有用.
對我很有用.

Exercise 3. Illustrative Sentences (Chinese)

1. 我早就知道他不來.

2. 這兒的地名你寫給他了没有？

3. 我不知道甚麼原因他又要來.

4. 要不是你説今天有晚會，我還不知道呢.

5. 他原來説叫我們早來. 誰知道我們來了他還没來呢.

6. 省長要到這兒來，報上有没有？

7. 到學校給校長問好.

8. 他明天晚上能不能到這兒來現在很難説.

9. 我去的原因是要看我姐姐.

10. 寫這張字畫的原來是個外國人.

11. 學生給校長一個外號叫"萬能先生."

12. 我的車能容五個人，兩個坐前頭，
三個坐後頭.

13. 我初學中國話的時候很難. 後來就
不難了.

14. 現在他們的日子很難過.

15. 原子能在大家天天的生活上很有用.

16. 中國古書外國人念很不容易.

17. 後天原子研究所為了原子能要開會.

18. 那條船很小. 容不下一百人.

19. 他到省城的時候從這裏路過.

20. 文學月報上有用湖南方言寫的小說
没有？

21. 你明天早上可以見省長.

22. 這個小木船容不下十個人.

23. 他說南華日報、上海晚報都不容易看.

24. 我在中西書店買了一本日語文法、一本英語文法.

25. 再見,毛先生.我們明年年會再見.

26. 他們家裏人太多,所以日子很難過.

27. 中國最大的高原在西北.

28. 我早晚要去看看萬里長城.

29. 要是你會說國語,張家口的土話就很容易懂了.

30. 那本書是不是很難念?…我想不會的,是白話文.

31. 我中國字寫不了.寫的太難看了.

32. 中國人過中國年都是在二月一號前後.

33. 我想明年到中國去，再不然就到日本去.

34. 那本書雖然是文言文，可是不難懂，我都會.

35. 要是你看見他請你對他說我問他好.

Exercise 4. Dialogues

1. 邊：今天早上為甚麼文小姐没來呢？
   錢：我也不知道甚麼原因他没來.
   邊：是不是他不知道這兒的路名呢？
   錢：他知道地名. 我前天寫給他了.
   5 邊：一會兒我們去看看他.
   錢：甚麼時候？
   邊：晚上. 再不然我們現在去？
   錢：我說最好還是晚上去. 白天他可能不在家.

2. 馬：後天是<u>張</u>省長的生日．你去不
　　去？

　萬：是嗎？要不是你説他過生日我
　　　還不知道呢．我們一塊兒去好
5 　　　不好？

　馬：好．

　萬：甚麽時候去？

　馬：他原來説叫我們早去，可是我
　　　想太早了不好．因為是晚會，
10　　我們晚上去．

　萬：好．晚上我到你家去．我們一
　　　塊兒去．再見．

　馬：晚上見．

3. 高：<u>馬大文</u>最近要離開省城了．

　毛：他到那兒去？

　高：他先到華南然後到華北．

　毛：他路過華中是不是？

5 高：不知道．現在很難説．

毛：他家裏人也去嗎？

高：就是他一個人去.

毛：馬大文離開省城了，報上有没
　　有？

5 高：有. 人民日報上早就有了. 前
　　天就有了.

4. 馬：張太太來了！請坐. 從那兒來？

張：我從家來看看你們. 近來生活
　　好嗎？

馬：比以前好了. 因為我們馬先生
5 　　給人家畫圖，錢比以前多了.
　　可是我們兒女多，過日子用錢
　　用的多.

張：是的. 人多日用就多. 現在過
　　日子不容易. 不過你比我還好，
10 　兒女還小，用錢的地方還少.
　　你看我那兩個女兒看見東西就
　　要買. 有用没用他們都要. 你
　　說這個日子難過不難過？

5. 毛：你説中文難念不難念？

   白：最初不容易，很難．不過後來
   　　就容易了．

   毛：你念過中國古書嗎？

   白：念過不多．古書很難懂．

   毛：古書，中國人念也不容易．

6. 田：你是研究原子能的嗎？

   文：對了．我是學原子能的．

   田：原子能對人很有用是不是？

   文：是的．現在我們知道原子能對
   　　我們生活上很有用，所以大家
   　　都研究．

   田：前年為了原子能西方國家開會．
   　　過年以後為了原子能又要開會
   　　了．

7. 高：那個過路的小姐是誰？

   南：是白美華小姐．你説他好看嗎？

   高：我説他不好看，太難看了．

8. 毛：中國的高原在西北是不是？

　　馬：是．你要去嗎？

　　毛：我想去．

　　馬：你甚麼時候去？

　　5 毛：現在很難説．早晚我要去一次．

9. 高：毛一文有一個外號．你知道嗎？

　　白：不知道．他外號叫甚麼？

　　高：我也不知道．

10. 方：那條船很大．能容一千二百人．

　　文：人家説那條船容不下一千二百人，就能容九百人．

11. 毛：張小姐，張先生、張太太甚麼時候走？

　　張：過年前後他們就要走．

　　毛：他們是開會去嗎？

　　5 張：是的．他們開年會．

12. 方：你的用人好不好？

毛：我這個用人很好。就是他的話
　　我不懂。他説他們那兒土話。

13. 萬：<u>張</u>小姐為甚麼到現在還没來呢？
　　　他是不是不來了？
　　錢：不會的。他説他來。

14. 萬：你看甚麼報？
　　路：我看<u>華北時報</u>。你呢？
　　萬：我看<u>中華晚報</u>。

15. 毛：<u>張</u>太太，你到那兒去？
　　張：我到中西書店給我女兒買書去。
　　毛：買甚麼書？
　　張：買<u>英語文法</u>還有<u>日語會話</u>。
　5 毛：<u>張</u>小姐英文、日文都念嗎？
　　張：是的。

Exercise 5. Narratives

1. 今天早上<u>張</u>先生對我説："今天晚上
　有一個晚會，你知道嗎？"我説："我

不知道. 這個晚會在甚麼地方開？
為甚麼有這個會？"張先生說:"名畫
家張大千前天來了. 他是從這裏路
過. 他明後天就要走, 所以大家就
5 在今天晚上開個晚會, 一來是大家
見見他, 二來是看看他近來畫的畫
兒. 晚會的地方原來要在生活書店.
因為生活書店地方小, 容不下, 所
以就在文學研究所的會所了."我說:
10 "原來是為了張大千開這個晚會. 我
也去看看他. 從前我在日本見過他.
我去的那天是他的生日."

2. 我明年要念大學了. 上大學要懂第
二外國語.為了念大學我要學日語、
英語.前天早上我到中西書店去,買
了兩本書. 在這一年裏我要用心念
5 書了,要不然可能明年念不了大學.

3. 萬先生研究中國古典文學. 他說:

"古典文學是古時候的語文. 初看的時候又有生字又看不懂. 不過要是用心研究, 就容易明白了."

4. <u>萬為英</u>是現在很有名的畫家. 他念初小的時候, 畫兒就畫的很好. 可是他也很用心念書. 他從初小到高小在學校裏圖畫都是第一. 校長、
5 先生都説以後可能他是個名畫家. 他因為家裏沒有錢, 所以在念初中的時候他就在一個畫報上畫圖, 為的是人家可以給他錢. 他念高中的時候, 一邊念書一邊學畫兒. 要是
10 人家有名畫他都想方法去看. 他初次畫畫兒的時候, 他畫了一張山水畫兒, 他畫的是西湖. 那張畫兒他畫的太好了. 要是你看那張畫兒你就想你是在西湖呢. 現在他是一個
15 大畫家了, 可是他最近畫的畫兒我

看不懂．前天我看見他一張畫兒．
初看是一條牛，再看是一條魚，再
看看原來是個人．我說他現在畫的
畫兒又難看又難懂．人家說他是學
5 現在西方國家最有名的大畫家呢．

5. 中國西北是高原，離海很遠，人口
不多．我從來沒去過高原．明後年
我想去西北高原研究高原人的生活．
然後我就寫一本書，書的名子就是
5 高原人的生活，再不然我在東方晚
報上寫一個小說，天天寫高原人的
生活．可是明後年是不是能去西北
高原呢，現在很難說．要是我明後
年不去，以後早晚我要去一次．

6. 高省長有一年從省城到上海去了．
他去上海的目的是要看看上海工人
的生活．高省長以前說過這省雖然
很小，可是省城裏工人很多．工人的

生活很不好.他們的日子很難過,原
因是他們的工錢太少,不能生活.他
說他那次到上海去看看的目的, 是
要想法子叫工人的生活過的好.

7. 一個外國學生學日文. 他說日文很
難念, 他不想再念了. 他對日文書
說:"再見了, 再見了."

8. 外邊有人叫門. 門裏頭的人問:"是
誰?"門外的人說:"是我. 我是問路
的. 請問有一個很有學問的人, 還
能寫字畫, 他家裏還有很多古今名
人字畫, 是在這裏嗎?"門裏頭的人
說:"請你說他的名字, 看我知道不
知道." 門外的人說:"他的名字是<u>高
一山</u>." 門裏頭的人開開門. 門外頭
的人說:"原來就是你. 你家就在這
裏. 我想買一張字畫. 以後我再來,
我就知道你這個地方了."

9. 萬先生是個畫家. 他看見了東西就能畫, 都畫的很好, 所以人家給他一個外號叫「萬能畫家」.

10. 張先生問我:"原子能學會今年的年會是不是不開了?" 我說:"不會的. 原子能學會的會長前天說過今年的年會要在大學開學的前後開會."

11. 從前毛木不會說國語, 就會說上海土話. 他天天看上海時報, 因為上海時報上有用上海土話寫的小說.

12. 我前天買了一本書.書裏都是現在畫家的名字. 那本書對我們學畫畫兒的很有用.

13. 一月一號是高小姐的生日. 前年一月一號我在高小姐家. 我對高小姐說:"今天是你最好的一個日子. 又過生日又過年."

14. 有一個外國人能看中文書. 他說：
"四書最不容易懂. 我看四書最初看
不懂. 後來有的懂了, 有的還是不
懂. 不懂的地方, 我就問高先生.
⁵最後我都可以看懂了." 他又說:"要
不是我問高先生, 到現在我還不能
都看懂呢."

15. 我要買生活畫報、人民畫報. 有人
說:"那很容易. 學校的對門有一個
書店, 那個書店書、報很多. 你可
以到那個書店去買. 不過學校門口
⁵那條馬路車很多. 你過馬路要小心.
最好你叫用人去買." 我說:"不用.
一會兒, 我去買."

16. 張家在河邊, 離城裏很遠. 前天早
上我從城裏叫車到張家去. 開車的
說:"前邊都是大水. 没法子走了."
所以我就没去.

17. 有一天我問<u>張大文</u>、<u>錢長木</u>：" 你們
學名以外誰有小名 ?"他們都不說他
們有沒有小名.

18. <u>馬</u>先生給我寫的那個人的人名、地
名誰知道都不對, 所以我沒法子到
那個人家裏去.

19. <u>邊</u>先生有很多古今名人小說. 有一
本小說寫的是兩個人的對話. <u>邊</u>先
生說這本小說最好.

20. 有一個外國人在河北省研究中國語
文. 他說他要在中國研究兩年. 今
年先學會話, 明年學中文, 後年離
開中國. 在離開中國以前, 他想去
5看萬里長城.

Exercise 6. Illustrative Sentences (English)

1. I knew long ago that he wasn't coming.
2. Did you write him the address here?
3. I don't know why [lit. what reason] he's coming again.

4. If it hadn't been for your mentioning that there's an evening meeting today, I[still] wouldn't have known about it.

5. He [actually] said that we should come early. Who would have thought [lit. known] that we would get there before he arrived [lit. we came but he had not yet come.]

6. Is it in the newspaper that the provincial governor is coming here?

7. When you get to school, give my best to the principal.

8. It's very difficult to say now whether or not he'll be able to come here tomorrow evening.

9. The reason for my going is to see my sister.

10. The one who wrote this scroll was actually a foreigner.

11. The students have given the principal the nickname "Mr. Can-do-anything."

12. My car can accommodate five people--two in front and three in back.

13. When I first studied Chinese, it was very difficult. Later it wasn't hard any more.

14. They're having a hard time making a living now.

15. Atomic energy is very useful in everyone's daily life.

16. It is very difficult for foreigners to read ancient Chinese books.

17. Day after tomorrow the Atomic Research Institute will hold a meeting on atomic energy.

18. That boat is very small. It can't hold a hundred people.

19. When he went to the provincial capital, he passed through here.

20. Does Literature Monthly have any fiction written in the Hunan dialect?

21. You can see the provincial governor tomorrow morning.

22. This little wooden boat can't hold ten people.

23. He says both the South China Daily and the Shanghai Evening Journal are hard [lit. not easy] to read.

24. I bought a Grammar of Japanese and a Grammar of English at the Sino-Western Bookstore.

25. Goobdye, Mr. Mao. We'll meet again at next year's annual meeting.

26. Their family is too large, so living is hard.

27. China's largest plateau is in the northwest.

28. Sooner or later I intend to go see the Great Wall.

29. If you can speak the National Language, the Kalgan dialect will be easy to understand.

30. Is that book hard to read?··· Not likely. It's in the vernacular language.

31. I can't write Chinese characters. I write very badly [lit. too ugly].

32. The Chinese celebrate Chinese New Year's about the first of February.

33. I plan to go to China next year. If not, I'll go to Japan.

34. Although that book is in the literary style, it isn't hard to understand. I can (read it) all.

35. If you see him, tell him I asked after him.

Supplementary Notes

知道 zhīdao "know" is often reduced to 知 in written style and in fixed expressions such as the proverb 路遠知馬力 "From a long trip one can tell a horse's strength" — i.e. Over a long period one can tell the quality of a person.

Lesson 23

1	2	3	4	5
科	課	考	試	已

6	7	8	9	10
經	表	常	夫	縣

1. 科 kē *   (1) subject (in school), course (of study), curriculum; (2) branch of medicine.

2. 課 kè   (measure for lessons)

3. 考 kǎo   (1) examine, take an examination (for a school or in a subject); (2) examination

4. 試 shì   try, test

5. 已 yǐ *   already

6. 經 jīng *   pass through

7. 表 biǎo   (1) a watch (timepiece); (2) table, list; (3) meter (in names of scientific instruments)

8. 常 cháng *   (1) regular, constant; (2) often

9. 夫 fū *   man

10. 縣 xiàn   county, district

11. 大 dài *   in 大夫 dàifu 'doctor, physician'

Special Combinations

1.	表店	biǎodiàn	watch store
2.	常常	chángcháng	(1) frequently ; (2) constantly
3.	大考	dàkǎo	(1) final examination ; (2) have a final examination
4.	大夫	dàifu	physician, doctor
5.	工夫	gōngfu	(leisure) time
6.	工科	gōngkē	engineering course, engineering department
7.	經過	jīngguo	(1) pass through ; (2) endure ; (3) after (as coverb)
		jīngguò	experience
8.	開刀	kāidāo	perform an operation, have an operation (VO)
9.	考古	kǎogǔ	(1) perform archaeological explorations ; (2) archaeological explorations, archaeology
10.	考古學	kǎogǔxué	archaeology
11.	考古(學)家	kǎogǔ(xué)jiā	archaeologist
12.	考上	kǎoshang	succeed in passing an examination (for admission to a school) (RV)
13.	考試	kǎoshì	(1) examine ; (2) examination
14.	課本(兒)	kèběn(r)	textbook
15.	科學	kēxué	(1) science ; (2) scientific
16.	科學家	kēxuéjiā	scientist
17.	人口表	rénkǒu biǎo	population table
18.	上課	shàng kè	go to class
19.	時常	shícháng	(1) frequently ; (2) constantly
20.	試試看	shìshi kàn	try (it) and see
21.	試用	shìyòng	try out, use on probation
22.	手表	shǒubiǎo	wristwatch
23.	圖表	tú-biǎo	charts and tables
24.	外科	wàikē	surgery

25.	文科	wénkē	liberal arts, humanities
26.	下課	xià kè	leave class
27.	縣城	xiànchéng	district capital
28.	縣長	xiànzhǎng	district magistrate
29.	小兒科	xiǎo'erkē	pediatrics
30.	小考	xiǎokǎo	quiz (N/V)
31.	已經	yǐjing	already
32.	月考	yuèkǎo	monthly examination

Who's Who and What's What

1. 東三省 Dōngsānshěng Manchuria (old name, used especially before the Japanese occupation in 1931, but also used informally after that)

2. 大刀會 Dà Dāo Huì Big Knife Society (antiforeign society whose murder of two missionaries led to German occupation of Shantung Province in 1898)

3. 小刀會 Xiǎo Dāo Huì Small Knife Society (offshoot of the Big Knife Society)

4. 考古學報 Kǎogǔ Xuébaò Chinese Journal of Archaeology

Supplementary Note

誰知道? is used in its literal meaning of "Who knows?" and also has a rhetorical usage with the meaning "Who would have known?" or "Unexpectedly". 我這次考試我想考的一定不好，誰知道考的還很好。 "I thought I had certainly done badly on this exam, but I unexpectedly did rather well".

Exercise 1. Buildups

考上大學

考不上大學

他考不上大學

1. 我的看法他考不上大學

這本書　　　　　　　　　　　　　　　　說外國話

這本書有用　　　　　　　　　　　　　學說外國話

這本書很有用　　　　　　　　　　是學說外國話

這本書在考古上很有用　　　　不是學說外國話

2. 這本書在考古上是很有用的　　3. 學語言學不是學說外國話

Exercise 2. Pitfalls

1. 他開車開的很好.　　　　　　　2. 他考不上大學.

他開刀開的很好.　　　　　　　　　在考古上有用.

3. 中國話他們都說的好.

這本書他們都說很好.

Exercise 3. Illustrative Sentences (Chinese)

1. 我天天下了課還要念書.

2. 我這個月走不了. 我下月走.

3. 你們中大有語言學這科嗎?

4. 我的看法他考不上大學.

5. 今年考大學的學生比去年還多.

6. 那本課本上的圖表畫的很好.

7. 上課以外就是在家裏念書.

8. 你們中文課本念到第幾課了？

9. 先有大刀會，後有小刀會．

10. 請你說一說見省長的經過．

11. 你這個方法很不科學．

12. <u>萬</u>大夫是外科大夫，不是小兒科大夫．

13. 中國的考古家也有學會嗎？

14. 今天的晚會你去嗎？…我沒工夫去．

15. 這個人口表上就有省城的人口，沒有縣城的人口．

16. <u>方</u>大夫今天早上要開三次刀．

17. 我們已經考試了．你們呢？

18. 我到表店給我姐姐買手表去．

19. 他下個月到湖南去考古．

20. 我們的研究生念文科的少，念工科的多．

21. 看<u>考古學報</u>不很難．

22. 他是中國最有名的科學家．

23. 東三省有很多人原來都是山東人．

24. 縣長是本地人．

25. 我們學校就有大考．沒有小考，也沒有月考．

26. 用這個法子好不好很難說．我們試試看．

27. 我初次看見他是在一九四三年遠東學會的年會上．

28. 他開車開的比我好．

29. 那個學會時常開會．下月又要開會了．

30. 他有沒有能力現在很難說．我們先試用兩天試試看．

31. 那個學會常常晚上開會的原因是因為白天大家都沒工夫．

32. 他不去開會的原因很多. 主因是他
    不想看見<u>馬</u>會長.

33. 我現在要走了. 再見, 再見.

34. 中文很難念. 近來我天天念中文,
    因為在過年前後要有一次考試.

35. 我想今天去, 再不然就是明後天去.
    我早晚要去一次.

Exercise 4. Dialogues

1. 張：<u>常</u>先生到法國去了嗎？

   古：没有. 我的看法他最近走不了.
       他要下個月走了.

   張：他為甚麼到法國去？

   5 古：他是科學家. 他到法國的主因
       是為了研究原子能.

   張：現在念科學的人很多，念文科
       的很少.

   古：可不是嗎！現在是科學第一.

2. 常：<u>方有文</u>是外科大夫嗎？

萬： 是的. 他是很有名的外科大夫.
　　 他開刀開的很好.

常： 你知道不知道，這兒有沒有好
　　 的小兒科大夫？

5 萬： 很難説. 有的好，有的不好.

常： 我的兒女多，常常要看大夫，
　　 所以我初到一個地方就先要問
　　 問有好大夫沒有.

3. 邊： 你念那科？

錢： 我念工科.

邊： 工科很難念是不是？

錢： 也不很難. 我説工科比文科容
5 　　易.

邊： 你天天下了課晚上還要念書嗎？

錢： 是，我晚上還要念.

邊： 你們有月考嗎？

錢： 沒有. 我們就有大考，可是年
10　　年開學以後先有一個小考.

4. 常：你們甚麼時候考試？

萬：我們已經考過了．你們呢？

常：我們馬上就要考了．

萬：你們學校有考古學這科嗎？

5 常：有．念考古的不少，也有研究
生念考古學．

萬：我姐姐想到遠大念考古學．

常：你姐姐是學考古的嗎？

萬：不是．他原來是學語言學的，
10 後來又學文學．現在又要學考
古學了．

常：他學過考古學嗎？

萬：没有．他没學過考古學．

常：你姐姐學校裏也有考古學是不
15 是？

萬：有．不過他要考遠大的原因是
因為有名的考古學家都在遠大
呢，所以我姐姐要考遠大念考
古．

5. 方： <u>張再文</u>考上中大了嗎？

　路： 考上了．這次考中大的學生有
　　　兩千五百多人．他說他是試試
　　　看，可是他考上了．

5 方： 他要念甚麼？

　路： 他要念語言學，還要研究方言．
　　　他的學問很好．時常在<u>大華晚
　　　報</u>、<u>中國語文</u>、<u>上海時報</u>上寫
　　　東西．

10 方： <u>張</u>小姐以後可能是一個語言學
　　　家．

　路： 可能．好．我要上課去了．再見．

　方： 再見．

6. 南： 今天早上我在大華表店看見一
　　　個手表很好看．

　邊： 你要買嗎？

　南： 我要買，可是没錢．我買不了．

7. 馬： <u>毛</u>先生，你有工夫嗎？

毛：没工夫．我畫圖表呢．

馬：你畫甚麽圖表呢？

毛：我畫課本圖表呢．

馬：你畫了幾課了？

5 毛：我已經畫到第二十五課了．

8. 張：你這個工人好不好，毛太太？

　毛：還不知道呢，試用兩天看看．
　　　這個工人有五個兒女．因為没
　　　有錢，日子很難過．没法子．
5　　所以離開家到縣城裏來．他家
　　　原來還是大地主呢．

9. 毛：張縣長開刀了．

　高：是嗎？那天開的刀？

　毛：前天．

　高：開刀的經過好不好？

5 毛：很好．

10. 華：你到學生中心經過中華書店嗎？

　邊：經過，經過．你要買書嗎？

華： 請你給我買一本<u>考古學報</u>.

邊： 好的.

11. 文：<u>方</u>先生，你那兒有今年的湖北
　　 省人口表嗎？

　方： 我没有現在的. 就有民國三十
　　 二年的.

　5 文： 你看看民國三十二年有多少人
　　 口？

　方： 有二千五百萬.

12. 馬： 從前中國有大刀會、小刀會.
　　 是不是都在東三省？

　高： 不是. 在山東省.

Exercise 5. Narratives

1. <u>方</u>先生從前念工科. 現在是一個科
　 學家, 研究原子. 他說："美國早就能
　 用原子能了. 上個月有一條大船, 是
　 用原子能的, 已經從美國到了英國."

2. 高先生是考古學家. 他近來寫了一
本書, 書名是考古學. 很多研究考
古的人都看過這本書, 都説這本考
古學在考古上是很有用的. 高先生
5 最近又在考古學報上寫過「我在東
三省考古的經過」. 看過的人都説很
好.

3. 一個念文科的學生説:"念文科没有
用. 我從考上大學文科以來, 天天
上課, 下課, 念課本, 從早到晚都
是念書. 念書以外, 就是考試—有
5 小考、月考、大考. 要是書念的好,
考試也都考的好. 請問, 有甚麼用?"
有人説:"你説念文科没有用, 你為
甚麼從前不考工科呢?"這個念文科
的學生説:"我没考上工科."

4. 現在的外科大夫都會開刀, 可是在
兩千年以前中國有一個人已經會開

刀了. 那個會開刀的人是中國古時
候有名的大夫，給一個有名的人開
刀.

5. 馬先生是文學家，也是語言學家.
他中西學問都好，能說英語、日語，
又會法文，還會中文，能說國語.
他也研究土話. 有人問他:"研究語
言學是不是學說外國話?"他說:"不
是. 研究語言學是用科學方法研究
語言，不是學說外國話."他寫了很
多中文書. 有國語課本、國語語法、
中文文法、中國語文的外來語. 他
常說:"研究語言,要用心研究語法.
比方說西方人學國語,本來不容易,
要是明白語法就容易了."

6. 田中原是小兒科大夫. 他說:"張大
為是外科大夫. 他開刀開的最好.
要是有人開刀的時候，我時常請張
大為來開刀."

7. 有一個縣長到省城去見省長. 省長
   對他説:"縣長要常常在縣裏, 不可
   時常離開縣城. 還有, 你的縣裏從
   前人口有多少? 最近是不是比以前
   5多了? 最好有個人口表給我看看."

8. 東方中學有一個先生能畫圖表. 從
   前學校裏圖表都是他畫. 近來没有
   工夫. 校長想再用一個能畫圖表的
   先生, 已經試用兩個人了. 這兩個
   5人畫的圖表都很難看,所以都没用.
   今天又有一個人,他説他能畫圖表.
   校長説:"先試試看. 要是畫的好,
   我們學校就用他."

9. 從前中國人念書, 在小的時候要念
   千字文. 這本書是文言的, 有一千
   個字. 現在中國小學生不念千字文
   了, 因為千字文是文言的, 又因為
   5這一千個字裏, 有的字不常用.

10. 中國語文研究所裏有兩個方言研究
會. 一個是湖南方言研究會, 時常
開會. 一個是河南方言研究會, 不
常開會. 前天研究所的所長對河南
方言研究會的會長說:"研究方言要
大家常常在一塊兒研究. 最好是時
常開會."

11. 古時候沒有民主國家, 後來人民知
道民主好, 人人想要民主, 所以近
來有很多民主國家.

12. 有一個高原水很少, 人口也不多.
有一次, 我到那個地方, 走了很遠,
從早到晚沒看見水, 也沒看見人.

13. 張先生是東方表店的主人. 他前天
對我說:"我最近買了很多手表. 你
要是有工夫, 請你來看看." 我說:
"我明後天到你的表店去. 要是有學
生用的手表, 我要買一個."

14. 在七八十年以前中國有個大刀會，
是在山東省． 大刀會以後又有小刀
會，也是在山東省．

15. <u>省名</u>　　　<u>人口(中華民國三十二年)</u>
　　山東　　　　　　三千八百萬
　　山西　　　　　　一千二百萬
　　河北　　　　　　二千九百萬
5　　河南　　　　　　三千二百萬
　　湖北　　　　　　二千五百萬
　　湖南　　　　　　二千八百萬

16. 上個月學校開學． 校長説今年的學
生太多，原來的地方容不下． 為了
大家都能念書，所以有的學生在白
天上課，有的學生在晚上上課．

17. 前天<u>華美晚報</u>上説<u>高</u>縣長要走了．
我説："不會的． <u>高</u>縣長在這縣裏，
人民都對他很好,他對人民也很好.

大家都説他是一個民主縣長. 我想
他不會走的."

18. 今天大華時報上説，我們知道現在
的地主給工人的工錢太少，工人的
日子很難過. 要是地主再不給工人
想法子，工人就活不了了.

Exercise 6. Illustrative Sentences (English)

1. I still have to study every day after leaving school.

2. I won't be able to leave this month. I'm leaving next month.

3. Does [your] Sun Yatsen University have a course in linguistics?

4. In my opinion he can't pass the examinations for college.

5. This year even more students are taking the exams for college than last year.

6. The illustrations and tables in that textbook are very well done.

7. Apart from going to classes, I just [i.e. I do nothing but] study at home.

8. What lesson have you got to in your Chinese textbook?

9. First there was the Big Knife Society, and later, the Little Knife Society.

10. Please tell about your experience in seeing the provincial governor.

11. This method of yours is very unscientific.

12. Dr. Wan is a surgeon, not a pediatrician.

13. Do Chinese archaeologists also have an association?

14. Are you going to this evening's meeting? ···I don't have time to go.

15. This population table has the population only of provincial capitals, not of district capitals.

16. Dr. Fang will perform [lit. have] three operations this morning.

17. We've already had our exams. How about you?

18. I'm going to the watch store to buy my sister a wristwatch.

19. He's going to Hunan next month to do some archaeological work.

20. Few of our graduate students (are) studying the humanities; many (are) studying engineering.

21. It's not difficult to read the Journal of Archaeology.

22. He's China's most famous scientist.

23. A lot of people in Manchuria were originally natives of Shantung.

24. The district magistrate is a local man.

25. Our school has only final exams. It doesn't have quizzes or monthly tests.

26. It's difficult to say whether it's all right to use this method. Let's try it and see.

27. The first time I saw him was at the annual meeting of the Far Eastern Association in 1943.

28. He drives better than I do.

29. That scholarly organization often has meetings. It will have another one next month.

30. It's hard to say now whether he has ability or not. Let's try him for a couple of days and see.

31. The reason why that scholarly organization often has evening meetings is that no one is free during the daytime.

32. There are many reasons why he isn't going to attend the meeting. The main reason is that he doesn't want to see Chairman Ma.

33. I'm leaving now. Goodbye.

34. Chinese is very hard [to study]. Recently I've been studying Chinese every day because we're going to have an exam around New Year's.

35. I'm going to go today or [else] tomorrow or the day after. Sooner or later I intend to go once.

Lesson 24

Exercise 1. Review of Single Characters

1. 萬	9. 科	17. 現	25. 常	33. 省	41. 問	49. 究
2. 試	10. 研	18. 給	26. 初	34. 百	42. 經	50. 名
3. 語	11. 再	19. 縣	27. 易	35. 晚	43. 懂	
4. 請	12. 用	20. 開	28. 畫	36. 過	44. 誰	
5. 時	13. 難	21. 早	29. 原	37. 夫	45. 方	
6. 道	14. 後	22. 最	30. 法	38. 古	46. 知	
7. 對	15. 考	23. 已	31. 課	39. 容	47. 候	
8. 活	16. 千	24. 主	32. 前	40. 叫	48. 表	

Exercise 2. Distinguishing Partially Similar Combinations
A. Same Character in Initial Position

1	2	3	4	5	6	7
以為	上山	開門	會說	外國	日本	名子
以前	上課	開車	會話	外號	日子	名字
以後	上學	開刀	會所	外科	日文	名人
以來	上次	開學	會長	外頭	日用	
以外	上月	開會				

8	9	10	11	12	13
時候	生字	問路	土話	考古	古書
時常	生活	問好	土人	考上	古典
時報	生日	問他	土地	考試	古今

14	15	16	17	18	19
原來	法子	對門	中東	大考	工人
原因	法國	對話	中西	大夫	工科
原子	法文	對了	中華	大水	工夫

20	21	22	23	24	25	26
離開	主人	圖書	看書	四書	中英	研究生
離家	主因	圖畫	看懂	四邊	中日	研究所

B. Same Character in Final Position

1	2	3	4	5	6
日報	以後	主人	地名	日子	科學家
時報	明後	用人	人名	法子	小說家
看報	然後	名人	小名	名子	語言學家
畫報	最後	女人	學名	原子	考古學家
晚報	前後	文人	有名	本子	

7	8	9	10	11	12
不用	比方	不過	會長	看法	開車
有用	地方	難過	所長	方法	火車
日用	東方	路過	省長	文法	叫車
試用	西方	經過	縣長	語法	馬車

13	14	15	16	17	18
從來	對門	後年	方言	圖畫	看見
近來	大門	過年	文言	字畫	再見
原來	叫門	前年	語言	畫畫	可見

19	20	21	22	23	24
法文	開學	在外	大考	工科	三角學
日文	大學	以外	小考	文科	考古學
語文	科學	海外	月考	外科	語言學

25	26	27	28	29	30
晚會	國語	對話	初次	從前	初小
年會	英語	會話	一次	以前	高小
學會	日語	白話			

31	32	33	34	35	36
工錢	過路	我的	前天	說話	請問
沒錢	馬路	目的	後天	對話	學問

37	38	39	40	41	42
用心	手表	地主	畫家	會念	小學生
小心	圖表	民主	人家	難念	研究生

43	44	45	46	47	48
畫兒	書店	大夫	上課	省城	白話文
女兒	表店	工夫	下課	縣城	千字文

49	50	51	52	53	54
中西	中美	難說	再不然	我的表	大刀會
東西	英美	小說	要不然	人口表	研究會

C. Same Character in Different Positions

1	2	3	4	5	6
早晚	現在	最初	高原	最好	手上
晚上	在家	初中	原來	好看	上課

7	8	9	10	11	12	13
手工	看法	最近	上課	學問	手工	買賣
工科	法國	近東	課本	問路	工錢	賣給

D. Reversibles

1	2	3	4	5
人名	畫圖	過路	文法	開會
名人	圖畫	路過	法文	會開

Exercise 3. Review of Special Combinations

All combinations appearing in this Unit other than those already reviewed in the preceding exercise are listed below :

1. 没法子	10. 為了	19. 山水畫兒
2. 不會的	11. 容不下	20. 遠東大學
3. 畫畫兒	12. 要不是	21. 人民畫報
4. 容易	13. 張大千	22. 萬里長城
5. 一會兒	14. 原子能	23. 日子難過
6. 知道	15. 外來語	24. 生活畫報
7. 過日子	16. 過生日	25. 考古學報
8. 小兒科	17. 東三省	
9. 大刀會	18. 小刀會	

Exercise 4. Excerpts from Actual Publications

The following sentences are taken from Act I of A Question of Face, by Lǎo Shè, a leading novelist and playwright.

1. 不要再說了.
2. 我不能去.
3. 大夫為甚麽不來？
4. 是他們大，還是我大？
5. 你不懂！
6. 他的錢是他的.
7. 你們不去？
8. 他知道你手裏没錢，他説給你五塊錢.
9. 他不是有錢的人.
10. 這很容易明白.
11. 不過，小姐今年多大了？
12. 他是我的女兒.

13. 請到這裏來.
14. 我們没看見他.
15. 我們能走路！

Exercise 5. Narratives

1. 我去中國畫學會的目的是要研究中國畫. 我以為在學會裏可以時常看看人家畫畫兒，再不然大家都在一塊兒研究畫畫兒. 可是最近没有人畫畫兒，也没有人來研究. 大家來到這裏，有的看看報，有的說說話，一會兒就都走了. 我想我在這裏没法子研究中國畫了. 我就去見田會長. 田會長對我說："以後我們要常常開研究會. 我還要時常請名畫家來給我們說說畫中國畫的方法，你就可以學中國畫了，是不是?"

2. 中國的萬里長城在中國的北方. 從河北省的東北邊經過四個省，到中國的西北. 雖然長城的名子叫萬里長城，可是就有四五千里長．

3. <u>田大海</u>是船上水手．他的工錢很少，
家裏人口很多，他不常在家．有一
天他在家裏，他太太說：“今天是你
過生日了．”<u>田大海</u>說：“我們過日子
都不容易，不用過生日了．”他的太
太說：“我們日子雖然難過，可是今
天是你生日，就是你的好日子，我
已經給你買東西了．給你！你看看！”

4. 一個買賣人對一個念書的人說：“你
說有「書」好呢，還是有「錢」好呢？”
念書的人說：“我是念書人，我說還
是有「書」好．你說呢？”買賣人說：
“我也說有「書」好．”念書的人心裏
想，買賣人心目中「錢」是第一，他
為甚麼說有「書」好呢？他問那個買
賣人：“你為甚麼也說有「書」好呢？”
買賣人說：“比方說，你有本<u>四書</u>，

你可以先念<u>四書</u>，念了以後，書能
再賣給人，所以我說有書好."

5. <u>邊一夫</u>到縣城去考南華中學，考上
了．他說:"我本來是試試看，誰知
道考上了."我說:"南華中學原來學
校地方很小，學生很多，這次又考
⁵上二百多人,容的下嗎?"<u>邊一夫</u>說:
"容不下了.我們現在在學校以外一
個地方上課."

6. 太湖四邊兒地土很好,有很多水田.
我家就在湖邊兒．我時常在湖邊畫
畫兒．我畫了很多山水畫．有一張
是「太湖的月」.有一張畫的是「湖山」.
⁵還有一張不是山水，是「海口的船」,
畫的是中國最大的海口——上海.

7. 我是學語言學的．我現在研究中國
語言裏的外來語．有人說:"西方人
學中國語文很不容易.中文很難念,

中國話很難說." 我說:"要是能用心
學, 也就不難了."

8. 水口山在湖南省. 那個地方的水力
很大. 我知道最近要用那兒的水力.
不知道現在已經用了沒有.

9. 有人說:"路遠知馬力." 這就是說,
在走遠路的時候就知道馬有沒有走
路的能力. 要是走很近的路, 不會
知道馬走路的能力.

10. 一個大夫為了要到中國去, 所以在
西東大學學中國話. 他雖然學過了
不少的中國話了, 可是他從來也不
說. 有一次先生用英文問他:"你為
甚麼學了中國話不說呢?" 他說:"我
不會說, 所以我不說." 先生說:"好.
現在我們兩個人說中國話. 你說一
說試試看." 他沒法子了. 他就說了,
說的很好.

11. 現在請看我們課本上第三課的地圖，
有一個小地方叫大山口．你們看看
是在那一省？

12. 張小姐在中華表店買了一個手表，
很好看．我問他多少錢，他說不到
二十塊錢．我想明天下課以後也去
買一個．

13. 我念考古學．念書以外要是有工夫
我還看書、報、甚麼的．現在我看
考古學報呢．這個學報上都是有名
的考古學家寫的東西．

14. 人家都說張大夫雖然是外科大夫可
是他不會開刀．要是有人要開刀他
都是叫毛大夫開．我說不會的，因
為上次我看見他給人家開刀了．

15. 東三省在中國東北邊．也叫東北．
地方很大，土地很好．日本人到東

三省以前我家就在東北一個縣城裏.
那個縣長很好. 一九三一年我們就
離開東北了. 那個縣長也離開了.
要不是為了日本人我們到現在可能
⁵不離開那裏.

16. 我念工科. 我姐姐念文科. 我們兩
個人都在一個大學念書. 我姐姐書
念的很好，年年考第一. 他天天下
了課就念書. 我對念書不很用心.
⁵要是小考、月考、大考我就用心念
念，不然我就不念. 不是說大話，
我雖然不用心念書，可是我會畫圖
表. 我常常給人家畫圖表. 我姐姐
要是有圖表，都是我給他畫.

17. 一個學生看書看不懂. 先生說:"你
最好上下文都看,要不然你看不懂."

18. 我女兒從來不說英文. 他雖然學過
了，可是他學不會. 我很想知道他

學不會的原因．是他不用心呢，還
是英文先生不好呢？

19. 船上用水手，都是要經過試用．在
試用的時候，要是能力好，就可以
用．要是能力不好，就不用．

20. 毛先生是科學家．近來他在科學研
究所研究原子能．他說："原子能很
有用，很多人都已經知道了．可是
甚麼是原子能？原子能有甚麼用？
5 很多人還不知道呢．我最近要寫兩
本書，一本是甚麼是原子能？一本
是原子能有甚麼用？我想這兩本書
是很多人想要看的．"

21. 在人口表上看那個縣裏人口很多，
可是大夫很少．就有兩個外科大夫、
一個小兒科大夫．

22. 一八九七年山東省有大刀會，後來
又有小刀會．不知道在那年大刀會、
小刀會都没有了．

23. 有一個外國學生研究中國語文. 有
人問他:"研究中國語文難不難?"他
説:"研究語文都不容易. 你問研究
中國語文難不難, 就看研究的人用
5 心不用心了.用心研究的人就不難,
不用心研究的人就以為很難了."

24. 有人問我:"你是一個外國人, 為甚
麼要學中國語文呢?"我對他説:"你
看一看地圖,中國是一個土地很大,
人口很多的國家. 我想你看過地圖
5 以後, 就知道我為甚麼要學中國語
文了."

UNIT V

Lesson 25

1	2	3	4	5
半	點	鐘	必	得

6	7	8	9	10
跟	事	業	往	實

1. 半　bàn *　　　　half, semi

2. 點　diǎn　　　　(1) a dot, a point ; (2) a bit, a little

3. 鐘　zhōng　　　(1) bell ; (2) clock ; (3) o'clock

4. 必　bì *　　　　must, have to

5. 得　dé　　　　(1) get, receive ; (2) get to (do something)
　　　de　　　　(see Supplementary Note 2)
　　　děi　　　　must, have to　(negative : búbì)

6. 跟　gēn　　　　with, and

7. 事　shì　　　　(1) thing, affair, event ; (2) work, job, task

8. 業　yè *　　　　occupation, business

9. 往　wàng, wǎng　toward

10. 實　shí *　　　　solid, real

11. 地　de　　　　(see Supplementary Note 2)

Special Combinations

1. 半路　bànlù　　　halfway

2.. 半天	bàntiān	(1) half a day ; (2) quite a while
3. 必得	bìděi	must, have to (negative : búbì)
4. 必要	bìyào	(1) necessary ; (2) necessarily ; (3) requirement, necessity
5. 大半(兒)	dàbàn(r)	(1) greater half ; (2) for the most part ; (3) most likely
6. 得到	dédào	get, acquire, obtain
7. 得了	déle	(1) OK, Enough!; (2) done, finished ; (3) No such thing!
8. 點心	diǎnxin	(1) refreshment, snack; (2) dessert
9. 多(一)半(兒)	duō(yi)bàn(r)	(1) greater half ; (2) for the most part ; (3) most likely
10. 工業	gōngyè	industry (narrower in scope than 實業 shíyè)
11. 工業學校	gōngyè xuéxiào	industrial school
12. 來往	láiwǎng	(1) come and go; (2) have contacts ; (3) coming and going
13. 上(一)半	shàng (yí) bàn	first half, upper half
14. 上半天	shàng bàntiān	forenoon, morning
15. 實話	shíhuà	the truth
16. 實力	shílì	actual strength (figurative)
17. 事實	shìshí	fact
18. 事實上	shìshíshang	in fact, as a matter of fact, actually
19. 實說	shí shuō	speak truthfully
20. 事業	shìyè	enterprise, occupation, career
21. 實業	shíyè	productive activity, industry (includes mining, commerce, etc.)
22. 實業家	shíyèjiā	industrialist, business man
23. 實業學校	shíyè xuéxiào	industrial school, technical school
24. 實在	shízài	real(ly), actual(ly)

25. 實在的	shízàide	(1) real, actual; (2) Really! (as isolated utterance)
26. 說實在的	shuō shízàide	(to) tell the truth
27. 往後	wǎnghòu	(1) toward the rear; (2) hereafter
28. 下(一)半	xià(yí)bàn	second half, lower half
29. 下半天	xià bàntiān	afternoon
30. 小時	xiǎoshí	an hour (M)
31. 心事	xīnshi	matters of the mind, cares, concerns
32. 一半(兒)	yíbàn(r)	a half
33. 一大半(兒)	yídàbàn(r)	(1) greater half; (2) for the most part; (3) most likely
34. 一點(兒)	yìdiǎn(r)	a little, a bit (See Supplementary Note 1)
35. 有事	yǒu shì	be engaged, be occupied
36. 有心事	yǒu xīnshi	be concerned about something
37. 鐘表	zhōng biǎo	clocks and watches
38. 鐘頭	zhōngtóu	an hour (more colloquial than xiǎoshí)

Exercise 1. Pitfalls

1. 你不用心念書.
   你不用念中文.

2. 不到中山路去.
   不到一里路遠.

3. 我在這兒有三個小本子.
   我在這兒有三個鐘頭了.

4. 我有一個本子要給他.
   我有一個月沒看見他.

5. 我們十個人都沒有書.
   我們十個鐘頭沒看書.

6. 張大文是研究原子能的學生.
   張大文是研究原子能的不是?

Exercise 2. Illustrative Sentences (Chinese)

1. 他不來的原因多一半兒為了有事.

2. 說實在的我得到他不少的學問.

3. 他在實業學校念的是那科？

4. 到工業學校不是很近，不到二里路
   嗎？

5. 你說實話，你現在有甚麼事？

6. 我說事實上沒有那個必要. 你說呢？

7. 從法國來了一個大實業家，他對我
   們說的是「法國二十年以來的實業」.

8. 我們家跟張家來往得很好.

9. 現在我離不開. 我的事太多了.

10. 這本書裏頭都寫的是甚麼？

11. 我上半天上學校的時候走在半路上
    看見毛校長了.

12. 他說了半天話我都不懂.

13. 你晚來半個鐘頭就看不見他了.

14. 比這個好一點兒的有沒有?

15. 我們下次考中文是從第十九課到第二十四課.

16. 我跟他們一點兒來往也沒有.

17. 我跟你一塊兒到鐘表店去好不好?

18. 那張地圖要是你不用的時候請你給我看一看.

19. 這本字典二十塊錢我說一點兒也不多.

20. 你說你跟萬小姐三個多月不見了. 我也是.

21. 我上半天念了三小時的英文.

22. 在美國的中國人多一半是從華南來的.

23. 他說要到中國去．我看事實上沒有那個可能．

24. 我明天下半天必得去見南長木．

25. 為甚麼這個湖裏沒有魚？

26. 路先生有甚麼心事，你知道嗎？

27. 英國的工業實力比不了美國．

28. 說實在的，他沒有到那裏去的必要．

29. 他們的事業大半都在華北．

30. 我往後一大半的時候要學國語．

31. 那六塊點心一半是你的，一半是我的．

32. 我得到了古先生不少的學問．

33. 我的心事都跟你實說了．

34. 得了！得了！不要說了．我都明白了．

35. 我們現在的生活比以前好得多．

Exercise 3. Dialogues

1. 常：你知道晚會甚麼時候開嗎？

　萬：九點鐘.

　常：還是在工業學校開嗎？

　萬：是的. 你幾點鐘去？

　5 常：八點半. 一會兒我跟你一塊兒
　　　去.

2. 張：錢一多為甚麼不上學了？

　華：他不念的原因多一半為了這次
　　　的考試.

　張：他考得不好嗎？

　5 華：不好. 說實在的, 他不用心念書.

3. 路：毛有為, 要是你下半天没事我
　　　們上山去好不好？

　毛：我有事.

　路：你有甚麼事？

　5 毛：我到鐘表店去買表.

　路：鐘表店很近, 不到一里路遠.

毛： 也得走半天呢.

路： 得了！我知道了. 你多半兒是
看<u>文</u>小姐去.

毛： 我實在是買表去.

4. 文： 你明天白天能到實業學校去嗎？

邊： 不能. 我要到語言學會去開會.

文： 是研究國語嗎？

邊： 是的，所以必得去.

5 文： 我以為你有工夫呢. 要是有事
就不必去了.

邊： 實業學校明天有甚麼事？

文： 從美國來了一個實業家，到實
業學校來. 要説一説「美國的
10   工業實力」.

5. 錢： 明天開會以後是不是要有一點
兒點心？

田： 對了. 最好有點兒點心.

錢： 誰去買呢？

田：高東明沒事. 他可以去.

錢：買中國點心還是買外國點心?

田：我想買一半兒中國點心，一半兒外國點心. 你說呢?

5 錢：很好. 甚麼時候去買?

田：明天上半天去買.

6. 高：到中心鐘表店往那邊兒走?

白：從這兒往西. 第三個路口兒第一家就是. 你要買表嗎?

高：是的. 我的表不走了. 我想再

5 買一個.

白：中心的鐘表都很好. 你甚麼時候去? 我跟你一塊兒去.

高：明天上半天好嗎?

白：下半天好不好?

10 高：好的.

7. 馬：東方學報是月報還是半月報?

萬：是半月報. 你沒看過嗎?

馬：我没有．裏頭寫的都是甚麼？

萬：文學、語言、小説、甚麼的．
這個半月報名子叫東方學報，
事實上西方文學跟科學有時候
也有一點兒．也可以説是中西
學報．

8. 邊：萬開華往這兒來已經有一個鐘
頭了．為甚麼還没到呢？這是
甚麼原因？

路：誰知道呢？是不是路過張先生
家，他到張家了？

邊：可能．他常跟我説最近有一個
月没看見張先生了．他説往後
必得常去看看張先生．

路：説實在的，他得到了張先生不
少的學問．

邊：可不是嗎！他實在得到張先生
不少的學問．

9. 田：前天早上我到研究所去．走在
　　　半路上看見張小姐了．他説他
　　　考上大學了．

　　文：他考的是那科？

5　田：他學原子能．

　　文：原子能很不容易學．

　　田：張小姐念書很用心．一天二十
　　　四小時他大半的時候都念書．

10. 錢：毛九城為甚麼現在還没來呢？

　　白：已經九點了，他一大半兒不來
　　　了．

　　錢：為甚麼不來呢？

5　白：可能他有事，不能來．

　　錢：我們去看看他？

　　白：得了．我看没有那個必要．

11. 萬：你近來是不是有心事？

　　文：我的心事不必説了．

　　萬：説實在的，你有甚麼心事？

文：我對你實説. 明年多半兒我没
　　法子念書了.

萬：是不是為了没錢？

文：是的, 没錢. 念大學很難.

5 萬：你可以跟<u>張</u>先生説, 請他給你
　　一點兒錢.

文：不能説. 我家跟他没來往.

12. 高：人家説你很有錢, 你的事業很
　　多. 又説這個地方的地都是你
　　的, 都説你是個大地主.

邊：不是的. 事實上這個地方的地
5 　我就有一點兒. 多半兒都是人
　　家的.

高：是嗎？

邊：是的. 這是事實. 我從來説實話.

Exercise 4. Narratives

1. <u>張</u>先生家離賣點心的地方不遠. 從
　前<u>張</u>先生常去買點心, 來往都是不

到半個鐘頭. 可是今天張先生又去
買點心, 去了有三個多鐘頭. 他的
太太問他是甚麼原因. 他說:"我去
買點心的時候, 在半路上看見馬校
長了. 馬校長要去買鐘, 叫我跟他
一塊兒去, 我就跟他去了. 到鐘表
店馬校長看了半天, 對我說:「這裏
的鐘表不很好, 我不在這裏買, 我
要到大華鐘表店去買. 你要是沒有
事再跟我去看看.」我說:「說實在的,
我有一點兒事, 不能再跟你去了.」
馬校長說:「好, 你不必去了.」我就
離開鐘表店, 去買點心. 到了賣點
心的地方, 賣點心的人說:「點心沒
有了. 你要是早來半小時還有.」所
以我雖然走了半天的路, 可是點心
也沒買."

2. 白先生去年都在遠東. 上半年在日

本，下半年在中國．他說今年他又
要去遠東，多半兒是常在日本，不
去中國了．

3. 有八九個美國學生到中文學會去開
會．他們多一半兒會說國語．有人
說："你們國語說得很好．你們在甚
麼地方學的?"他們說是在中國學的．
5 他們學國語的時候很用心．上半天
學說話，下半天念中文．他們念過
千字文、四書．

4. 有七八個人要坐白先生的車上山．
白先生說："我的車太小，七八個人
坐不下．我姐姐有一個大一點兒的
車．我想大半兒能坐七八個人．我
5 們可以坐我姐姐的車上山．"

5. 上次在學生中心開晚會，來的人很
多．一大半是外國學生．他們雖然

是外國人,可是多半會説中國話,説
得都很好.

6. 田先生從前在實業學校研究工業,
   現在是有名的實業家. 他説:"西方
   有很多國家是工業國家. 東方的工
   業國家就很少了."

7. 高先生對我説:"我家裏有一張名人
   字畫. 明天早上你要是没有事, 請
   到我家來看看." 我問他:"明天早上
   幾點鐘?"他説:"最好早上九點鐘."
   5 我説:"九點鐘我有事. 後天早上可
   以嗎?"高先生説:"後天早上這張字
   畫就不在我家了, 因為已經賣給人
   家了." 我説:"明天早上我實在有事,
   没法子來. 要不然我明天晚上七點
   10 鐘來." 高先生説:"好."

8. 毛先生説:"明後天要考國語. 這次
   考試是從第一課到第十八課. 又考

會話，又考語法，還考寫字，太難
了."我說:"我說一點兒也不難. 不
是我說大話，我都念會了. 還有，
你說還要考寫字. 我想不會的，因
為我們還沒學過寫字呢."毛先生說:
"這本書我就念了一半.上一半已經
念過了，下一半一點兒也沒念呢.
我都對你實說了,你說你都念會了,
誰知道你是說實話呢還是說大話呢?"

9. 我這兩天因為家裏的事很難過. 今
天方以文問我是不是有心事. 我的
心事我不想跟他說. 說實在的，跟
人家說一點兒用也沒有，所以也不
必對人家說.

10. 我家跟田家對門.以前來往的很好.
後來不知道為甚麼他們不跟我們來
往了. 可以說現在兩家沒來往. 最
近他們看見我們都不說話了. 雖然

現在他們對我們不好，我想可能以
後兩家又有來往了.

11. 毛學明說他有很多事業. 我看他是
說大話呢. 他說的事業在事實上都
是張先生的.他不過天天都去看看，
他就說是他的事業了.

12. 我從張先生那裏得到一本書. 這本
書很有用. 我必得用心研究研究.
張先生說:"我知道你有看這本書的
必要，所以我先給你看. 要是你不
用的時候，你再給我."

13. 文學半月報上的小說大半是文言的.
我以前看不懂，可是我常常看，近
來我有一點兒懂了.

14. 我是一個美國人. 從到中國以來我
多半看中文報. 比方日報、晚報、
畫報我都看.以外我還看考古學報、
文學月報、甚麼的.

15. 要是看一個國家有沒有實力，第一
必得去看這個國家在工業上有實力
沒有.看一個國家的工業很容易看，
因為工業是實在的東西，人人都能
5 看見.

16. 田子文是西東大學的研究生. 他有
一個兒子一個女兒. 田子文又研究
中國國語又研究日本語言. 他念書
最用心，天天手上離不開書. 有時
5 候一邊走路一邊看書. 有一天在上
課的時候他的國語課本不見了. 他
心裏想，這本書多半在女兒手裏，
再不然就是在兒子手裏. 他又想，
今天早上來大學的時候是先到書店，
10 買了兩本書，然後到大學. 這本書
也可能在書店. 他就到書店對書店
裏人説："請問，我有一本國語課本
不見了. 今天早上我來買書，可能

是在這裏. 你看見了沒有?"書店裏
人説:"是不是這本?"他看了那本書
以後説:"就是這本. 我原來以為在
家裏呢. 這本書要是不見了, 我又
5 得買一本. 可是現在我手上沒錢,
沒法子買."

17. 從前中國的中學生要是念過中學以
後想要念工科, 有的念大學工科,
有的念工業學校. 在工業學校裏學
的東西, 雖然比在大學裏學的少,
5 可是都很有用.

18. 那個地方地土好, 山水好. 從前有
很多土人, 近來那裏的土人, 有的
是水手, 有的是工人. 現在他們都
有生活的能力了.

19. 中華日報、中文學報都是中文的.
我念中文雖然有三年了, 可是還不
能看中文報. 張先生説:"你不要以

為看中文報很難. 你可以時常看.
有不懂的地方, 你來問我."

20. 高經國是英國人. 他上次到中國是
在一九三三年, 也就是中華民國二
十二年. 那是他頭次到中國, 也是
頭次離開英國到海外去. 高先生是
5 從英國坐船, 在中國一個大海口下
船. 又坐火車到了一個地方, 就在
那裏念大學. 那個大學有不少外國
學生, 都會說中國話. 因為高先生
也會說, 所以大家在一塊兒都說中
10 國話. 高先生說, 這裏是學中國語
文的最好的地方, 一來是先生好,
二來是所有的學生都說中國話. 他
本來要在這裏念兩年, 可是後來他
念了不到一年就走了. 高先生為甚
15 麼走了呢? 高先生没說明原因. 大
家都不明白為甚麼. 有人說高先生

到他本國念書去了，在本國念書又
不用很多錢，又離家近，要不然高
先生不會離開中國的．

21. 我到這裏來念中文有三個月了．本
地人看我是外國人，會説中國話，
他們常問我為甚麽要學中文．我跟
他們説我學中文為的是要看中文書、
⁵報．

22. 中華民國二十六年，因為日本人到
了華北，所以有很多人都到華西去
了．我們家裏人也都到華西去了．
在那裏八年我們又到了華東．

Exercise 5. Illustrative Sentences (English)

1. The reason for his not coming (is) most likely that he is engaged.
2. To tell the truth, I learned a lot from him.
3. What course is he taking at the industrial school?
4. Isn't it close to the technical school, less than two miles (away)?
5. Tell the truth, what do you have to do now?
6. I say that actually there's no need of that. What do you think?

7. A big industrialist has come from France ; he spoke to us on industry in France in the past twenty years.

8. Our family gets along very well with the Zhang family.

9. I can't leave now. I've too much to do.

10. What's [written] in this book?

11. [When] going to school this morning, I saw Principal Mao after I'd gone halfway.

12. He talked for a long time, but I didn't understand a thing.

13. If you come half an hour later, you won't be able to see him.

14. Do you have one a little better than this one?

15. Our next exam in Chinese will be from lesson 19 to lesson 24.

16. I don't have any contacts with them at all.

17. How about my going with you to the clock and watch store?

18. When [and if] you aren't using that map, please let me have a look.

19. I think $20 is not at all too much for this dictionary.

20. You say that you and Miss Wan haven't seen each other for over three months. Me neither.

21. I studied English (for) three hours this morning.

22. The majority of the Chinese in America come from South China.

23. He says he wants to go to China. I think, as a matter of fact, that there is no possibility of that.

24. Tomorrow afternoon I must go to see Nan Changmu.

25. Why are there no fish in this lake?

26. Do you know what's worrying Mr. Lu?

27. England's industrial power can't compare with (that of) the United States.

28. To tell the truth, he has no need to go there.

29. The majority of their enterprises are in North China.

30. Hereafter I will (spend) the greater part of my time studying the National Language.

31. Of these six pieces of dessert, half are yours and half are mine.

32. I acquired quite a bit of knowledge from Mr. Ku.

33. I'll tell you truthfully all that I'm concerned about.

34. All right! All right! Don't say anything more. I understand everything.

35. [Our] life today is much better than in the past.

Supplementary Notes

1. 一點兒也 and 一點兒都 are used with negative verbs to express the idea "not at all": 我一點兒都不懂 "I don't understand anything at all". 我一點兒錢也没有 "I don't have any money at all". 英文一點兒也不難 "English isn't at all difficult".

2. The syllable <u>de</u> is used in various ways, including the following:
   (1) as a general subordinating particle:
   　(a) Tāde-shū　　　　　　'his book'
   　(b) Tā-qù-de-shíhou　'when he goes'
   (2) as a particle in adverbial expressions of manner and in resultative verb compounds:
   　(a) Tā-shuō-de-hěn-hao　'He speaks very well.'
   　(b) Tā-kàndejiàn　　　　'He is able to see.'
   (3) as a suffix for adverbs modifying a following verb:
   　　Shízàide-shuō　'frankly speaking'

All three uses are frequently written with the character 的. However, modern usage is increasingly tending to distinguish the three <u>de</u> by using 的 for the first, 得 for the second, and 地 for the third. Thus the preceding sentences would be written as follows:

   (1) (a) 他的書

   　　(b) 他去的時候

   (2) (a) 他説得很好

   　　(b) 他看得見

   (3) 實在地説

Note that in the last expression, while the suffix <u>de</u> may be written either as 的 or 得, in its post-verbal use, as in <u>shuō shízàide</u> (which occurs more frequently than <u>shízàide shuō</u>), only 的 can be used.

Recent materials published in the PRC tend to be more consistent in observing the distinctions noted above. Hence our usage in the Supplementary Lessons and Simplified Characters will also be uniform in accordance with that in the PRC. However, in the main lessons, in order to provide practice in the variant usages that students will encounter, we shall use 的 interchangeably with 得 and 地.

Lesson 26

1	2	3	4	5
別	才	當	應	該

6	7	8	9	10
每	差	更	教	朝

1. 別　bié*　　(1) other, different; (2) don't!

2. 才　cái*　　(1) talent; (2) just, then and only then, not until;
   (3) only, merely

3. 當　dāng*　　(1) at (time or place); (2) ought to, should

4. 應　yīng*　　ought to, should

5. 該　gāi　　ought to, should

6. 每　měi*　　(1) each; (2) every time

7. 差　chā, chà　differ by (such-and-such amount), be short, lack

8. 更　gèng*　　still, still more

9. 教　jiāo, jiào　teach (a person or subject)

10. 朝　cháo*　　dynasty

11. 〇　líng　　zero

Special Combinations

1. 別的　biéde　　other, another

324

2.	別人	biéren	other people, others
3.	才好	cái hǎo	be best (used after a sentence, often paired with zuìhǎo at beginning of a sentence)
4.	差不多	chàbuduō	(1) almost the same (RV); (2) almost all right, not bad (RV); (3) almost, approximately (AD)
5.	差一點兒	chà yìdiǎr	(1) lack a bit; (2) almost
6.	初學	chūxué	study for the first time
7.	常年	chángnián	(1) for many years; (2) annual, (in) ordinary years; (3) regular; (4) permanently
8.	當初	dāngchū	at the beginning
9.	當地	dāngdì	on the spot, at the place in question, local
10.	當然	dāngrán	natural(ly), of course
11.	當時	dāngshí	(1) at the time in question; (2) at once, immediately
12.	當天	dāngtiān	on the same day, on the day in question
13.	當中	dāngzhōng	middle, in the midst of (often in the construction zài…dāngzhōng)
14.	高才生	gāocáishēng	greatly talented student
15.	教法	jiāofǎ	teaching method(s)
16.	教給	jiāogěi	teach to
17.	教科書	jiàokēshū	textbook
18.	教書	jiāo shū	teach
19.	教學	jiāoxué*	teach
20.	教學法	jiāoxuéfǎ	teaching method(s)
21.	口才	kǒucái	eloquence, speaking ability
22.	人才	réncái	talented person
23.	說不上	shuōbushàng	(1) can't be said (to be); (2) can't say for sure, perhaps
24.	說法	shuōfǎ	way of speaking, orally expressed view
25.	說給	shuōgěi	tell to
26.	天才	tiāncái	talent

27. 想法 xiǎngfǎ way of thinking, viewpoint
28. 寫法 xiěfǎ way of writing
29. 寫給 xiěgěi write to
30. 學生會 xuésheng huì student council
31. 應當 yīngdāng ought to, should
32. 應該 yīnggāi ought to, should
33. 最多 zuìduō (1) be most numerous; (2) at most
34. 最少 zuìshǎo (1) be fewest; (2) at least

Who's Who and What's What

1. 三國 Sān Guó Three Kingdoms (Period) (220-280 A.D.) A period of struggle among the kingdoms of Shǔ, Wèi, and Wú, the story of which is told in a popular historical novel of that name translated by C.H. Brewitt-Taylor under the title Romance of the Three Kingdoms. (See chart, p.346)
2. 六朝 Liù Cháo Six Dynasties (229-589 A.D.)
3. 南北朝 Nán Běi Cháo Northern and Southern Dynasties (386-589 A.D.)
4. 明朝 Míng Cháo Ming Dynasty (1368-1644 A.D.)

Exercise 1. Pitfalls

1. 他們學校有學問的先生不很多.
   他們學校有學問好的先生没有?

2. 這本書買得到嗎?
   這本書也得買嗎?

3. 離中國有三千里.
   離現在有三千年.

4. 從中國到這兒來.
   從民國九年以來.

Exercise 2. Illustrative Sentences (Chinese)

1. 我們今天考英語語法跟英語會話.

2. 他教初中三國文. 他的教學法很好.

3. 你們學校有學問好的、教中文的先生沒有？

4. 他去年在這兒不過兩三天. 我的想法他今年可能在這兒日子多一點兒.

5. 我們前天大考了. 我的中文考一百.

6. 先生教到他們所有的字都會了，他才不教了.

7. 我學中文一天最少學四個鐘頭，最多學十個鐘頭.

8. 那個外國人能用中文寫書. 一個外國人能用中文寫書可見他的學問很好.

9. 我們最好用別的教學法才好.

10. 這個縣是從1920年才有的.

11. 這本書你看得明白看不明白？

12. 他雖然書念得很好，可是說不上是
一個高才生.

13. 我沒來以前那個事你說給他了嗎？

14. 別人的想法以為學中國話沒有用.

15. 這兩本教科書，那本好？…都差不
多.

16. 我們學生會每月開一次會.

17. 我初學中國話的時候就用這本教科
書.

18. 中國南北朝的時候跟西方國家有沒
有來往？

19. 三國在六朝以前還是在六朝以後？

20. 他有教書的天才.

21. 明朝到中國來的外國人不少.

22. 你們每天學過的字當時要會了.

23. 我每個月最少差不多要用兩百塊錢.

24. 毛先生每天教給我們五個字的寫法.

25. 那本教科書不是我的，是別人的.

26. 他不會常年在這裏. 最多他在這裏三個月.

27. 方一山當初念初中的時候就很有口才.

28. 中文不容易學. 文言文當然更不容易了.

29. 從這裏到上海要是坐火車當天就到了.

30. 這本書要是為了外國人看，應該有英文說明.

31. 人名、地名你都應當寫給他.

32. 坐在當中的那個就是<u>馬</u>縣長.

33. 他的說法是初學外國語言要先學文法. 你說對嗎?

34. 這本書在當地買不到.

35. <u>路大文</u>對原子能很有研究. 他實在是個人才.

Exercise 3. Dialogues

1. 邊: <u>常</u>先生還教書嗎?
   萬: 還教書.
   邊: 他在那兒教書?
   萬: 他在第三中學教高中三國文.

2. 馬: 我們前天已經考試了.
   路: 都考甚麼了?
   馬: 就考英語會話了. 別的還沒考呢.

路： 你有語言天才. 你會話是不是
　　 考了一百？

馬： 差不多.

路： 說實在的, 你有天才. 每次考
5　　 試, 不必說, 當然第一都是你.

馬： 得了！

3. 毛： <u>田為文</u>是我們學校的高才生.

文： 我知道他姐姐書念的比他更好.
　　 年年考第一.

毛： 他姐姐書念得好, 口才也好.
5　　 他們兩個人都是好學生.

4. 錢： <u>毛</u>先生去年到山東有甚麼事？

華： 他是一個考古學家. 當然是考
　　 古去了.

錢： 他去年到這兒來了, 當天就走
5　　 了. 不知道今年他最多能在這
　　 兒多少日子？

華： 我的想法他可能在這兒日子多

一點兒. 他也說過往後要常年
在這兒, 不到別的地方去了.

錢: 我想去看看他.

5. 白: 邊大有請我到他家去. 我不想
去.

張: 我說你應該去. 人家請你為甚
麼不去呢? 要是你沒工夫去,
你得跟邊大有說明你不去的原
因.

白: 你說有這個必要嗎?

張: 我說應當說給他才好.

6. 應: 張先生買了一張畫兒別人說是
南北朝的, 可是也有人說是明
朝的.

常: 要是南北朝的離現在最少有一
千三百年了. 要是明朝的不過
就有五六百年.

7. 馬：錢先生的教學法實在好.

　高：他用甚麼教法呢?

　馬：他每次上課以後，先不叫我們
　　　看課本. 他先給我們説一次，
5　　　然後才叫我們看教科書.

　高：他用甚麼方法教寫字呢?

　馬：初學的時候他先教我們寫法，
　　　然後他寫給我們看. 他寫了以
　　　後，當時就叫我們寫. 要是我
10　　　們寫法不對，他再教給我們.
　　　他教到我們所有的生字都會了，
　　　他才不教了.

8. 張：那個小兒科大夫好不好?

　文：很好.

　張：他是在當地學的嗎?

　文：是. 他當初在中大學的. 現在
5　　　是最有名的小兒科大夫.

9. 馬：那三個小姐裏頭那個是你姐姐?

高：坐在當中的那個是我姐姐.

馬：你姐姐比那兩個小姐都好看.

高：我姐姐説不上好看, 可是書念得好.

5 馬：人家都説你姐姐是個人才.

10. 張：那個外國人對中國文學很有研究. 他現在研究六朝的文言文呢.

文：六朝的文學很不容易. 外國人

5 去研究六朝文學, 可見他的學問很好了.

張：他很用心研究. 每天他用六個鐘頭研究六朝時候的文學.

11. 先生：方又文, 你説三國在南北朝以前還是以後呢？三國有多少年？

方：三國在南北朝以前. 三國有

5 六十年.

先生：南北朝有多少年呢？

　方：南北朝有二百多年.

先生：明朝呢？

　方：明朝是從一千三百六十八年

5　　　到一千六百四十四年. 有二

　　　百七十多年.

12. 文：前天我上學的時候，車走在半

　　　路上不走了. 差一點兒晚了.

　白：你的車常常不走嗎？

　文：没有. 這是第一次.

Exercise 4. Narratives

1. 我在中學教書. 我教學已經二十多

年了. 現在我教國語. 我的教法是

先教課本裏的生字，然後再教課本

裏的對話. 教生字的時候，叫學生

5先看字典. 要是學生看不明白，我

再教給他. 教對話的時候也是叫學

生先念，要是學生不會念，我再教
給他．學生都說這是最好的教學法．
我用這個法子雖然說不上是最好的，
可是我想這個法子對學生很好．

2. 張大文念書很有天才，可是他上課
的時候常常跟別人說話，又時常看
別的書．學生會的會長說給校長了．
有一天，校長對他說："上課的時候
5 應當用心，不要跟別人說話，也不
要看別的書．從前我們學校有個學
生書念得很好，是個高才生．後來
他在上課的時候不用心，常跟人家
說話，常看小說．最後他的書念的
10 很不好．這是一個實在的事實．我
們學校以後不要再有這個事才好．"

3. 我有一本很好的中國國語課本．當
初我在中國學國語的時候，當地有
很多國語教科書．在所有教科書裏，

最好的就是這本國語課本，我當時
念的也就是這本書．教我念這本書
的是張先生．他一邊教我念書上的
字，一邊教我字的寫法．他很會教
書，口才也好．現在我在美國，每
次看到這本國語課本，就想到張先
生了．

4. 張先生有兩個兒子，都是人才．大
兒子從前在實業學校念書，現在是
個實業家．二兒子當初在大學念文
科，後來不念文科，在工業學校念
書，現在在外國研究工業．人家都
說張先生有兩個好兒子．

5. 有一個學校前天開學，當天就上課
了．學生對先生說："以前開學的時
候，當天都不上課．多半是開學第
二天上課．這次學校也沒說明，為
甚麼當天就上課呢?"先生說："開學
就應該馬上上課．這是當然的事."

6. 我們這個縣城是個古城. 有人說在
五百多年以前從明朝的時候就有這
個縣城. 可是前天來了三個人都是
考古的. 當中還有一個有名的考古
5 學家. 他們給我一本<u>考古學報</u>, 在
<u>考古學報</u>上的說法, 這個縣城不是
從明朝的時候才有的, 是在一千五
百多年以前, 差不多是六朝以前三
國的時候, 要不然就是南北朝時候
10 就有這個縣城. 所以他們的想法是
必得來到這個縣城實在的看看. 要
是他們常年在這兒, 能在當地得到
一點兒古時候的東西才好.

7. 先生對學生說:"你們看這是東三省
的人口表. 東三省在中國的東北.
當初人口最少. 後來從山東省、河
北省去了很多人. 現在東三省的人
5 口也不少了."

8. 張文天是外科大夫. 他開刀很有名.
   當地人都知道他. 他初學小兒科.
   後來他想, 外科大夫太少了, 他應
   該學外科, 所以他又學外科了.

9. 高子才在學校教書. 本來不會畫圖
   表. 有一天, 下課以後, 校長叫他
   畫兩張圖表. 高子才說:"我沒畫過
   圖表. 我試試看." 他畫了以後, 校
   5 長說:"這兩張圖表畫的都好. 以後
   我們學校的圖表都請你畫."

10. 鐘表店的人說:"我們的鐘表都很好,
    手表更好. 要是你買手表, 當時給
    一半錢,就可以先試用四十八小時.
    要是你不買, 你已經給的那一半錢
    5 表店再給你."

11. 每次小考、月考張家文都說他考得
    不好, 我都說我考得很好. 前天大
    考, 張家文又說他考得不好, 我還

是説我考得很好. 後來張家文考第
一，我考第二. 有人説:"張家文每
次都説考得不好. 為甚麽考第一了
呢?"我説:"張家文每次考試考得好
5 不好從來不實説. 我説的都是實話."

12. 在七八十年以前,山東省有大刀會,
後來又有小刀會. 這兩個會都是因
為當時有很多國家想要中國的土地,
所以山東人民才有了這兩個會.

13. 從前中國人，很多人用心念文學.
當時他們的想法以為文學是最有用
的. 後來知道工業、實業在事實上
更有用，所以中國人也在工業上、
5 實業上用心了.

14. 前天我從家裏往學校去. 我是開我
姐姐的車. 走在半路上,車不走了.
没法子,我走路去的.差一點兒晚了.

15. 毛先生從一九三〇年到一九三四年
在這四年當中，他的事業很多了，
很有實力．在我們這一縣的土地、
買賣、甚麼的差不多都是他的．他
₅還有很多條大船．他實在是一個大
實業家．他雖然是很有名的實業家，
可是他一點兒學問也沒有．說實在
的，實業家也不必有學問．

16. 我這兩天心裏頭很難過，因為我姐
姐說了明年我不要念書了，叫我學
買賣．今天馬天才來了．他問我是
不是有心事，可是我的心事我不想
₅對別人說．他問了我半天，我也没
跟他說．他走了以後我想，人家大
家都念書，我因為没錢就不能念書
了，我一會兒跟我姐姐說上半天我
念書，下半天我學買賣．

17. 我是一個外國學生．我學中國語言．

我天天用一大半的時候學中國話.
外國人學中國話最難的是語法. 雖
然現在的語言學家寫的書用科學方
法說明語法，可是還是很難學.

18. 我的表是我姐姐的，可能有二十五
年了，常常不走. 人家都說我的表
可以請考古學家考古了，所以我必
得買一個了，可是我不知道得用多
5 少錢，也不知道到那個表店去買.

19. 從前中國人的看法是兒子要有學問，
也要有名，女兒不要有學問，最好
不念書，應該在家裏，不能到外邊
去. 從民國以來，女人也念大學了，
5 可是多一半念文科. 我姐姐考大學
他考上工科了. 人家都說女人念工
科沒有用.

20. 我是高中三的學生. 大考以後我要
考大學了，可是這裏的學生多，大

學少，所以在這裏考大學很難．我
要考中大工科．大家都說遠大工科
很好，可是比別的學校更難考．考
得上考不上，我試試看了．

21. 今天學校考試．我應該早一點兒到
學校去，可是現在已經八點鐘了，我
得馬上走了．

22. 這本書我念了一大半兒了．下半兒
沒念的我想明天念．姐姐說："你現
在為甚麼不念呢？你是不是有心事？
要是你有心事，你可以說，我給你
想法子．"我說："我沒心事．往後你
不要常說我有心事．"

23. 一個考古學家、一個科學家在一塊
兒說話．考古學家說："我研究的東
西都是以前的東西，對科學我是一
點兒也不懂．"科學家說："我對科學

雖然知道一點兒，可是對考古學也是不懂."

24. 高先生是一個有名的實業家．他的事業很多．去年他到這兒來，經過一個縣城．有人說應該去看看這個縣的縣長．高先生說:"我這次沒有看他的必要．下次再看他."

Exercise 5. Illustrative Sentences (English)

1. We're having an exam today on English Grammar and English Conversation.

2. He teaches third-year lower middle school Chinese. His teaching methods are excellent.

3. Does your school have any scholarly teachers of Chinese?

4. He was here for only two or three days last year. In my opinion it's possible that he will be here somewhat longer this year.

5. We had a final exam day before yesterday. I got a hundred in Chinese.

6. The teacher taught until they had mastered all the words, and then he stopped teaching. (Note pattern: V dào X bù/méi V le 'V until X and only then not V any more')

7. I study Chinese at least four hours a day, and at the most, ten.

8. That foreigner can write books in Chinese. (From the fact that) a foreigner can write books in Chinese, it can be seen that he is very learned.

9. It would be best if we used some other teaching methods.

10. This district has been in existence since 1920. (The date is pronounced yī jiǔ èr líng nián.)

11. Can you read this book with understanding?

12. Although he is good in his studies, he can't be said to be a talented student.

13. Did you tell him about that matter before I came?

14. In the opinion of other people [they think that] it's useless to study Chinese.

15. Of these two textbooks, which is better? ···They're both about the same.

16. Our student council holds one meeting each month.

17. I used this textbook when I first studied Chinese.

18. Did China have any intercourse with Western countries at the time of the Northern and Southern Dynasties?

19. Was the Three Kingdoms (period) before or after the Six Dynasties?

20. He has a talent for teaching.

21. Quite a few foreigners came to China during the Ming Dynasty.

22. The characters that you study each day you should (also) master the same day [lit. that time].

23. Each month I have to spend a minimum of about $200.

24. Each day Mr. Mao teaches us the way to write five characters.

25. That textbook isn't mine; it's someone else's.

26. He won't be able to be here permanently. He'll be here for three months at the most.

27. From the beginning, when he was studying in lower middle school, Fang Yishan had quite a bent for speaking.

28. Chinese is not easy to study, and the literary style is of course even less easy.

29. If you go from here to Shanghai by train, you can get there the same day.

30. If this book is intended for foreigners to read, it should have an explanation in English.

31. You should write both the name and the address for him.

32. The one sitting in the middle is District Magistrate Ma.

33. His view [lit. way of saying] is that in beginning the study of a foreign language, one should first learn grammar. Do you think [lit. say] that's right ?

34. This book can't be bought at the place in question.

35. Lu Dawen has done a lot of research in atomic energy. He certainly is a talented person.

Chronological Chart

1949	Rénmín Gònghéguó
1911	Zhōnghuá Mínguó
	Qīng
1644	
	Míng
1368	
1280	Yuán
	Sòng
960	
907	Wǔdài Shíguó
	Táng
618	
589	Suí
	Nán Běi Cháo
420	
265	Jìn
220	Sān Guó
AD 0	
BC	Hàn
206	
221	Qín
	Zhànguó
403	
	Chūnqiū
772	
	Zhōu
1028	
	Shāng
1500	

Lesson 27

1	2	3	4	5
病	貴	姓	吃	飯

6	7	8	9	10
館	或	者	談	代

1. 病　bìng　　(1) be sick; (2) sickness, illness

2. 貴　guì　　　(1) expensive, dear; (2) your (honorific)

3. 姓　xìng　　(1) surname; (2) have the surname

4. 吃　chī　　　eat

5. 飯　fàn　　　(1) cooked rice; (2) food, a meal

6. 館　guǎn*　establishment

7. 或　huò*　　(1) either, or; (2) perhaps

8. 者　zhě　　　(verb suffix indicating doer of an action)

9. 談　tán　　　chat, discuss

10. 代　dài*　　generation

Special Combinations

1. 報館　bàoguǎn　　newspaper office

2. 本事　běnshi　　　(special) ability, something one is good at

3. 病人　bìngrén　　　sick person, patient

347

4.	朝代	cháodài	dynastic period, dynasty
5.	吃飯	chī fàn	eat [food]
6.	吃飯館(兒)	chī fànguǎn(r)	eat in a restaurant (colloquial)
7.	吃小館(兒)	chī xiǎoguǎn(r)	eat in a small restaurant (colloquial)
8.	飯車	fànchē	dining car
9.	飯館(兒)	fànguǎn(r)	restaurant
10.	飯店	fàndiàn	hotel (one serving meals)
11.	古代	gǔdài	antiquity, ancient times
12.	貴姓?	guìxìng?	what is your (sur)name?
13.	好吃	hǎochī	tasty, delicious, good to eat
14.	或是	huòshi	(1) perhaps, or, or else, otherwise; (2) either…or (used twice)
15.	或者	huòzhě	(1) perhaps, or, or else, otherwise; (2) either…or (used twice)
16.	或者是	huòzhě shi	(1) perhaps, or else; (2) it may be that, perhaps is
17.	家常飯	jiāchángfàn	home cooking, plain food (such as one gets at home)
18.	近代	jìndài	modern period, contemporary period
19.	開飯	kāi fàn	serve a meal
20.	看病	kàn bìng	(1) attend a sickness; (2) see a doctor
21.	毛病	máobing	(1) defect; (2) bad habit
22.	生病	shēng bìng	become sick
23.	時代	shídài	epoch, period, era
24.	談話	tán huà	chat, converse
25.	談天(兒)	tán tiān(r)	chat, gossip
26.	談心	tán xīn	converse about personal matters, have a heart-to-heart talk
27.	圖書館	túshūguǎn	library
28.	晚飯	wǎnfàn	dinner, supper
29.	現代	xiàndài	modern period, contemporary period

30.	小館(兒)	xiǎoguǎn(r)	small restaurant
31.	姓名	xìngmíng	name (surname and given name)
32.	學者	xuézhě	scholar
33.	要飯	yào fàn	beg for food
34.	要飯的	yàofànde	beggar
35.	有病	yǒu bìng	be sick, have an illness
36.	早飯	zǎofàn	breakfast
37.	中飯	zhōngfàn	lunch

Exercise 1. Pitfalls

1. 我天天吃中國飯.
   我天天吃飯館兒.

2. 我跟他說話.
   我跟他很好.

3. 外國字典很貴.
   外邊吃飯很貴.

4. 他們不在家吃.
   中飯不在家吃.

Exercise 2. Illustrative Sentences (Chinese)

1. 你飯後吃點心嗎?

2. 他們一個月給我四百塊錢工錢.

3. 你就在這兒念書還是想到別的學校去念書?

4. 他病好了沒有？…他的病還沒好呢.

5. 吃飯館兒很貴. 我每天飯錢用的不少.

6. 我跟他很好. 没話不談.

7. 我或者今天晚上在會上看得見他.

8. 邊大夫八點鐘前後到這兒來給我看病.

9. 他不是要飯的，他是賣報的.

10. 現代中國這本書貴不貴？

11. 大夫説我一兩天不吃飯病就會好的.

12. 到上海的火車甚麼時候開？有飯車嗎？

13. 四百年前是甚麼朝代？

14. 我不是教書的. 我是研究生.

15. 他因為吃多了生病.

16. 你坐三號車可以在學校大門口下車.

17. 他來的目的是要買一條水牛.

18. 我們家每天晚飯都是八點鐘開飯.

19. 我不吃早飯. 中飯在小館兒吃，或者在家吃.

20. 我說家常飯比飯館兒的飯好吃. 你說呢？

21. 門口有個要飯的.

22. 現代是原子時代.

23. 那個學者最近寫了一本書，書名叫湖邊談話.

24. 中國古代三國的時候有一個很有本事的開刀大夫姓華.

25. 我的車雖然很貴，可是時常有毛病.

26. 報館、圖書館、飯店、甚麼的都在那條路上.

27. 你們先寫姓名然後再看書.

28. 我就能跟他談天兒,不能跟他談心.

29. 他寫的<u>近代語文</u>跟<u>中國現代語法</u>我都看過.

30. 他今天没來. 或者是有病了.

31. 你貴姓?⋯我姓<u>馬</u>.

32. 大夫說那個病人活不了了.

33. 他常年教我中文.

34. 我問他貴姓, 他說他姓<u>張</u>.

35. 我問<u>萬</u>先生知道不知道甚麼地方有書店. <u>萬</u>先生說他說不上那裏有書店.

Exercise 3. Dialogues

1. 應: <u>馬</u>太太生病了你知道嗎?
   毛: 是嗎? 我不知道他病了. 看大夫了嗎?

應：沒看，他現在好一點兒了.

毛：應該請大夫看看才好.

2. 高：前天我跟馬大文我姐姐三個人
去吃飯館兒. 我的車走在半路
上有了毛病了，不走了. 我們
三個人下車走路去的. 走了有
一個鐘頭.

白：甚麼毛病？

高：不知道. 本來一點兒毛病也没
有.

3. 張：文太太，你上那兒去？

文：我到張大夫那兒看病去.

張：這兩天病人很多. 我大女兒也
病了.

4. 華：我們去吃個小飯館兒好不好？

方：好. 到那兒去吃呢？

華：我們到一個北方小館兒去吃.

方：好的.

華：這兒有一個小館兒叫萬年小館
　　兒，或者我們到華北飯店？

方：我們不要到華北．華北是大飯
　　館兒，太貴了．到萬年小館兒
　　去吃．又好吃又不貴，在那兒
　　吃飯的一大半兒是學生．還有，
　　那個飯館兒雖然叫小館兒，可
　　是地方很大．飯後可以在那兒
　　談談天．

5. 應：你家不在這兒．每天你在那兒
　　吃飯呢？

文：我早飯、中飯都在學校吃．晚
　　飯我在外邊兒吃．

應：外邊兒吃飯很貴．你一年飯錢
　　也用不少了．

文：可不是嗎！我都是吃最小的小
　　館兒，要不然錢用的太多了．

6. 白：你姓甚麼？

路：我姓<u>路</u>．我叫<u>路國才</u>．

白：你是那兒人？

路：我是河北人，先生．

白：我就是要用一個北方工人．你

5　　以前在那兒？

路：我從前的主人也是一個英國人．
　　現在他到日本去了．

白：我這兒的事很容易．就是我一
　　個人．我每天晚飯吃中國飯．

10路：好的．先生請問你，每天早飯、
　　中飯、晚飯都是甚麼時候開飯？

白：早飯八點鐘，晚飯七點鐘．中
　　飯不在家吃．晚飯大半兒都在
　　家吃．我一個月給你一百塊錢

15　　工錢．

路：好．明天早上我來試試看．

7. 文：<u>馬子才</u>，你病好了嗎？

馬：好了．已經好了一個月了．

8. 毛： 小姐貴姓？

　 張： 我姓張．你是毛先生嗎？

　 毛： 我是毛為文．張小姐甚麼時候
　　　 到這兒的？

5 張： 我來九個月了．

　 毛： 你就在這兒還是想到別的地方
　　　 去呢？

　 張： 今年過年或者是明年我到華南
　　　 去．

9. 錢： 應文長，你有中國現代語法這
　　　 本書没有？

　 應： 我没有．你要看嗎？

　 錢： 是．

5 應： 你到圖書館去看看．

　 錢： 圖書館在那兒？我還不知道呢．

　 應： 就在中華報館西邊兒．

10. 南： 你見過萬有實先生嗎？

　 邊： 是不是那個很有名的學者萬先
　　　 生？

南：是的．

邊：見過，可是沒說過話．

11. 路：這張畫兒是甚麼朝代的？

古：有人說是南北朝的．

路：我說不可能是南北朝的．

古：南北朝的畫兒現在買的到嗎？

5 路：買不到，時代太遠了．

12. 文：你看門口兒又來一個要飯的．

華：為甚麼天天有要飯的到這兒要
飯呢？

13. 張：我坐火車差不多一天沒吃飯了．

高：不是有飯車嗎？

張：飯車上東西太貴，也不好吃．

14. 馬：張東生為甚麼今年不來上學呢？

毛：他有病，不能念書．病好了再
念書．

馬：他有甚麼病？

毛：大夫都不知道他生的是甚麼病.

馬：他病了多少日子了？

毛：差不多有三個月了.

15. 張：馬有為, 你教給我一點兒英文好不好？

馬：我能教你嗎？

張：你當然能教我了.

5 馬：我們得每天下課以後學.

張：當然了. 你在那兒教我呢？

馬：學校或是我家都可以.

16. 毛：先生, 你是不是遠大的研究生？

文：不是. 我是教書的. 我在第一中學教書.

17. 錢：你吃中飯了嗎？

田：沒有.

錢：走. 到我那兒吃中飯去. 吃家常飯為的是談談心.

田：家常飯更好吃．我們没有家的
　　人天天想吃家常飯．

18. 馬：那張山水畫是甚麼朝代的？
　　白：是明朝的．我還有我姐姐最近
　　　　畫的畫兒．請你看看．
　　馬：畫的太好了．你姐姐又能寫，
　5　　　又能畫．近代文學、古代文學
　　　　又都有研究．

Exercise 4. Narratives

1. 我在美國常吃中國飯．有的時候吃
飯館兒，有的時候在張先生家裏吃．
今年我到了中國，差不多天天吃中
國飯．我是早上八點鐘吃早飯，多
5 半在家吃．中飯大半在學校吃．晚
飯或是在家吃，或者是吃小館兒．
晚上十點鐘前後我還要吃一點兒點
心．飯館兒飯雖然好吃，可是我還
想吃張先生家裏的家常飯．

2. 錢大文有病了. 他去看病. 當時看
   病的病人很多, 大夫没工夫給錢大
   文看病. 有人問錢大文是甚麼病.
   他説吃飯以後就病了,可能吃多了.
   5 那個人説要是因為吃多了生病, 最
   好今天就吃少一點兒, 或者是不吃
   東西, 病就會好的, 没有看大夫的
   必要.

3. 上次我坐火車到上海去. 我在飯車
   上吃飯的時候,火車已經到上海了.
   我才下車, 火車馬上就開了, 差一
   點兒我下不了火車.

4. 毛子文很有天才, 也有口才. 從前
   念書的時候就是學校的高才生. 現
   在他是有名的實業家, 在實業上很
   有實力. 他的事業很多. 今天是實
   5 業學校請毛子文對學生説話. 他説
   了兩小時的話, 以後他就來看我.

我以前跟毛子文常有來往. 今天我
要請他吃中飯. 他説他没工夫, 他
上半天來的, 下半天在當地還有事,
當天晚上就要走. 他又説往後可能
5 常來.

5. 中國人寫姓名的時候, 是先寫姓,
然後再寫名字. 比方有一個人姓馬
名字叫天實, 他寫他的姓名就寫馬
天實.

6. 我們學校的晚飯是每天晚上七點鐘
開飯. 今天晚上因為要開晚會, 所
以六點鐘就開飯了.

7. 中國的飯館兒, 吃飯的人都是吃過
了飯才給飯錢. 日本的飯館兒, 有
的地方是先給飯錢然後吃飯.

8. 今天我在圖書館看書. 坐在我前邊
兒有兩個人談話. 離我很近的地方

又有兩個人一邊看報一邊談天. 我
想, 到圖書館來為的是看書,不應該
在這裏談天.

9. 張大田是個要飯的. 當初很有錢.
從小就不用心念書, 也没本事, 可
是毛病很多. 每天在大飯店吃飯用
錢很多. 買東西, 都是買最貴的.
5 每月用的錢太多. 從一九五〇年到
一九六〇年十年的工夫就没錢了,
當然就得要飯了.

10. 中國從古代到現代當中有很多朝代.
有的朝代很長, 有的不長. 比方説,
明朝這個朝代是從一三六八年到一
六四四年, 有二百七十多年, 是近
5 代最長的朝代.

11. 馬先生是個學者. 教書差不多有五
十年了. 他的教法很好. 近來研究

六朝文學，也研究南北朝的文學．
有人說他是六朝文學家．

12. 馬路上有賣報的．我要買前天的<u>華</u>
<u>美晚報</u>．賣報的說："我就有當天的
報，你要是買前天的報，必得到報
館去買．"

13. <u>田</u>小姐跟他姐姐都在一個學校裏教
書，都教國語．<u>田</u>小姐的教學法是
不用教科書．他姐姐說教書應該用
教科書．他們每天都在學校吃中飯．
5 有一天<u>田</u>小姐說："我不想吃中飯了．"
他姐姐說："你為甚麼不吃飯了呢？
是不是有甚麼心事?"<u>田</u>小姐說："我
沒有心事．"他姐姐說："你說你沒有
心事，可是你為甚麼不吃飯？我想
10 你還是有心事．你要說實話．"<u>田</u>小
姐說："我實在沒有心事．我說的是
事實．"他姐姐說："要不然你是生病

了."田小姐説:"我也没生病. 得了！
得了！你不要問了. 我吃中飯去."
他姐姐説:"説實在的，我看你還是
有心事. 你是不實説. 你要是實説
⁵了我或者給你想個法子."田小姐説：
"是嗎？我不是有心事.我是想,教國
語應該不應該用教科書."

14. 有人問我:"你貴姓?"我説:"我姓張."
我又問他，他説他也姓張. 我們兩
個人都姓張. 可能五百年前我們還
是一家呢.

15. 我是個教書的. 我在文華中學教國
文. 我教五十二個學生. 在這五十
二個人裏頭，有的書念的很好，有
的書念的很不好.

16. 前天我在學生會看見毛大文了. 我
們兩個人在一塊兒談話. 他説他最

近又買了很多書，他的書現在差不
多有一千本．我說我的書最少，字
典在外最多也不過二十本．

17. 很多人以為中國近代才有外科大夫，
可是事實上，中國古時候就有外科
大夫了．比方說三國時代就有很有
名的一個外科大夫．

18. 我就會說中國話，不很會寫中國字．
我的名字是錢為時．我雖然會說我
的名字，可是不知道寫法．我得請
張先生寫給我．

19. 張一力要到日本去了．我的看法他
不是去念書，因為他在日本有很多
買賣．他雖然沒說明為甚麼去日本，
我的想法他不會念書的．比方說要
是念書去，為甚麼九月不去，現在
才去呢？

20. 前天下半天工業學校來了一個外國
工業家. 校長請他對學生說話. 他
說了很多話. 他最初說工業要有人
才, 當中說工業應當有實力, 最後
5 說到「鐘表工業」.他說的是法文.
學生多一半能懂法文, 所以他說的
話學生多一半明白. 學生說:"他說
得很好. 可以得到很多學問. 不知
道他幾點鐘走. 要是有工夫, 再請
10 他說一點兒西方的工業." 校長說:
"這個外國工業家今天有事.當地還
有別人請他說話呢."

21. 我初學國語的時候, 張先生說要先
念中國字. 有人說張先生的說法很
對, 有人說他的說法不對. 我也是
說張先生的說法不對, 因為我是要
5 學說話, 不是要念書.

22. 高知遠要離開他的家了. 家裏有人

問他，要甚麼東西？他説："我就要
那條水牛．別的東西我都不要．上
次我已經説給你們了．要是你們能
給我那條水牛，今天就給我才好．"

Exercise 5. Illustrative Sentences (English)

1. Do you have dessert after a meal?

2. They give me wages of $400 a month.

3. Will you study just here, or do you plan to go elsewhere to study?

4. Has he recovered yet from his illness?···He isn't over his illness yet.

5. Eating in restaurants is expensive. I spend quite a bit on food every day.

6. I'm on very good terms with him. There isn't anything that we don't talk about.

7. Perhaps I'll be able to see him at the meeting this evening.

8. Dr. Bian will come here about 8:00 to see me [lit. see my illness].

9. He's not a beggar. He's a newsboy.

10. Is the book Contemporary China expensive?

11. The doctor says I'm likely to get better if I don't eat for a day or two.

12. When does the train for Shanghai leave? Does it have a diner?

13. What dynasty was it four hundred years ago?

14. I'm not a teacher. I'm a graduate student.

15. He became ill because he overate.

16. If you take the No. 3 car, you can get off at the main gate of the school.

17. His reason for coming is to buy a water buffalo.

18. In our home, dinner is served every day at eight o'clock.

19. I don't eat breakfast. I eat lunch in a little restaurant or at home.

20. I think [lit. say] home cooking is tastier than restaurant food. What do you think?

21. There's a beggar at the door.

22. This is the age of the atom.

23. That scholar has recently written a book, the title of which is Lakeside Chats.

24. [In ancient times] at the time of the Three Kingdoms there was a very skillful surgeon named Hua.

25. Although my car was very expensive, it's constantly breaking down.

26. The newspaper offices, libraries, restaurants, etc., are all on that street.

27. First write your surnames and given names, and afterwards read.

28. I can talk with him only (about inconsequential matters). I can't talk with him about personal matters.

29. I've read both the Contemporary Language and the Modern Chinese Grammar that he's written.

30. He didn't come today, perhaps he's sick.

31. What's your name?···My name is Ma.

32. The doctor says that that patient can't survive.

33. He has taught me Chinese year after year.

34. I asked him what his name was, and he said it was Zhang.

35. I asked Mr. Wan if he knew where there was a bookstore. Mr. Wan said that he couldn't say for sure.

Lesson 28

1	2	3	4	5
定	告	訴	如	果

6	7	8	9	10
飛	機	意	思	價

1. 定　dìng　　(1) definite ; (2) make definite, decide on ; (3) order (goods)

2. 告　gào*　　tell, inform

3. 訴　sù, sòng*　　make known

4. 如　rú*　　(1) as ; (2) if

5. 果　guǒ*　　(1) fruit ; (2) result, outcome

6. 飛　fēi　　to fly

7. 機　jī*　　(1) mechanism, machine ; (2) opportunity

8. 意　yì*　　(1) idea ; (2) meaning ; (3) intention

9. 思　sī*　　think

10. 價　jià*　　price

Special Combinations

1. 比如　　　bǐrú　　　　　(1) for instance ; (2) let us suppose, if

2. 不好意思　bùhǎoyìsi　　be embarrassed

369

3.	不如···好	bùrú···(hǎo)	not equal to (in pattern A bùrú B (hǎo) 'B is better than A' or 'It is better to B than to A.')
4.	不如不	bùrú bù	would be best not to (do something), better not
5.	不一定	bù yídìng	(1) uncertain ; (2) not necessarily, not definitely
6.	大意	dàyì	general idea
7.	得意	déyì	(1) pleased with oneself ; (2) successful, prosperous(refers to accomplishments)
8.	地價	dìjià	price of land
9.	定價	dìngjià	(1) fix a price (VO); (2) fixed price, list price
10.	定錢	dìngqian	a deposit (on a purchase)
11.	飛機	fēijī	airplane
12.	告訴	gàosu	tell, inform
13.	果然	guǒrán	sure enough (very emphatic)
14.	機會	jīhui	opportunity, chance
15.	價目	jiàmu	price
16.	價目表	jiàmu biǎo	price list
17.	價錢	jiàqian	price, cost
18.	課文	kèwén	text
19.	賣價	màijià	selling price
20.	没(有)意思	méi (yǒu) yìsi	uninteresting
21.	如果	rúguǒ	if
22.	如意	rúyì	(1) accord with one's wishes, be satisfying ; (2) satisfied(refers to wishes)
23.	生意	shēngyi	way of making a living, business
24.	説不定	shuōbudìng	(1) can't say for sure ; (2) perhaps
25.	説定	shuōdìng	say for sure, be definite
26.	書價	shūjià	price of books

27. 水果   shuǐguǒ   fruit

28. 往下   wàngxià   (1) toward the bottom; (2) continue doing something (when followed by a verb)

29. 要價   yàojià   asking price

30. 一定   yídìng   certain(ly), sure(ly)

31. 一定要   yídìng yào   (1) definitely want; (2) insist on (doing something)

32. 意見   yìjian   opinion, view

33. 意思   yìsi   (1) idea, thought; (2) meaning

34. 意外   yìwài   (1) unexpected; (2) unexpected event, accident

35. 用法   yòngfǎ   way of using, use (N)

36. 用意   yòngyì   intention, purpose

37. 有用意   yǒu yòngyì   have a (special) reason (for doing something)

38. 有意思   yǒu yìsi   (1) be interesting; (2) have an idea

39. 原價   yuánjià   original price

40. 主意   zhúyi   (1) determination, decision; (2) suggestion, idea

Note on Titles of Publications

Titles of books and articles in Chinese often contain fixed expressions comparable to English On···, The Question of···, Studies on···, History of···, etc. Study the following examples of titles of actual publications.

說「的」	On de
再說「的」	More on de
談文學的教法	On the Teaching of Literature
也談「的」字的用法	Also on the Uses of the Character de
文學常談	Frequent Chats on Literature
文法兩問	Two Questions of Grammar
中國人口研究	Studies on the Population of China

Exercise 1. Pitfalls

1. 他說這本書好.
   他說坐飛機好.

2. 他們都寫的好.
   他們都寫的了.

3. 這是一個很好的機會.
   這是一個坐船的機會.

4. 我坐了三天船.
   我坐了三次船.

Exercise 2. Practice in Reading Titles

The following list contains the titles of twenty books and articles on Chinese which are included in <u>Bibliography and Glossary for Chinese Grammar,</u> by William S. Y. Wang and Lillian Liu. Give an acceptable English translation for each title.

1. 中國現代語法
2. 說「給」
3. 教不教語法？
4. 語文常談
5. 中國語文研究
6. 「呢，嗎」的用法
7. 說「是…的」
8. 能，可，會，得
9. 中國文法
10. 人民文學
11. 語言研究
12. 國語文法
13. 說「所以」
14. 後邊的說明前邊的
15. 中學語法教學
16. 初中語文課本
17. 談字的教學
18. 語法三問
19. 說「差一點」
20. 也談「好」字的用法

Exercise 3. Illustrative Sentences (Chinese)

1. 我告訴他的目的是叫他也知道.

2. 前天的會張先生談的是現代文學.

3. 他病好了再到中國去.

4. 我很少有機會跟他談談.

5. 我們原價是五塊錢. 現在賣價是四塊半.

6. 你說坐飛機好，我們就坐飛機. 我沒意見.

7. 今天開會多半是沒意思. 說不定我不去.

8. 坐飛機不如坐船好.

9. 還是坐飛機好. 要不然該晚了.

10. 他才下了飛機就去看張校長.

11. 你如果走路到那兒太晚了.

12. 你一定要去，我就跟你一塊兒去.

13. 他叫我去是有用意的. 他的意思是叫我見見<u>錢</u>先生.

14. 對那個事我沒主意了.

15. 我不明白「了」字的用法.

16. 對這個事你有甚麼主意？

17. 他今天一定要請我吃飯，我實在不好意思.

18. 你給他一點兒定錢沒有？

19. 現在坐飛機很少有意外.

20. 明天下半天我不一定到學校去.

21. 他說<u>文心</u>這本書有意思. 今天我買了一本看看. 果然很有意思.

22. 你看看價目表就知道書價多少了.

23. <u>馬</u>先生的生意近來不很好.

24. 最近地價很貴. 張先生那塊地要賣.
他要價五千塊錢.

25. 這裏書的價錢都是定價.

26. 我們現在說定是明天上半天去還是
明天下半天去.

27. 華大文, 你說一說這課書的大意.

28. 馬先生近來在生意上很不得意.

29. 請你們現在寫生字. 從第五課往下
寫, 寫到第七課.

30. 中國人以前吃家常飯, 吃飯以後很
少吃水果.

31. 比如我有機會到中國去我一定去看
看萬里長城.

32. 萬先生近來有很多不如意的事.

33. 我念國語課本,先念生字後念課文.

34. 如果你手邊有地圖，你可以看看地
圖就知道太湖是在華東了.

35. 我對姐姐說我要坐飛機到上海去.
姐姐說:"可以."

Exercise 4. Dialogues

1. 張: 你到中國去坐飛機還是坐船?

南: 大半兒坐飛機. 本來想坐船.
坐船很有意思，可是如果坐船
到那兒太晚了,人家都開學了.

5 張: 你十五號一定走了?

南: 十五號不一定走的了，可是二
十號我一定走.

張: 你告訴文先生了嗎?

南: 我還沒機會跟他說呢.

2. 常: 你到那兒去?

邊: 我看毛小姐去. 他近來有很多
事不如意, 他生病了.

常：毛小姐有病了！請大夫看了嗎？

邊：看過了．

常：如果你再去看他我跟你一塊兒
　　去看看他．

5 邊：好．

常：你說我要是看他去買點兒水果
　　還是買點兒點心好呢？

邊：你不必買東西．

常：看病人去應該買點兒東西．

10 邊：你一定要買就買點兒水果好了．
　　我去以前一定告訴你．我們一
　　塊兒去．

3. 白：那條大木船多少錢？

毛：原價本來是三百五十塊錢．後
　　來他們賣價是三百二十塊錢．

白：那條船三百二十塊錢不太貴．

4. 高：我們吃飯館兒去好不好？

錢：好．我也想吃飯館兒了．我們

到那兒去吃？

高：到大華飯店去吃好不好？

錢：不吃大華. 他們的價錢太貴了.
我們不如去吃個小館兒. 價錢
不貴，東西好吃. 大華的東西
很貴，可是他們的東西不一定
比小館兒的好吃.

高：所以他們的生意不好呢.

錢：你對門兒的山東小館兒好不好？

高：不好. 人家都說不好. 前天我
去試試，果然不好吃. 不如不
去，在家吃家常飯了.

5. 華：明天晚上八點鐘實業學校有個
會.

張：甚麼會？

華：實業學校請了一個實業家來談
話.

張：我不想去. 没意思. 你去嗎？

華：原來我也不想去．毛校長一定
　　叫我去．他說他叫我去是有用
　　意的，為的是叫我見見那個實
　　業家，所以不好意思不去．比
5　如你沒事你也去，好不好？

張：現在我沒主意了．你說我去不
　　去呢？

華：去，去．談的是現代工業，對
　　我們工科學生很有用．

10 張：好，我也去．

華：說定了．你不能不去了．

張：好．你還沒告訴我在那兒呢？

華：就在實業學校．

6. 錢：現在這兒的地價貴不貴？

白：不很貴．這兩三年以來都差不
　　多．你要買地嗎？

錢：我沒錢買地．是一個姓張的叫
5　我給他問問．

白：得了！得了！你說姓張的叫你
　　問，說不定是你要買.

錢：我跟要飯的差不多了. 我還有
　　錢買地嗎？

7. 文：那塊水田你要不要買？

田：多少錢？

文：要價不高. 二千九百塊錢.

田：兩千九不很貴. 可以買.

5 文：如果你想買我有個意見. 你先
　　給他一點兒定錢，因為很多人
　　要買那塊水田，要不然別人就
　　買了.

8. 路：我看張為民近來很得意是不是？

南：當然了. 他的事很好，省長對
　　他也好，所以他很得意.

9. 先生：第九課課文的大意你們都懂
　　　　了嗎？

學生：有的懂了，有的不懂.

先生：以後不懂的地方，你們要問
　　　我.

學生：先生,我們第九課念了以後是
5　　　考試呢還是往下念第十課呢?

先生：我們念了第十課再考.　你們
　　　還有不懂的沒有？現在問.

學生：先生，我不明白「了」字的
　　　用法.

10先生：到時候了.　下次再告訴你.

10. 邊：是不是所有的書上都有價目？

錢：有的書上有，有的沒有.　要是
　　你想知道書價多少，你跟書店
　　要一張價目表,那上頭有定價.

11. 毛：張文明到湖北去.　為甚麼不坐
　　飛機坐船呢？

白：他說坐船的意外比飛機少.

毛： 現在飛機很少有毛病．不會常
　　　有意外．

12. 錢： 我這次坐了七天火車．我每天
　　　中飯、晚飯都到飯車去吃．
　　田： 飯車上的東西不好吃．
　　錢： 這次很意外，飯車上的飯很好
　5　　吃．
　　田： 飯車上的飯好吃這是意外的事
　　　了．

Exercise 5. Narratives

1. 我要買車．張先生來告訴我，田先
生的車要賣，價錢不貴．我就跟張
先生去看田先生的車．田先生說這
個車他買的原價很貴，現在的賣價
5 是八百塊．我說："這個車很好．八
百塊錢要價不貴．我一定買了．不
過，我要在後天給錢．今天要不要

先給一點兒定錢?"田先生説:"我們
説定就可以了. 不必給定錢."

2. 我跟姐姐要一塊兒去日本. 我姐姐
的意思是坐船去, 我想坐飛機. 我
説:"我們没坐過飛機. 這是一個坐
飛機的機會." 姐姐説:"坐船很有意
思, 價錢又不貴. 還有, 如果坐飛
機要是有了意外那就更不好了." 我
説:"坐飛機不一定都有意外. 不過,
你説坐船好, 我也没意見. 我們就
坐船好了."

3. 我在圖書館裏看見一張中國朝代圖.
這張圖很好. 從古代到現代所有的
朝代圖上都有.每個朝代有多少年,
圖上也有.

4. 我是一個賣水果的. 近來生意很不
好. 有時候賣五六塊錢, 有時候賣
一兩塊錢. 説不定有時候没人買.

5. 有人說:"念書能懂大意就可以了.
不必每一個字都懂." 我的意思是念
書必得都懂. 如果念了半天不都懂,
不如不念了.

6. 有一天我跟錢先生在小館兒裏, 一
邊吃飯一邊談天. 在那裏坐了三個
鐘頭, 不好意思再坐了, 我們就走
了. 走在路上, 錢先生說:"我們不
如到時代書店去看看書, 如果有原
子能的用法我想買一本." 我說:"你
這個主意很好, 我也想買書呢."

7. 在書店買書如果不知道書價, 應當
先看看書上有沒有價目. 要是沒有,
再看圖書價目表. 圖書價目表上一
定有定價.

8. 我對文先生說:"明天學生日報在報
館裏開會. 我們必得有一個人去.
或是你去, 或者是我去. 最好是你

去．比如你有事，就是我去."文先
生說:"明天開會多半是有用意的．
你比我有本事．我看我去不如你去
好."

9. 前天我在大華飯店吃飯，吃的太多
了．當時我就想，我不應該吃多了，
要是吃多了，該生病了，還得去看
病．今天我果然有病了．不想吃東
5 西，就吃水果．我想以後要是我再
吃飯館兒我得小心一點兒．

10. 張先生要買一塊地．我跟他說近來
這裏的地價很貴，如果沒有買的必
要，最好現在不必買地．

11. 張力子是一個有名的學者．他教書
教了差不多四十年．現在他在一個
大學教近代中國文學．他教書以外
每天就是寫書．他常對人說他最得
5 意的事就是寫書．

12. 有一天張先生來跟我談話. 他說要
跟我談談心, 他有點兒不如意的事
要告訴我. 張先生才說到這裏, 有
人來了. 張先生看來人了, 他就不
5 往下說了. 他說:"我先走了. 或者
明天或者是後天我再來."

13. 我們國文先生的教學法很不好, 所
以大家都說國文沒意思. 他天天上
課就教給我們課本上的課文. 我們
請他說給我們一點兒課本以外的東
5 西. 他說一定要念課本, 別的不是
必要的.

14. 前天學生會開會. 張會長對大家說
話說的很有意思. 後來又有一個人
對大家說話,說的話又長又沒意思,
所以很多人都走了.

15. 我每年一定從中國到英國去一次,
每次都是坐船經過地中海. 有一次

船又走到地中海，我在船上吃早飯
的時候，看見了一個人．這個人我
從前見過，可是我不知道他的姓名，
我又不好意思問他貴姓．後來他說
5 他姓高，上次我們見過了．他又說
很有意思我們前後見過兩次，都是
在這條船上，都是船走在地中海．

16. 張先生想請我吃飯．他的目的是要
跟我談談．我說："不必你請我了．
我請你吃中飯或者晚飯．我們去吃
小館兒，沒有別人，就是我們兩個
5 人."我們就到萬年小館兒去吃北方
飯．

17. 學校裏的先生對學生說："一個文明
國家的人民在坐車、坐船的時候，
要先請女人坐下．走路的時候也要
請女人先走．不然，那就不是一個
5 文明國家的人民了."

18. 有一個文學家去年寫了五本書，他
在報上寫的東西在外．有人說他寫
書的時候一邊寫一邊跟人家說話．
可見他寫書是很容易的．

19. 有一個要飯的在路上要飯．要了半
天，没有人給他．他看見一個小學
生，離他不遠，一邊走一邊吃東西．
他就對小學生要東西吃.小學生說：
5 "我的東西已經吃了一半了.還有一
半兒可以給你吃."

20. 田先生告訴我他這次是坐火車來的.
他在火車上坐了二十多個鐘頭．他
說往後不坐火車了．一來在火車上
没意思，二來在半路上想吃東西必
5 得在飯車上吃．飯車上的飯不好吃，
所以以後他不想坐火車了．他要坐
飛機了．

21. 有一個病人坐人力車去看病. 到了
大夫的門口, 大夫不在家. 這個病
人說:"我往後不來這裏看病了, 因
為這個大夫常常不在家."

22. 張大有的家離這兒三里, 是在一條
小河的西邊. 他有一條水牛、一塊
水田. 這條水牛每天早上跟張大有
到水田裏去, 晚上就跟張大有到家
裏來. 前天張大有說他的水牛有病
了, 活不了了. 他的心裏很難過.

23. 有一個實業家, 事業很多, 也很有
實力. 在他的事業裏, 最大的是鐘
表工業, 最小的是手工業. 他說：
"實業在事實上雖然有大有小, 可是
都是事業."

24. 今天早上我念英文的時候, 毛文華
來了. 他說:"得了,得了！別念了.
我們到外頭去走走." 我說:"後天我

要考英文. 我才念了上半本，還有
一大半没念." 他説:"不要念了，你
已經念了一半兒了. 明天再念好不
好?"没法子. 我就跟他一塊兒到外
⁵頭去了. 這次英文大半兒考不了一
百.

25. 我問華長木近來有心事嗎？ 他説：
"誰告訴你我有心事?"我説:"你有
心事為甚麼不對我實説呢? 我從來
有事都對你説實話. 説實在的， 你
⁵是不是有心事?"他才説:"没心事.
我想家了."

Exercise 6. Illustrative Sentences (English)

1. My purpose in telling him was to have him know about it, too.
2. What Mr. Zhang spoke about at the meeting day before yesterday was modern Chinese literature.
3. He'll go to China after he has recovered.
4. I very rarely have a chance to talk to him.

5. Our original price was $5. The selling price is now $4.50.

6. If you say it's better to go by plane, then let's go by plane. I don't have any objections [lit. any opinions].

7. Today's meeting will most likely be uninteresting. Perhaps I won't go.

8. It would be better to go by boat than by plane.

9. It would be better to go by plane after all. Otherwise you're bound to be late.

10. He went to see Principal Zhang as soon as he got off the plane.

11. If you go there on foot, you'll be too late.

12. If you insist on going, then I'll go along with you.

13. He had a special reason for having me go. His idea was to have me see Mr. Qian.

14. I have no idea how to deal with that matter.

15. I don't understand the use of the character le.

16. What suggestions do you have [regarding this matter]?

17. He insisted on inviting me to eat today. I certainly was embarrassed.

18. Did you give him a small deposit?

19. Nowadays planes rarely have accidents.

20. I'm not sure about going to school tomorrow afternoon.

21. He said that the book The Heart of Literature was very interesting. I bought a copy today and read it. Sure enough, it was quite interesting.

22. If you look at the price list, you can see [lit. know] what [lit. how much] the book prices are.

23. Mr. Ma's business hasn't been very good lately.

24. Recently land prices have been very high [lit. expensive]. That plot of land belonging to Mr. Zhang is for sale. His asking price (is) $5,000.

25. Book prices here are all fixed prices.

26. Let's say definitely now whether we go tomorrow morning or tomorrow afternoon.

27. Hua Dawen, tell (us) the general idea of this lesson.

28. Mr. Ma has been quite unsuccessful in business recently.

29. Please write the new characters now. Write (those) from lesson 5 to
     lesson 7.

30. Previously the Chinese rarely ate fruit after a home-cooked dinner.

31. If I had the opportunity to go to China, I would certainly go to see the
     Great Wall.

32. Mr. Wan has recently had many disagreeable things (happen to him).

33. In studying the National Language textbook, I study the new characters
     first and afterwards read the text.

34. If you have a map at hand, you can see [from the map] that Lake Tai
     is in East China.

35. I told my sister that I wanted to go Shanghai by plane. She said: "OK."

Lesson 29

1 2 3 4 5

6 7 8 9 10

1. 客 kè guest
2. 氣 qì (1) air ; (2) anger ; (3) angry (with)
3. 喜 xǐ* glad
4. 歡 huān* joyous
5. 間 jiān, jiàn* space between, interstice, interval
6. 簡 jiǎn* simple
7 單 dān* (1) single ; (2) a list
8. 票 piào ticket
9. 員 yuán* (1) member ; (2) (suffix like English <u>er</u> in 'teacher')
10. 元 yuán* (1) primary ; (2) Yuán dynasty (1260-1368); (3) dollar
11. 當 dāng be (in the role of)
12. 角 jiǎo* dime
13. 道 dào* say (See below, no.7)

Special Combinations

1. 別客氣 bié kèqi That's all right!, Don't mention it!, Please don't
   bother !

2. 不客氣   bú kèqi   (1) impolite ; (2) Don't mention it !

3. 不要客氣   bú yào kèqi   Don't mention it ! Don't stand on ceremony,
                             Make yourself at home

4. 船票   chuán piào   boat ticket

5. 大事   dàshì   major event, major happening

6. 單子   dānzi   a list

7. 道喜   dàoxǐ   offer congratulations (VO)

8. 店員   diànyuán   clerk in a store

9. 歡喜   huānxi   like, be fond of, be pleased (less common)

10. 會客   huì kè   receive guests, see visitors

11. 簡單   jiǎndān   simple

12. 簡寫   jiǎnxiě   abbreviate, write in abbreviated fashion

13. 簡易   jiǎnyì *   short and simple, abridged (used often in book
                             titles)

14. 價目單   jiàmu dān   price list

15. 教員   jiàoyuán   teacher

16. 開單子   kāi dānzi   make out a list

17. 客船   kèchuán   passenger boat

18. 客氣   kèqi   polite, courteous, kind

19. 客人   kèren   guest

20. 力氣   lìqi   strength

21. 賣票員   màipiàoyuán   ticketseller

22. 民間   mínjiān   (1) among the people ; (2) folk-(e.g. mínjiān
                             wénxué 'folk literature')

23. 難得   nándé   hard to get, hard to meet with, rare

24. 年表   niánbiǎo   historical table of dates and events

25. 氣力   qìli   strength

26. 請客   qǐng kè   invite guests

27. 生氣   shēngqì   become angry (VO)

28. 時間   shíjiān   time

29. 思想   sīxiǎng   thoughts, thinking

30. 天氣　tiānqi　　weather

31. 喜歡　xǐhuan　　like, be fond of, be pleased (more common)

32. 喜事　xǐshì　　an occasion for joy (e.g. wedding, birth)

33. 小事　xiǎoshì　　minor event, minor happening

34. 中間　zhōngjiàn　middle

35. 主客　zhǔkè　　main guest, guest of honor

Who's Who and What's What

1. 客家　Kèjiā　　Hakka (a major dialect of Southeast China)

2. 元朝　Yuán Cháo　Yuan or Mongol Dynasty (1280-1368)

3. 五四　Wǔ Sì　　May Fourth (Student demonstrations of May 4, 1919, against the Versailles Treaty, marking the beginning of the national and cultural upsurge known as the May Fourth Movement)

4. 七七　Qī Qī　　Marco Polo Bridge Incident of July 7, 1937 (Japanese attack near Peking, initiating the 1937-1945 war between China and Japan)

5. 九一八　Jiǔ Yī Bā　Mukden Incident of September 18, 1931 (Japanese attack which led to the seizure of Manchuria)

Note on Conventional Dates

There are a number of major events in recent Chinese history which are dated by a special formula using only numerals to express the month and day. Frequently the conventional date alone is cited, without further amplification, since the abbreviated formula is supposed to evoke in the mind of the reader the event to which the date refers (much as The Fourth does in the case of Americans). A few of the most important conventional dates are given in this lesson.

Note on Expressing Prices

The expressions we have learned so far concerning prices (e.g. wǔkuài sān-máo qián ' $5.30') occur most often in speech and sometimes in writing as well. There are also other forms which are rarely spoken but are the preferred way of writing prices. These forms use 元 yuán for 'dollar' and 角 jiǎo for 'dime.' The following expressions for '$5.30' show the contrast :

五塊三(毛錢)　(spoken style)

五元三角　　　(written style)

There is another written form which is much like English except that in place of a dollar sign before the money expression the character 元 is used after it :

5.30 元　'$5.30'

This is read as wǔkuài sān. We do something similar in English when we read $5.30 not as 'dollar sign five period three zero' but as 'five dollars and thirty cents.'

Exercise 1. Pitfalls

1. 他當然也是教員.
   他當了三年教員.

2. 天氣不好我就不去了.
   天氣不好不如不去了.

3. 我很喜歡見馬縣長.
   我很少看見馬縣長.

4. 中國話也很難說.
   他來不來很難說.

Exercise 2. Practice on Spoken versus Written Styles

In the following list items 1-10 represent prices in spoken style; items 11-20 represent prices in the written style. Translate into English and re-write 1-10 in the written style (in two ways) and 11-20 in the spoken style.

1. 三塊三毛錢
2. 兩塊五
3. 四毛錢
4. 兩塊八
5. 九塊二毛錢
6. 六毛

7. 五毛錢   14. 四元五角

8. 二十七塊四   15. 五角

9. 四塊九   16. 0.10元

10. 三毛   17. 二角

11. 三元七角   18. 20元

12. 3.70元   19. 三元二角

13. 二十六元四角   20. 1.30元

Exercise 3. Illustrative Sentences (Chinese)

1. 外國人能寫中文書是很難得的.

2. 你對張校長説的話有意見没有?

3. 在這兒買, 到日本的飛機票當地錢要多少?

4. 我們現在不要跟馬先生説話. 他的氣很大.

5. 如果説他不用心不如説他不喜歡念書.

6. 五四時代以前很少用白話文.

7. 我們當教員的應當常常研究我們的教學法.

8. 研究原子能的用意是為了人在生活上可以用原子能.

9. 天氣不好不如不去了.

10.「簡易」的意思就是説又簡單又容易.

11. 我念書以外的時間都畫畫兒.

12. 到中國去，坐飛機雖然日子少，可是我還是喜歡坐船.

13. 每一課書先生都用簡單的話説説大意.

14. 毛先生已經當了三十年教員.

15. 學中文必得先學説話然後再念書才好.

16. 你考第一我太為你歡喜了.

17. 今天晚上我請你吃飯.····別客氣了.你常請我太不好意思了.

18. 他請那五個客人裏誰是主客？

19. 賣票員說那條客船的船票已經都賣了．買不到了．

20. <u>馬</u>先生人太好了．對人很客氣，我從來沒看見過他對別人不客氣．

21. 那本<u>民間小說</u>價目單上的價錢是「一元三角」，可是店員說一塊六一本．

22. 中國古時候有很多大思想家．

23. 你的名字你會不會簡寫？

24. 不知道甚麽原因省長會客以後很生氣．

25. 雖然他今年才十三，可是他很有力氣．

26. 那個病人病了一年了，一點兒氣力也沒有了．

27. 你想要買的東西都開單子了嗎？

28. <u>中國大事年表</u>上有七七跟九一八嗎？

29. 簡太太生兒子了. 我們得給他道喜.

30. 我近來比以前更没時間了. 文校長
大事、小事都問我.

31. 你看湖中間那條小船上是不是没有
人?

32. 你看看那張單子上有没有書的價錢.

33. 高先生說學國語應當先念書. 你看
他的說法對不對?

34. 從前中國人的看法是女人不必念書.

35. 這本簡易日語課本是不是你的?

Exercise 4. Dialogues

1. 簡: 明天晚上我請你吃飯. 你有時
間嗎?

文: 不要客氣了.為甚麽要請客呢?

簡: 毛大元到美國去要走了, 所以
我想大家在一塊兒談談.

文：毛大元是主客．他以外還有別
　　的客人嗎？

簡：有你、我、還有張文小姐．我
　　也請了我們的國文教員馬先生．
5　　因為馬先生最喜歡毛大元，所
　　以也請他來跟我們一塊兒談談．

2. 田：張太太，你上那兒去？

　　張：我給人家道喜去．你呢，田太
　　　　太？

　　田：我去買水果．誰家有喜事？

5　張：高家．高太太又生了一個兒子．
　　　　他很歡喜．

　　田：又生個兒子！我也應當去道個
　　　　喜才好．

3. 馬：你有甚麼事？

　　萬：我要見省長．

　　馬：現在開會呢．請你明天再來．

　　萬：明天甚麼時候？

馬： 他每天會客有一定的時間.

萬： 幾點鐘?

馬： 每天上半天九點到十一點.

4. 白： 這兒有教書教得好的英文先生
沒有?我想學英文.

邊： 馬文英先生可以教給你. 他是
一個很難得的先生. 他教的書
當天學了當天就會. 最好你買
一本簡易英語看看. 馬先生教
初學的學生都是用這本書.

5. 張： 你到日本去要坐那條船?

錢： 我想坐日本客船.

張： 票價貴不貴?

錢： 不很貴. 我看價目單上最貴的
船票是當地錢三百五十塊錢.

張： 現在天氣好. 坐船是很有意思.

6. 田： 今天我們上課的時候馬先生的
氣很大. 上課以後他第一個先

問我元朝有多少年. 我說不知
道. 他又問方有為元朝土地大
還是明朝土地大. 方有為也不
知道. 馬先生很生氣. 他說高
5　中二沒有一個好學生.
　文：馬先生從來對人很客氣. 我沒
　　看見過他對人不客氣或者生氣.

7. 路：張太太, 你好?
　張：好. 路太太, 你好? 我上個月
　　病了一次. 現在走路還沒力氣
　　呢.
　5路：是嗎? 甚麼病? 我一點兒也不
　　知道, 所以也沒看你去.
　張：別客氣.

8. 毛：你兒子現在有事了嗎?
　田：有了. 在一個書店裏當店員.
　毛：你的兒子比我的兒子好. 你看
　　我那個兒子初小念了三年就不

念書了. 他力氣很大. 我想叫
他在船上當水手去.

田： 雖然不喜歡念書, 可是有氣力
也是他的本事. 他現在一定很
高了.

毛： 跟你兒子差不多. 前天別人告
訴他有個地方考賣票員, 我說
他一定考不上. 果然没考上.

9. 簡： 民間文學跟五四時代這兩本書
寫的好不好？

方： 很好. 寫的很簡單, 可是很有
思想.

10. 萬： 張文元, 這是誰開的單子？我
都看不懂.

張： 單子上都是簡寫的字, 所以你
看不懂.

萬： 這六個字是甚麼？

張： 是 "先給一半定錢."

11. 簡：中國人用白話文是從甚麼時候?

    文：是從五四時代.

    簡：五四在中國文學思想上是一個
    大事, 不是一個小事.

12. 張：今天我差一點兒來晚了.

    錢：為甚麼?

    張：我的車走到中山路中間兒不走
    了. 我就想坐火車. 我到那兒
5   火車就要開了. 没買票就上火
    車, 到了車上才買車票. 要是
    來晚了太不好意思.

13. 先生：張一山, 你説元朝在明朝以
    前還是在明朝以後?

    張：   在明朝以前.

    先生：元朝這個朝代有多少年?

5   張：   八十八年.

    先生：中國在元朝的時候土地大不
    大?

張：　　元朝的時候中國土地最大.

14. 教員：你們看中華民國大事年表上,
　　　　在一九一九年中國有甚麼大
　　　　事?

　　學生：是五四.

5　教員：一九三一呢?

　　學生：是九一八.

　　教員：一九三七呢?

　　學生：是七七.

　　教員：五四、九一八、七七你們知
10　　　　道都有甚麼事嗎?

　　學生：知道.上次先生說給我們了.

15. 外國人：甚麼叫客家話?

　　中國人：客家話就是客家人說的話.

　　外國人：甚麼地方有客家人?

　　中國人：中國的東南兩三省有客家

5　　　　人.

　　外國人：甚麼叫客家人?"客家"是

甚麼意思？

中國人：客家人的意思就是説不是
本地人，是客人的意思．

外國人：他們都是甚麼朝代到東南
的？

中國人：在三國以後他們從別的地
方到那兒的．

Exercise 5. Narratives

1. 中國在明朝以前是元朝．元朝從一
二八〇年到一三六八年，有八十八
年．元朝這個朝代雖然不長，可是
土地最大．從古到今土地最大的朝
代就是元朝．

2. 馬校長要到英國去了，所以我們學
校的教員大家請他吃飯．我們大家
是主人，就是校長跟他太太是客人，
也是主客．我們吃飯以後還有點心
跟水果．馬校長跟他太太兩個人都

説我們太客氣. <u>馬</u>校長還説:"我有
個意見. 要是你們再請客就請我吃
家常飯好了."

3. 今天<u>白</u>家有喜事. 我去道喜看見<u>邊</u>
先生了. 他近來事業很得意. 他説
最近他又買了一條大客船.

4. 我是一個外國學生. 我念了差不多
有三年中文了. 中國話不容易説,
中國書很難念, 中國字更難寫. 我
雖然能看中文書, 可是中國人寫的
5 字, 我有很多看不懂, 因為中國字
有很多的寫法, 比如簡寫的字, 我
們外國人就看不懂. 中國字雖然很
難, 可是學中文很有意思.

5. 我是一個教中文的. 我很喜歡研究
六朝文學. 我教書以外的時間都研
究六朝文學. 六朝是中國古時候六

個朝代. 這六個朝代是在南北朝時
代的前後, 六朝文學就是這六個朝
代當時的文學.

6. 中國在三國時代人才最多. 當時的
中國有三個國, 每一個國都有不少
人才. 有的很有天才, 有的有口才,
有的學問很好.

7. 高省長會客以後很生氣. 他說:"有
一個縣長說了半天話, 還沒說明白
大意是甚麽. 後來我請他不要往下
說了, 請他在這一兩天寫給我. 這
個縣長話都說的不明白, 一定沒有
本事."

8. 張先生對田先生說:"現在書價太貴
了. 我用五塊錢買了一本簡易國語
會話, 價錢很貴, 不知道好不好.
請你看看." 田先生看了以後說:"這

本書的用意是為了容易念，所以很
簡單．事實上不一定容易念．還有，
這本書課文裏頭生字用法、語法都
沒有說明．我看這本書沒意思，沒
5 有用．不如不買."

9. 路邊有三個小飯館兒．中間的飯館
兒主人是客家人，生意很好．有一
天，有兩個客家人從別的地方來．
他們走路走了一天，沒有力氣再走
5 了．他們想在這個小飯館兒吃點東
西再走，飯館主人說："你們沒有力
氣再走了．今天晚上就在這裏，不
要走了，明天再走．我們都是客家
人，不要客氣."

10. 有人告訴我，買東西的時候一定要
叫店員開單子，在單子上寫東西的
價錢．我問他如果買車票、船票也
叫賣票員開單子嗎？他說車票、船

票上頭都有價錢，不必開單子．

11. "不如意事常八九"這是中國民間常
說的話．這個說法的意思是一個人
不如意的事多，如意的事很少．

12. 我在學生會看見毛小姐．他說要到
日本去．他又想坐船又想坐飛機．
他沒有一定主意．我告訴他坐飛機
很有意思，票價也不貴．我也說給
5　他，學生會裏有飛機票價目表．他
先去看了價目表，就買飛機票去了．
後來有人告訴我，這個小姐買了飛
機票以後又有個想法，他想坐飛機
要是天氣不好可能有意外，他還是
10　坐船走了．

13. 張先生要到外國去．他有很多東西
都要賣．他寫了一個價目單．價目
單上的價目有原價，有賣價．單子

上有一塊地，地價不貴，地的定價
是一千五百元．他說他賣的東西要
價都很少，因為他說不上是那天走．
他想在他走以前，東西一定要賣了
5才好，所以他的東西價錢都不貴．

14. 中文有文言文，有白話文．從前常
用文言文，不常用白話文．從五四
以後，才常用白話文．五四時代在
中國文學思想上不能說是小事．

15. 九一八、七七這兩個日子，在中華
民國大事年表上都是大事．九一八
是一九三一年九月十八日，這天日
本想要中國的東北．七七是一九三
5七年七月七日，這天日本想要中國
的華北．

16. 我是美國人．我會說中國話，也能
看中文書、報．我心裏想如果有機

會，我一定要去中國．到了中國，
可以在當地買一點兒古典文學的書，
可以看見中國的學者，還可以去看
看中國古代的長城．

17. 從日本到這裏的飛機多半是早上八
點鐘到．有一次差不多八點半了，
飛機還沒到．有人問我現在幾點鐘
了，為甚麼飛機還沒到，是不是飛
機有了意外？我告訴他，飛機沒到，
不一定有了意外，或者現在飛機就
要到了．

18. 方先生要學國語．我告訴他學國語
要有好的教科書．我說："我當初學
國語念過一本書很好．這本書的名
子我說給你，你可以去買一本．不
過，現在在當地能不能買到，就很
難說了．你可以試試看."

19. 今天早上中文學會開會的時候，大
家有很多意見．馬會長説，他的意
思要在今天晚上再開一次會，研究
研究．大家都説馬會長的意思很好，
5 很多的意見當然都要研究研究．馬
會長説："我們就説定今天晚上再開
一次會．晚上的會，可能還有從外
國來的客人．他們是來看看中文學
會．如果大家喜歡跟他們談談，這
10 也是個好機會．"

20. 我已經到了中國了．我下了飛機以
後，就看見馬先生、馬太太他們已
經來了，我就跟他們一塊兒坐車到
他們家裏去．中國地方很好，人很
5 客氣．到了這兒第二天我就到大學
去了．他們看我是外國學生，用英
文跟我説話．我就告訴他們，我會
説中國話，我是來念中文．後來又

看見兩個小姐，他們說我中國話說
的很好．他們問我為甚麼要到中國
來念書．我說給他們原因．他們明
白我是來研究中文的．那兩個小姐
⁵問我的話都很有意思．我問他們要
不要到美國去念書．他們兩個人說
如果有機會當然喜歡到外國去．最
後他們還問我在美國念書的中國女
學生有多少．我說我不知道，因為
¹⁰在美國我很少看見中國小姐．

21. 邊先生要請田先生吃飯．田先生說：
"我明天就走，沒有時間了．不要客
氣了．你不必請我吃飯了．"邊先生
說："你別客氣．你要走了，我們應
⁵該在一塊兒談談．今天晚上到我家
吃晚飯．"田先生說："好，我就不客
氣了．今天晚上我一定來．"

22. 我想請一個人教給我寫中國字．有

人説馬先生常年教外國人寫中國字.
他的教法很好,他很會教初學的人.
我就去請馬先生教我寫中國字. 馬
先生果然教的很好. 馬先生説他的
學生當中有一個高才生學了不到一
年, 寫的中國字比中國學生寫的還
好.有人説有好先生當然有好學生.

23. 我買了一塊地.我知道那塊地很好,
價錢也不貴, 我就當天給了定錢.
後來我才知道要不是我當天給了定
錢, 差一點兒別人買去了.

24. 現在有很多國家已經知道原子能的
用法. 近來報上説中國買了一條用
原子能的大船. 説不定以後所有的
大船都用原子能了.

25. 毛文元是一個工人. 他每小時的工
錢是一元二角, 有時候一元五角.

有一天他跟他姐姐説他要去當船上
水手. 他姐姐説:"水手的工錢很少.
你為甚麼要當水手呢?"他對他姐姐
説:"當水手有意思, 可以去很多地
方, 也有機會到外國去看看, 所以
我要當水手."

Exercise 6. Illustrative Sentences (English)

1. It is very rare for foreigners to be able to write books in Chinese.

2. Do you have any opinion about what principal Zhang said?

3. How much is it in local currency if you buy a plane ticket for Japan here?

4. Let's not talk to Mr. Ma now. He's in an awful temper.

5. Rather than say he's not studious, it would be better to say he isn't willing to study.

6. Before the May Fourth Period little use was made of literature in the vernacular language.

7. We [who are] teachers should constantly examine our teaching methods.

8. The purpose in studying atomic energy is that people can use atomic energy [in their lives].

9. If the weather's bad, it would be better not to go.

10. The meaning of jiǎnyì is [to say that] (something) is both simple and easy.

11. My time apart from studying is spent in drawing.

12. Although it takes less time [lit. fewer days] to get to China by plane, I still prefer to take a boat.

13. For each lesson the teacher explains the general idea in simple words.

14. Mr. Mao has already been a teacher for thirty years.

15. In studying Chinese, it is best to learn to speak first and then to learn to read.

16. I'm awfully pleased [for you] that you came out first on the exam.

17. I'm asking you to dinner today. ⋯ Don't be polite. You often ask me. It's [too] embarrassing that you invite me (so) often.

18. Who is the main guest of the five guests that he's invited?

19. The ticket seller says that all the tickets for that passenger boat have already been sold. You can't buy any more.

20. Mr. Ma is an awfully nice person. He's very polite toward people. I've never seen him impolite toward others.

21. The price of Folk Literature (as given) on the price list is $1.30, but the clerk says it's $1.60 per volume.

22. In ancient times, China had a lot of great thinkers.

23. Can you write your name in abbreviated form?

24. I don't know why [lit. what reason] the provincial governor became very angry after receiving visitors.

25. Although he's only thirteen this year, he's very strong.

26. That patient has been sick for a year. He doesn't have a bit of strength left.

27. Did you make a list of all the things you would like to buy?

28. Does the Chronological Table of Outstanding Events in China have (the dates) 7-7 and 9-1-8?

29. Mrs. Jian has given birth to a son. We must congratulate her.

30. Recently I've had even less time than before. Principal Wen asks me about all matters, big or small.

31. Look, isn't that little boat in the middle of the lake empty [lit. without people]?

32. See if the book prices are on that list.

33. Mr. Gao says that in studying the National Language, one should first learn to read. Do you think he's right?

34. It used to be the Chinese view that girls did not need to study.

35. Is this Abridged Textbook of Japanese yours?

Lesson 30

Exercise 1. Review of Single Characters

1. 朝	9. 飯	17. 該	25. 考	33. 才	41. 往	49. 得
2. 喜	10. 間	18. 思	26. 定	34. 或	42. 員	50. 跟
3. 點	11. 實	19. 病	27. 簡	35. 客	43. 別	
4. 告	12. 氣	20. 談	28. 鐘	36. 每	44. 代	
5. 更	13. 半	21. 價	29. 元	37. 吃	45. 意	
6. 貴	14. 果	22. 差	30. 當	38. 如	46. 必	
7. 單	15. 應	23. 歡	31. 訴	39. 事	47. 票	
8. 業	16. 飛	24. 姓	32. 館	40. 機	48. 教	

Exercise 2. Distinguishing Partially Similar Combinations

A. Same Character in Initial Position

1	2	3	4	5	6
實在	教給	開會	客人	三元	小姐
實話	教法	開車	客氣	三國	小時
實力	教書	開飯	客船	三角	小心
實說	教學	開門	客家	三民	小館
實業					

7	8	9	10	11	12
說給	飯店	六元	水手	別走	簡寫
說明	飯車	六朝	水果	別的	簡單
說法	飯館	六角	水田	別人	簡易

13	14	15	16	17	18
意思	半天	鐘表	如果	往後	初中
意見	半路	鐘頭	如意	往下	初學
意外					

19	20	21	22	23	24
得到	定價	主客	價目	説話	必得
得了	定錢	主因	價錢	説定	必要

25	26	27	28	29	30
難看	民間	應當	姓毛	最少	吃飯
難得	民國	應該	姓名	最多	吃魚

31	32	33	34	35	36
比方	價目表	上那兒	説不上	差一點	有意思
比如	價目單	上半天	説不定	差不多	有用意

B. Same Character in Final Position

1	2	3	4	5	6
説法	中飯	大事	書價	主意	書名
教法	早飯	本事	定價	用意	地名
想法	要飯	有事	要價	生意	姓名
用法	晚飯	心事	原價	大意	有名
方法	吃飯	小事	票價	得意	學名
看法	開飯	喜事			
文法					
語法					

7	8	9	10	11	12
多半	點心	毛病	還是	現代	圖表
大半	小心	看病	要是	時代	年表
上半	談心	有病	可是	近代	鐘表
下半	中心	生病	或是	朝代	手表

13	14	15	16	17	18
客氣	白天	雖然	大家	開會	往後
生氣	當天	不然	客家	機會	以後
力氣	半天	果然	人家	不會	前後
天氣	談天	當然	國家	學會	然後

19	20	21	22	23	24
説給	六朝	飯館	表店	人才	時間
寫給	元朝	小館	書店	口才	民間
教給	明朝	報館	飯店	天才	中間

25	26	27	28	29	30
請客	客人	華中	船票	法子	當地
會客	病人	初中	車票	單子	本地
主客	人人	當中	買票	刀子	土地

31	32	33	34	35	36
實話	工業	學者	不如	小時	容易
白話	實業	或者	比如	當時	簡易

37	38	39	40	41	42
教員	必得	説定	多少	過年	最初
店員	難得	一定	最少	常年	當初

43	44	45
水果	人口表	吃飯館
如果	價目表	圖書館

C. Same Character in Different Positions

1	2	3	4	5	6
一點	天才	應當	飛機	意思	知道
點心	才好	當年	機會	思想	道喜

7	8	9	10	11	12
簡單	貴姓	來往	道喜	當初	實在
單子	姓名	往北	喜歡	初學	在家

13	14	15	16	17	18
九元	比如	用法	難得	先生	思想
元朝	如果	法文	得走	生氣	想家

D. Reversibles

1	2	3
喜歡	四五	氣力
歡喜	五四	力氣

Exercise 3. Review of Special Combinations

The special combinations studied in this unit which have not appeared in the preceding exercise are reviewed below.

1. 工業學校
2. 不要客氣
3. 說實在的
4. 實業學校
5. 沒有意思
6. 不好意思
7. 很有意思
8. 事實上
9. 下半天
10. 實在的
11. 有心事
12. 教科書
13. 不一定
14. 要飯的
15. 有意思
16. 別客氣
17. 開單子
18. 賣票員
19. 上半天
20. 高才生
21. 學生會
22. 教學法
23. 或者是
24. 南北朝
25. 不如不
26. 家常飯
27. 一定要
28. 不客氣
29. 九一八
30. 實業家

Exercise 4. Excerpts from Actual Publications

The following passages occur in Vol.4 of the <u>Selected Works of Máo Zédōng</u> (Mao Tse-tung). Translate into English.

1. 這對不對呢？

2. 談了四十三天．

3. 還談甚麼呢？

4. 中國是甚麼人的中國？…中國是中國人民的．

5. 這是一個很好的說明．

6. 中國人民也有手．

7. 這是很明白的．

8. 我們在山上，他在水邊．

9. 現在他要下山了．

10. 是沒有可能或很少可能的．

11. 在我們手裏，在人民手裏，不是很好嗎？

12. 人民說：是．

13. 這一次我們去很好．

14. 我是地主．

15. 這已經有了說明．

Exercise 5. Narratives

1. 我是去年離開美國到日本的．日本很有意思．我在那兒差不多有兩個月．我去過不少的地方．日本的山水很好看．在美國的時候，就有人告訴我日本山水好．果然很好．我喜歡看山水．比如有工夫或是天氣好的時候，我都到外頭去看山水．

我到過日本一個圖書館，那裏中國古典文學的書不少．我也看了日本的工業．現在日本也是現代的工業國家了．日本地方不很大，可是人口很多．當然他們要想法子到別的地方去了．到外國去的日本人，多半都到南美去．

2. 我在中山中學念書．我們的國文先生很好．我們都喜歡他，一來他書教的好，二來他對學生很客氣．他從來不生氣．他對國文的教法很好．每一課書他用簡單的話先說說大意，然後再教我們課文，當時就明白了．還有，他每次教我們生字的時候，一定用一點兒時間教給我們中國字簡寫的方法．他對文學很有研究．他常在報上寫民間文學的東西．我們都很喜歡看．他寫的東西很有思想．他是很難得的先生．

3. 我雖然會說中國話，可是我不會念
中國字．有一次我去買船票，那個
賣票員是客家人，他不懂國語，我
也不會客家話．他給了我一張船票
5 價目表，我看了半天也不明白．我
的本事就是會說中國話．這個時候
我心裏想，學中國話必得說話跟念
字一塊兒學才好．我當初的看法是
學語言沒有學字的必要．現在我知
10 道要是學中國話也要學中國字．

4. 我因為家裏沒錢，沒法子，就不念
書了．因為我有力氣所以當工人．
我已經當了二年工人了．在這二年
當中我沒有看書的機會．白天、晚
5 上都當工人，為的是得一點兒工錢．
我看見人家別的學生天天上學，心
裏很難過．不知道我還有沒有機會
再念書了．

5. 張先生要買毛家那塊地. 那塊地又
好, 賣價又不很貴, 所以很多人想
買. 我就告訴張先生:"如果你一定
要買那塊地, 最好先給一半錢, 或
者給點兒定錢才好, 要不然別人就
要買了."

6. 我在書店看見一本書, 書上有古今
朝代的人名、地名, 對我很有用.
我很想買, 可是太貴了.

7. 前天學校開會. 因為我有事所以没
去. 今天我看見邊為城, 我問他開
會的經過.他説:"你没去很好.我前
天晚上也不如不去了. 這次的會不
如上次. 很多人都有意見,都説話,
説的都没有意思."

8. 張先生是個學者, 有學問, 有思想,
對人很客氣.他從來不跟別人生氣.

他常説:"我是人, 人家也是人, 所以我對別人應當客氣."

9. 國家最難得的是人才. 中國四書上説過 "才難." 這意思就是説人才最難得.

10. 中國元朝的時候, 東方人跟西方人的來往比以前多了, 所以東方文明到了西方, 西方文明也到了東方.

11. 我最喜歡寫中國字. 在我心目中中國字最好看. 當初我才學中國字的時候, 教我寫字的是田先生. 他的教法最好. 他先寫給我看. 他一邊寫一邊説明應該在甚麼地方用力. 他寫了以後才叫我寫. 我當時的想法, 以為字寫的多才能好. 可是田先生説寫字不一定要寫的多, 一定要每一個字都用心寫, 每次最多寫

十個字，都會了以後再往下寫．他
這個方法果然很好．現在人家看見
我寫的字，都說很好，也有人說我
有寫字的天才．

12. 圖書館有一本原子能跟現代的工業．
這本書寫的都是事實．書上說，現
在已經不是手工時代了，現在是原
子時代了．我們應當知道原子能的
用法．現代的工業必得用原子能了．

13. 有一次我坐船，船走到大海的中間
有了毛病，不能走了．船上的人都
沒主意了．有一個水手去看船是甚
麼毛病．他看了以後，他就說船有
毛病，他沒明說是甚麼毛病．他說
在這個地方這個時間可能有來往的
船．後來果然有個船來了．我們就
上了別的船．

14. 張先生說："「話到口邊兒要說一半．」

意思是說，一個人在說話的時候要
小心，話不要說的太多了."

15. 中國在明代的時候有人去過海外，
到過西方很多地方．這個人前後去
了七次．第一次是在一四〇五年，
最後一次是在一四三二年．第一次
去的時候，有六十二條船，二萬八
千多人．

16. 人民日報上說從前的中國不是民主
國家，現在的中國是人民民主國家，
國家的大事、小事都是為了人民，
人民是國家的主人．

17. 張先生的女兒在高小念書．他要學
日文．他說他因為看地圖上中國離
日本很近，又因為他姐姐現在在日
本念書，他也想去日本念書，所以
他要學日文．

18. 一個文學家在一年裏寫了三本書，
每本書最少都有七八萬字．有人說
他的寫書能力太好了．他說："我手
邊兒上書很少．有時候必得到圖書
5 館去看書，多半是看古今人名、地
名，用了不少時間，要不然我一年
可以寫四五本書."

19. 一個美國學生念中文有五年了．他
有兩本中文小說．一本是高原，一
本是海口．他說這本高原是白話的，
容易看，要是看不懂，看看上下文
5 就懂了．這本海口是文言的，他一
點兒也不懂.

20. 我家在城外頭，離城裏頭有五六里
路．因為我們有很多水田，所以有
二十多條水牛．我雖然現在念書，
可是下課以後也要給水牛吃東西甚
5 麼的.

21. 高先生是中學校長，也是書店的主
人．有一天高先生家裏有喜事．學
校裏的教員跟書店裏的店員都來道
喜．高先生對他們説：“請大家別客
5 氣，都在這裏吃飯．”有一個教員對
高先生説：“今天是高先生你最歡喜
的日子．你叫我們在這裏吃飯，我
們就不客氣了，都在這裏吃飯了．”

22. 有一個外國人要買一張中華民國大
事年表．他想在年表上看看五四、
七七、九一八都在那年．張先生説：
“我有一本簡易國語課本．課本裏
5 有五四、七七、甚麼的．我給你這
本課本．你看看課本就知道了．不
必買大事年表了．”

23. 毛文貴很有氣力．他在一個客船上
當水手．他説在船上當水手，在天
氣好的時候很有意思，如果天氣不

好就没意思了.

24. 學校要開學了. 我要去買上學用的
東西. 因為要買的東西太多, 所以
我先在家裏開單子. 姐姐看見我這
張單子, 他問我:"這張單子上的東
西要用多少錢?"我説:"書的價錢我
知道, 因為我手裏有一張圖書價目
單. 別的東西我就不知道是多少錢
了."

25. 馬縣長不喜歡請客, 也不喜歡別人
請他. 有一次有人請客, 請的客人
有馬縣長還有別人.馬縣長是主客,
可是馬縣長没去.

UNIT VI

Lesson 31

1	2	3	4	5
把	出	進	回	內

6	7	8	9	10
拿	但	連	只	冊

1. 把　bǎ*　　(1) take ; (2) (measure for objects with handles, such as knives)

2. 出　chū*　　(1) to exit ; (2) to put out, produce (e.g. money, books)

3. 進　jìn*　　(1) advance ; (2) enter

4. 回　huí　　(1) to return ; (2) a time, a turn (same as 次 cì)

5. 內　nèi*　　interior

6. 拿　ná　　take, take hold of

7. 但　dàn*　　but

8. 連　lián*　　(1) even; (2) (a surname)

9. 只　zhǐ*　　only, merely

10. 冊　cè*　　(1) volume : (2) booklet

11. 點　diǎn　　to check over, call (a roll)

12. 給　gěi　　(often used before main verb in bǎ construction ; see Illustrative Sentence 1)

Special Combinations

1. 冊子   cèzi   pamphlet, booklet, notebook
2. 出城   chū chéng   go out of a city
3. 出國   chū guó   go abroad
4. 出路   chūlù   (1) a way out (of a problem), way of escape, outlet ; (2) career opportunity
5. 出口   chūkǒu   (1) exit (N); (2) export (N/V)
6. 出力   chū lì   put forth effort
7. 出毛病   chū máobing   develop trouble, develop a defect
8. 出門   chū mén   (1) go out (of the house);(2) go away from home, travel
9. 出錢   chū qián   pay out money
10. 出事   chū shì   have an accident
11. 出外   chū wài   go (a long distance) from home
12. 出現   chūxiàn   appear, become manifest, materialize (concrete)
13. 出主意   chū zhúyi   make a suggestion
14. 但是   dànshi   however, but
15. 點名   diǎn míng   call a roll, call out a name on a roll
16. 點名冊   diǎnmíngcè   a roll, roster
17. 過去   guòqu   (1) pass by ; (2) passed by, past ; (3) deceased ; (4) in the past
18. 回國   huí guó   return to one's native country
19. 回家   huí jiā   return home
20. 回頭   huí tóu   (1) turn the head ; (2) at the turn of a head, (in) a moment
21. 進門   jìn mén   enter a door
22. 進口   jìnkǒu   import (N/V)
23. 進出口   jìnchūkǒu   import and export (N/V)
24. 看出(來)   kànchu(lái)   distinguish, make out, perceive, realize (RV)

25.	口號	kǒuhào	slogan
26.	連…都	lián…dōu	even, even including
27.	連…也	lián…yě	even, even including
28.	名冊	míngcè	list of names, roster
29.	拿給	nágei	bring to, hand to
30.	拿主意	ná zhúyi	make a decision
31.	拿走	názǒu	take away
32.	内人	nèiren	(my) wife (less used in PRC)
33.	實現	shíxiàn	(1) become manifest, become reality (abstract), (2) practical manifestation, practical reality
34.	手冊	shǒucè	handbook
35.	説出(來)	shuōchū(lái)	speak out, reveal, divulge (RV)
36.	想出(來)	xiǎngchū(lái)	figure out, devise
37.	校車	xiàochē	school car, school bus
38.	學本事	xué běnshi	acquire an ability (by study)
39.	以内	yǐnèi	within (a certain time or space)
40.	只好	zhǐ hǎo	can only, cannot but, the best thing is to

Note on Numbering of Volumes

The characters 冊 cè and 本 běn are both used in numbering volumes. 本 běn 'volume' is a larger division than 冊 'volume' or 'part.' It is possible to have a běn of several cè but not viceversa.

Besides the ordinary numbers for 'one,' 'two,' and so on, the characters 上 shàng 'top,' 中 zhōng 'middle,' and 下 xià 'bottom' are used to number items in a set or series. Either by themselves or in combination with běn or cè they designate the volume number in a set of books. If the set consists of only two volumes, the designations are;

上本 shàngběn or 上冊 shàngcè 'vol. I'

下本 xiàběn or 下冊 xiàcè 'vol. II'

If the set consists of three volumes, the designations are:

上本 <u>shàngběn</u> or 上冊 <u>shàngcè</u> 'vol. I'

中本 <u>zhōngběn</u> or 中冊 <u>zhōngcè</u> 'vol. II'

下本 <u>xiàběn</u>   or 下冊 <u>xiàcè</u> 'vol. III'

Thus 下本 <u>xiàběn</u> and 下冊 <u>xiàcè</u> are ambiguous, meaning either 'vol. II' or 'vol. III' depending on whether they designate the last volume in a two-volume or a three-volume series.

Exercise 1. Illustrative Sentences (Chinese)

1. 他把水果都給吃了.

2. 你想到中國去幾年？

3. 他念書來，一年就回國.

4. 我的車常出毛病.

5. 我到中國來了已經五年了.

6. 這是應該的，不客氣.

7. 你那本小説給我看看. 一會兒給你.
   ⋯我看過了. 給你得了.

8. 現在我沒工夫告訴你. 回來再説.

9. 先生一定看出來你的書没念.

10. 這條路上每天過來過去的車很多.

11. 我們學校從來就没有過外國學生.

12. 我跟<u>張</u>先生學了不少的本事.

13. <u>田</u>先生最近過去這幾天他都不在家.

14. 我一會兒還來. 回頭見.

15. 那個開車的甚麼車都能開.

16. <u>近二十年的中國</u>上冊是前年寫的. 中冊是去年寫的, 下冊還沒寫呢.

17. 你把那本<u>中國地名手冊</u>拿給我.

18. 他這回寫的是甚麼教科書?

19. 我想來想去但是想不出好法子來.

20. 他有五年多沒回國.

21. 我內人是客家人, 所以他會說客家話.

22. 我每天回家進門以後一定要先吃一點兒點心.

23. 先生為甚麼沒點我的名? 是不是點名冊上沒有我的名字?

24. 他出主意明天早飯以後大家出城上西山.

25. 你的事我出錢出力都可以, 但是我不能給你拿主意.

26. 我姐姐今天很生氣因為我把水果都

給吃了, 客人來了連一個都没有了.

27. 一個學校的校車出事了. 車裏頭坐了十五個人. 連一個也没活, 連賣票員、開車的都在內.

28. 他們從前説出的口號現在實現了.

29. 我問萬先生他的進出口生意好不好. 他説進口生意很好, 出口生意不很好.

30. 前天張先生跟我談天兒. 他説這個月以內他要出國, 因為在本國没有出路, 只好出國.

31. 近來我們這條路上出現很多要飯的. 天天出門就看見他們.

32. 誰把我在大華書店買的那本書給拿走了?

33. 是誰出的主意, 把人名冊給校長了?

34. 因為我要出外了, 我得買一本小冊子, 把學校裏所有學生的姓名都寫上.

35. 有錢的，飯吃不了．没錢的，飯吃
不上．

Exercise 2. Dialogues

1. 錢：<u>張機</u>要出國了，你知道嗎？

   田：我不知道．他甚麼時候走？

   錢：這個月以內他就走了．

   田：他是到美國去嗎？

   5 錢：是的．

   田：他去幾年？

   錢：他開會去，一年就回來．

   田：原來他是開會去．我以為他去
   念書呢．

2. 簡：今天早上從日本到中國的飛機
   出事了．

   邊：是嗎？在那兒出事了？

   簡：在河北．飛機上五十七個人連
   一個也没活．

邊：所以我從來不坐飛機．飛機最
　　容易出事．這次的意外是不是
　　因為天氣不好？

簡：或者天氣不好，或者是飛機有
　　毛病．現在還不知道．

3. 華：馬先生，你到英國來有多少年
　　　了？

馬：我來了已經二十五年了．

華：在這二十五年裏頭你回國幾次
　　了？

馬：我連一次都沒回去過．我很想
　　回家看看，可是沒機會．

華：馬太太想不想回去呢？

馬：我內人他每年都說要回去看看，
　　但是從來也沒回去過．我們明
　　年一定回家去看看．華先生，
　　你離開家多少年了？

華：我才來．我到這兒沒幾天．

4. 連：<u>張有為</u>來了，請進來．

   張：你有第二冊的<u>高中國文</u>沒有？
       給我看看．

   連：有．你的呢？

5 張：前天<u>錢有山</u>來了．他把我的<u>國
       文</u>給拿走了．

   連：他最喜歡拿人家的書了．上次
       他把我的字典也給拿去了．

5. 錢：<u>華</u>太太，你上那兒去了？

   華：我出城去了．

   錢：<u>華</u>先生好嗎？

   華：好．他又出門兒了．

5 錢：<u>華</u>先生常出門兒．

   華：可不是嗎！有時候連過年都不
       在家．有時候進門兒馬上又得
       走．

   錢：<u>華</u>先生為甚麼常出門兒呢？

10 華：多半是為了生意．

錢：華先生是甚麼生意？

華：他是進出口．錢先生呢？

錢：他是出口生意．進口生意很少．

華：錢先生也常出門兒嗎？

5 錢：不．他很少出門兒．他說往後
　　他還要跟華先生學本事呢．

6. 田：張先生，為了我的事你又出錢
　　又出力．

　張：應該的．不客氣．

　田：書多少錢買的？我把書錢給你．

5 張：錢不多，不必給我了．你是不
　　是坐車回學校？

　田：是．一會兒校車從這兒經過．
　　回頭我坐校車回去．

7. 學生：先生，沒點我的名．

　先生：你叫甚麼？

　學生：我叫路國為．

先生：點名冊上沒有你的名字．現
　　　在我給你寫上．

8. 年：今天晚飯我們吃甚麼？
　　萬：我想不出來．你說呢？
　　年：我們到萬年飯館兒去吃魚好不
　　　　好？
　5 萬：好．我很喜歡吃魚，但是我有
　　　　三個月沒吃了．晚上幾點鐘？
　　年：七點鐘好嗎？
　　萬：好．回頭我們在萬年館兒見．
　　年：回頭見．

9. 華：請你把那本<u>文學手冊</u>拿給我．
　　文：在那兒？
　　華：就在那本<u>語言學報</u>上．那本小
　　　　冊子就是．

10. 文：這是誰出的主意，把書都給拿
　　　出去了？

田： 毛先生叫我拿到外頭去的，我
　　 只好拿走.

文： 毛先生為甚麼叫拿走？

田： 我也不知道.

11. 連： 我來晚了一個鐘頭因為我的車
　　 出毛病了. 你叫我來有事嗎？

　 簡： 我近來心裏很難過.

　 連： 我看出你有心事了. 你說出來

5　　 我給你拿個主意.

　 簡： 我說出來你也想不出法子來.

　 連： 不一定. 或者我能想出法子.

12. 張： 你過去這兩年裏頭寫了幾本書
　　 是不是？

　 高： 我也沒寫幾本. 只寫了兩本教
　　 科書跟一本小說.

5 張： 你寫的甚麼教科書？

　 高： 我寫的高中國文上冊跟中冊.
　　 本來想再寫下冊的，可是到今
　　 天也沒實現.

13. 錢： 我有一年多沒事了. 我得想個
    出路.

    田： 你有本事, 一定有法子.

    錢： 我去看<u>毛</u>先生, 請他給我想法
5   子.

    田： 他最近不在本地. 出外了.

14. 馬： 山上最近每天晚上出現一條大
    水牛, 走來走去的. 不知道是
    誰家的.

    南： 是不是<u>張</u>家的?

5   馬： 我想不是. <u>張</u>家的牛不會出來
    的.

15. 先生： 民國初年的時候中國有個口
    號兒, 是「有飯大家吃」. <u>張</u>
    <u>一文</u>, 你說這是甚麼意思?

    學生： 意思是, 如果有飯每一個人
5   都應該吃, 不應該有的人飯
    吃不了, 有的人沒飯吃.

Exercise 3. Narratives

1. 他從小的時候離開了家，差不多有
   五十多年才回來．他說的話雖然還
   是本地話，可是他的頭已經白了．
   人家不知道他是誰，就問他："你這
   5 個客人是從甚麼地方來？"

2. 中國人在「七七」的時候有一個口
   號是：「有錢出錢，有力出力」．這個
   口號的意思是說大家為了國家，有
   錢的就應該拿出來錢，有人力的就
   5 應該拿出來人力．

3. 張先生是個買賣人．他的生意是進
   出口．他喜歡看進出口手冊．他說
   這本小冊子很有用．他又說進出口
   生意裏最好的是出口，因為出口生
   5 意容易拿到錢．要是把出口的東西
   上了船，就可以拿到錢了．進口生
   意就不容易了．東西進口以後，必

得想法子把東西賣出，然後才拿到
錢．

4. 萬先生在上課的時候從來不點名，
也不看點名冊．他説，點名要用時
間，不如把點名的時間用在教書上．
學生都説萬先生這個説法很對．

5. 今天早上到學校晚了．先生點名的
時候我還沒來呢．我把來晚了的原
因説一説．我是開車來的．走在半
路上，車出毛病了，不走了．沒法
子．只好走路到學校了．

6. 前天考英文的時候馬大方有一個字
想不出來．他回頭問後邊的人，在
這個時候田校長進門來了．田校長
或者看出馬大方要問別人，他就在
離馬大方不遠的地方坐下了．這回
馬大方沒法子再回頭了．只好用心

再想. 想了一會兒, 把以前想不出
來的字也想出來了.

7. 在學校地裏頭出現了一把刀. 張先
生要把這把刀拿走. 他想拿給考古
家看看. 我說應當先給校長看. 張
先生說, 先給考古家看了, 回來再
5 說. 有人說, 說不定張先生很喜歡
這把刀. 過了一會兒張先生回來了.
他說已經請考古家看過了. 可能是
一把古刀. 可是, 是甚麼朝代的連
考古家也說不出來.

8. 邊先生、毛先生兩個人談天.邊先生
問毛先生家裏所有的事誰拿主意？
毛先生說:"說實在的, 都是我內人
拿主意." 邊先生說:"你太沒本事了,
5 為甚麼叫太太拿主意呢?"毛先生說:
"你說我沒本事, 請問你呢?"邊先
生說:"我家的大事必得我拿主意.

如果是小事，才是我內人拿主意."
毛先生説:"可是我再請問你，你家
大事多呢還是小事多呢?"邊先生説：
"我家從來就沒有過大事."

9. 今天我們學校的校車在路上出事了.
出事的原因，有人説是開車的回頭
跟人談話，没看見車前邊有人過路.
有人説是過路的人不小心，連校車
5 都没看見. 又有人説車有毛病. 大
家説了半天，也不知道誰説的對.

10. 萬先生在上個月回國來了. 他是坐
飛機回來的. 他下了飛機就説:"我
出國三年了. 今天回到本國，我很
喜歡. 我在外國的時候，有人給我
5 出主意，叫我長在外國. 我説我在
外國的目的是研究科學，學點兒本
事，我在外國最多三年，一定回國.
現在果然在三年以內回來了. 我説
出的話實現了."

11. 張文喜是張先生的兒子. 很有思想.
他很喜歡科學. 現在在高中三念書.
他念了六年中學, 每年第一都是他.
他想以後他念大學他一定學科學.
5 可是因為張先生是個買賣人, 他想
他原來只念過二年書, 他也很有本
事, 不必用很多錢念大學, 所以不
想叫他兒子念大學. 張文喜把這事
告訴我了, 我就跟張先生說:"這個
10 時代應當叫兒子念大學. 還有, 你
的兒子書念的很好,他又喜歡科學,
應該叫他學科學. 如果研究原子能
甚麼的, 對國家人民都有用." 我說
了半天, 後來張先生没話說了. 只
15 好說:"叫他念, 叫他念."

12. 高先生家在城裏頭, 毛先生家在城
外頭. 高先生常出城看毛先生, 毛
先生也常進城. 有一天高先生出城

去看毛先生. 毛先生没在家, 出門
兒了. 毛太太告訴高先生, 毛先生
出門兒已經有半個月了, 原因是最
近過去這幾個月, 毛先生在家裏没
5 事, 所以他出外去想點兒出路. 高
先生問毛太太甚麼時候毛先生才回
來, 毛太太説毛先生説了, 兩個月
以後才回家.

13. 先生叫學生念課文. 學生念了一半
説:"往下的我不會念了." 先生説：
"你已經念的一半兒也都念的不對.
往後你一定要用心念."

14. 前天高如山説的話太不客氣了. 他
的想法也不對, 所以我有點兒生氣.
今天高如山到我家來説是來拿書.
我看他來的用意不是來拿書, 是來
5 看我還生氣不生氣了.

15. 我知道馬先生是客家人，一定喜歡
吃客家飯．我對馬先生說：＂明天我
請客，請你吃客家飯館．＂馬先生說：
＂明天客人還有誰？＂我說：＂你是主
客，還有兩三個人．你一定得來．＂

16. 前天我生病了．我的姐姐請大夫來
給我看病．大夫說這個病三天以內
就可以好．

17. 有一次我在飯車上吃中飯．有一個
人過來問我：＂貴姓？是不是在大學
念書？到過大華報館沒有？＂我不知
道這個人是甚麼用意．我說：＂我姓
白…＂他又往下說：＂是的，你是白
文生先生．上個月我在大華報館看
見過你．我們說過話了，所以我知
道你在大學念書．＂

18. 張先生是一個有國家思想的學者．
他寫了一本書，從五四寫到七七，

中間也寫出九一八．他寫的這本書
名子叫<u>近五十年的中國跟日本</u>．不
到三個月<u>張</u>先生就把這本書給寫出
來了．

19. 東方書店的店員來看我．他說：“我
們店主明天晚上在大美飯店請你吃
晚飯．還有別的客人，你是主客．
先來問你有工夫沒有．”我說：“你們
5 的店主請我吃飯我很想去．大家可
以談談心．但是明天晚上我有事，
沒法子到大美飯店去．請你回去對
你們店主說．”店員說：“請你別客氣，
你說一個日子好不好？”

20. 有兩個外國學生在中國念書，都歡
喜吃中國飯．他們每天吃中國飯館
或者在<u>張</u>先生的家裏吃家常飯．他
們說在<u>張</u>家吃吃晚飯最有意思，不
5 只飯好吃，在開飯以前還可以說說
中國話．

21. 我跟我姐姐天天在家裏看書．今天
我對我姐姐說:"我們每天在家裏看
書太没意思了．明天上半天或是下
半天我們到湖邊去走走好不好?"姐
姐說:"明天天氣好不好誰知道呢？
要是天氣好，我們可以到湖邊去走
走."

22. 先生問學生誰能說出「代」字的用
法．有一個學生說這是「朝代」的
「代」,也是「時代」的代.又有一個學
生說「古代」的「代」、「近代」的「代」
也是這個「代」字.

23. 我跟毛先生前天晚飯的時候一塊兒
去吃小館.那個小館我是頭一次去.
他們的生意很好，我們在那裏有一
個鐘頭也没有地方坐.

24. 我前兩天生病，不想吃東西，一點
氣力也没有．今天張先生來看我，

問我那個大夫給我看病．我說我不
想看大夫．張先生說:"你為甚麼有
病不看大夫呢?"我說:"我最不喜歡
看大夫."

25. 我小的時候在没上學以前，很喜歡
看書上的畫兒，所以常常拿別人的
書．有一次我姐姐學校要考試國文
了，我把我姐姐的國文給拿走了.
5 我姐姐還以為他的國文在學校呢.
時候已經很晚了，他到學校去拿，
可是那本書不在學校裏．他回來以
後看見我手裏的書就是他的，他很
生氣.

Exercise 4. Illustrative Sentences (English)

1. He ate up all the fruit.

2. How many years do you plan to be in China?

3. He's come in order to study; after one year he will return to his country.

4. My car often breaks down.

5. It's already five years since I came to China.

6. This is something I should (have done for you). Don't thank me.

7. Let me have that novel of yours to read. I'll give it (back) to you soon. ⋯ I've already read it. I'll give it to you (as a present) [and that's that].

8. I don't have time to tell you about it now. We'll speak further when I come back.

9. The teacher will certainly realize that you haven't studied.

10. There are a lot of cars going back and forth on this street every day.

11. Our school has never had any foreign students.

12. I learned quite a lot [of abilities] from Mr. Zhang.

13. In the [very recent] past few days Mr. Tian hasn't been at home.

14. I'll come again in a little while. See you soon.

15. That driver can drive any car.

16. Vol. I of China in the Past Twenty Years was written year before last. Vol. II was written last year. Vol. III hasn't been written yet.

17. Hand me that Handbook of Chinese Place-Names.

18. What textbook has he written this time?

19. I've thought and thought but can't think of a good way.

20. He hasn't been back to his own country in over five years.

21. My wife is a Hakka, so she speaks Hakka.

22. Every day after returning home [and entering the door] I [certainly must] have a snack.

23. Why didn't the teacher call out my name? Isn't my name on the roll?

24. He suggested that after breakfast tomorrow everyone go out of the city to the Western Hills.

25. I can put out money and effort on your behalf [lit. your matters], but it's impossible for me to make decisions for you.

26. My older sister got very angry today because I ate up all the fruit, and when guests came, there wasn't any [lit. even one] left.

27. A school bus [of a school] was in an accident.   There were fifteen

people in the bus.   Not a person survived   including even the ticket seller and driver.

28. The slogan that they raised [lit. spoke out] in the past has now materialized.

29. I asked Mr. Wan how his export-import business was. He said that the import business was fine but that the export business wasn't so good.

30. Mr. Zhang was chatting with me day before yesterday. He said he was leaving the country within the month because he had no career opportunities in this [lit. his own] country, so the only thing to do was to leave the country.

31. Recently a lot of beggars have appeared on our road. I see them every day when I go out.

32. Who took away that book I bought at the Great China Bookstore?

33. Who made the suggestion to give the list of names to the principal?

34. Because I'm going away, I must buy a little notebook to write down the names of all the students in school.

35. Those who have money can't eat (all the food they have). Those who don't have money can't (get food to) eat. (Note the different meanings conveyed by the resultative verb endings liǎo and shàng.)

Lesson 32

1	2	3	4	5
作	做	直	真	跑

6	7	8	9	10
快	慢	錯	錄	版

1. 作 zuò   (1) do, make ; (2) be (in the role of)

2. 做 zuò   do, make (often used interchangeably with the preceding character, but it is sometimes preferred with more concrete objects)

3. 直 zhí   straight

4. 真 zhēn*   true, real

5. 跑 pǎo   (1) run ; (2) hurry, hasten

6. 快 kuài   (1) fast, quick ; (2) soon

7. 慢 màn   slow

8. 錯 cuò   (1) mistake ; (2) wrong, mistaken (used often as second element in compound verbs, as in No. 22 of Special Combinations)

9. 錄 lù*   (1) to record ; (2) a list

10. 版 bǎn*   an edition

Special Combinations

1. 不錯 bú cuò (1) not bad, quite good; (2) not mistaken, right

2. 初版 chūbǎn first edition

3. 出版 chūbǎn publish

4. 出版家 chūbǎnjiā publisher (a person)

5. 出錯 chū cuò(r) make a mistake

6. 錯字 cuòzì incorrect character

7. 大作 dàzuò (your) great work (polite expression)

8. 當作 dàngzuò treat as, consider as

9. 工作 gōngzuò work (N/V)

10. 工作者 gōngzuòzhě worker (in a particular field of endeavor)

11. 古版 gǔbǎn old edition

12. 簡直 jiǎnzhí simply, directly, concisely

13. 開快車 kāi kuàichē drive fast

14. 快車 kuàichē (1) fast vehicle; (2) express train

15. 名作 míngzuò famous work

16. 目錄 mùlù (1) catalogue; (2) table of contents

17. 內容 nèiróng contents

18. 前進 qiánjìn (1) make progress, advance; (2) progressive

19. 圖書目錄 túshū mùlù book list, book catalogue

20. 外文 wàiwén * foreign language

21. 寫不上來 xiěbushànglái can't remember how to write (RV)(<u>shàng-lái</u> is also used with 'say,' 'read', etc.)

22. 寫錯 xiěcuò write incorrectly, make a mistake in writing

23. 一直(的) yìzhí(de) straight ahead, straight through (in reference
　一直(地)   to time or place); constantly, always

24. 原版 yuánbǎn original edition

25.	再版	zàibǎn	second edition, reissue (N)
26.	真的	zhēnde	(1) real(ly); (2) Really!
27.	真話	zhēnhuà	the truth
28.	作法	zuòfǎ	method of doing something, plan of working
29.	做飯	zuò fàn	cook food, prepare a meal
30.	作工	zuò gōng	do work (usually physical labor)
31.	作家	zuòjiā	writer
32.	作買賣	zuò mǎimai	be in business
33.	作甚麽?	zuò shénmo?	(1) do what?; (2) for what purpose, why?
34.	作生日	zuò shēngri	celebrate a birthday
35.	作生意	zuò shēngyi	do business, trade
36.	作事	zuò shì	do work (usually mental work), do something
37.	作文(兒)	zuò wén(r)	write an essay
38.	作用人	zuò yòngren	be a servant (not used in PRC)
39.	作者	zuòzhě	author
40.	作主	zuòzhǔ	assume a responsibility

Note on Editions of Books

The edition of a Chinese book is indicated by the following terms:

初版　chūbǎn　'first edition'

再版　zàibǎn　'second edition'

三版　sānbǎn　'third edition'

The fourth and subsequent editions follow the pattern of 'third edition.' If a date is given, it precedes the edition number:

一九六一年初版　'first edition 1961'

一九六二年再版　'second edition 1962'

一九六三年三版　'third edition 1963'

If the place of publication is inserted in this formula (betwen date and edition) it indicates that an earlier edition was published elsewhere:

一九六二年上海再版　'second edition Shanghai 1962'

Exercise 1. Illustrative Sentences (Chinese)

1. 我原來沒有買那本古版書的意思.

2. 你一直地往北走三里路就到了.

3. 前進書店出版的都是科學用的書.

4. 邊先生是個名作家，我一點兒也不知道.

5. 你買初版的一定錯不了.

6. 要是把小說當作教科書念一定很有意思.

7. 現在做買賣的真有錢.

8. 先生,「飛機」的「飛」字我簡直寫不上來.

9. 請你看看我作的文兒有沒有錯兒.

10. 初版是在上海出版的. 再版也是在上海出版的嗎?

11. 你的大作中文版的、外文版的都有嗎?

12. 目錄上寫的是上冊六元二角下冊四元八角.

13. 科學工作者明天要開一個大會.

14. 書店的人說那本書初版的没有幾本了，可是再版的就要出版了.

15. 作用人的要出力給人家作事.

16. 我今天原來没意思念書，可是明天要考試了，没法子.

17. 再版的内容比初版的好，所以貴一塊錢.

18. 有幾個作家明天給出版家張先生作生日.

19. 那個字我看錯了，我把「直」字當作「真」字了.

20. 他當校長的時候，學校裏先生、學生都喜歡他.

21. 點名冊上先生把我的名字給寫錯了.

22. 他這次考國文一定得一百, 他寫的字連一個也不錯.

23. 那本書雖然是名作, 但是錯字太多了.

24. 馬先生現在作生意了. 出口生意、進口生意他都作.

25. 他在這兒作工已經三年了. 從來不出錯.

26. 你說你連中學都念不了了, 是真話嗎? … 是真的.

27. 路太太給我們說做中國飯的方法.

28. 他天天出城去作甚麼?

29. 你知道不知道文學手冊的作者是誰?

30. 今天毛先生到我們家來了. 我從學校跑回家去, 但是他已經走了.

31. 不要開快車. 快車很容易出事.

32. 他的作法不對. 他没告訴我就把我的書給拿走了.

33. 華先生出外了. 他家裏的事是華太太作主.

34. 現在幾點鐘了? 我的表慢了.

35. 進出口生意就是買賣東西.

Exercise 2. Dialogues

1. 張：明天萬文華作生日. 請没請你?
   文：没有. 我一點兒也不知道.
   張：真的嗎?
   文：當然是真的. 我從來都説真話.

2. 華：錢實的工作好不好?
   高：不很好. 他每天在工作的時候
       跟別人説話. 還有, 他作事常
       出錯兒. 説真的, 簡直不是一

個好的工作者.

華：你說的一點兒也不錯. 他事作
的不好，我是知道的. 我本來
想有機會告訴他這個作法不對，
可是一直的也沒看見他.

3. 邊：你的大作<u>中國文學</u>中文版的出
版了是不是?

南：已經出版了. 初版的沒有幾本
了. 再版的又快出版了.

5 邊：人家都說這本書的內容很好.

南：我想那是客氣話.

邊：這本大作要不要出英文版?

南：英文版我想以後再說.

邊：我想你還是馬上出外文版，因
10　為你是名作者,這本書是名作,
一定也有很多外國人要看.

4. 簡：<u>白</u>先生，我該走了.

白：不. 吃了晚飯再走.

簡：不要客氣了. 我還得出城到一
　　個出版家那兒，談我那本<u>文學</u>
　　<u>手冊</u>出版的事.

白：我内人馬<u>上</u>就做飯，我們很快
　　就吃飯了.

簡：好,我不客氣了,就在這兒吃了.

5. 路：我看中文圖書目錄上有一本<u>張</u>
　　<u>直文</u>寫的<u>國文研究</u>. 不知道這
　　本書内容寫的好不好？

　　華：我想錯不了，因為<u>張直文</u>是名
　　學者又是名作家. 他的書出版
　　以後很多人要買. 他寫書，都
　　是用很容易懂的語文. 把那本
　　書當作小説看很有意思.

6. 張：<u>文開華</u>，<u>毛</u>先生不在家嗎？
　　文：<u>張</u>先生來了. 請進來坐. 我們
　　先生出外了，三天才回來.

張：我想把毛先生的古版四書拿去
　　看看.

文：張先生，最好毛先生回來你跟
　　毛先生說. 我是做用人的，就
5　　能做工，不能做主.

7. 錢：毛初民真有錢. 天天跑到大飯
　　館兒去吃飯.

　邊：現在做生意的最有錢了.

　錢：他做甚麼生意?

5 邊：他是出版家.

　錢：出版事業也是生意嗎?

　邊：當然是生意了.

8. 張：你作文考的好不好?

　馬：不好. 我考的時候以為沒錯兒.
　　出來以後才知道錯字太多了.
　　你呢?

5 張：別問我了. 我的錯字更多. 很
　　多字，考試的時候我都寫不上

來了. 連點名的「點」我也寫
錯了.

9. 張： 毛過山要到英國去作甚麼?
　　馬： 他說他去作買賣.
　　張： 很多人說他思想很前進.
　　馬： 人家都說,但是事實上他不是.

10. 田： 前天我看外文書店的圖書目錄
　　　　上有原版山河, 我馬上跑到那
　　　　兒去買, 沒有了.
　　高： 你到文人書店試試看.
　5 田： 我去過了. 他們也沒有了.

11. 外國人： 我雖然學了三年的中國話,
　　　　　　可是還是說的很慢.
　　中國人： 我說你說的不很慢.
　　外國人： 你客氣. 我說的太慢了.
　5　　　　　還有, 連很簡單的話有的
　　　　　　還都說不上來呢.

12. 南：簡中明，你喜歡開快車嗎？

簡：我不喜歡開快車．出事的機會
多．

南：你給我姐姐開車就好了．我每

5　次開車他必得説幾次："開的慢
一點兒．不要開快車．"

Exercise 3. Narratives

1. 張校長有兩個得意學生．這兩個人
在念書的時候就很有天才，現在都
已經做事了．一個是作家，書寫的
很多，都是名作．一個是出版家，

5　出版的書都是現代科學用的書．有
的是中文的，有的是外文的．張校
長説："他們兩個人，一個寫書，一
個出版，這是我心裏最喜歡的事．"

2. 田先生教學生作文．田先生説："作
文的方法是要先有了意思，然後把

你的意思寫出來. 在寫一個意思的
時候, 要一直寫下去. 中間不要又
寫別的意思. 還有, 作文兒不要寫
錯字."

3. 馬文海前天到圖書館要看人民畫報.
他不知道人民畫報在甚麼地方, 他
先去看圖書目錄. 在目錄上果然有
人民畫報.目錄上還寫的有中文版、
5 外文版. 外文版裏頭有英文版、日
文版、法文版. 馬文海把英文版的
人民畫報拿出來看. 他説這本畫報
内容很有意思.

4. 有一本書, 初版有錯字. 後來再版
就没有錯字了, 所以買這本書的人
都要買再版的, 不買初版的. 田先
生前天買這本書, 把初版的當作再
5 版的, 他就買了一本. 回家以後,
才知道是買錯了.

5. 張學先是個買賣人．他作生意的作
法，是對客人很客氣，東西價錢又
不貴，所以他的生意很好．他說他
的賣價只是比原價多一點兒．他所
有東西的定價，一定比別人的價目
少．買東西的人看看價目表就知道
了．他真是會作買賣．

6. 馬先生有一本原版的古書．他說是
很難得的．有人說是元朝的，有人
說是明朝的．還有人說，那本書是
不是真的古版很難說，說不定是現
代的人做的．

7. 一個出版家對一個作者說："你的大
作我看過了，真好．如果出版，一
定有很多人看．我有一個主意，馬
上出版．"那個作者說："我想我寫的
內容太簡單，只是寫個大意．如果
有時間，我還要寫一點兒然後再請
你出版．"

8. 錢先生說:"馬小姐作事又快又好.
從來不出錯兒，真是一個最好的工
作者. 以後大事、小事都要請馬小
姐作." 馬小姐說:"我喜歡作事. 作
事可以學本事. 不過事作的太多可
能出錯兒. 如果出錯兒很不好意思."

9. 有一個人因為沒有錢去作用人. 他
的主人對他很好. 他的主人說:"當
用人的用力氣給我們作工，我們應
該對他客氣. 有人簡直把用人當作
牛馬，一點兒也不客氣."

10. 學校的事是校長作主.
家裏的事是家長作主.
人民的事呢，是誰作主?
人民的事，人民作主.

11. 去年我原來沒意思買地. 有人告訴
我有個好機會，有人要出國，他有

兩塊地要賣，要價不貴．當時我內
人看出這兩塊地不貴，他就作主買
了．今年地價貴了，我就寫個價目
單把這兩塊地賣了．真想不到賣價
5 比我買的原價多一千塊錢．我說：
"這是我內人的好主意."

12. 明天是田校長的生日．學校裏的教
員要給田校長作生日．今天開單子，
買作生日用的東西．單子上的東西
都買來了，都給了田校長．田校長
5 說："大家太客氣了．為了我生日的
小事，大家用了很多錢．我太不好
意思了."

13. 一直往前走，不要想回頭！
前進一定有大路，
回頭連小路都沒有．

14. 我問姐姐："你作甚麼呢?"姐姐說：

"我做飯呢. 今天張家有喜事, 應該去道喜. 我們在家吃點兒簡單的飯, 就到張家道喜." 我說:"人家有喜事多半兒請客, 請吃飯. 我們可以到張家吃飯." 姐姐說:"張家今天不請吃飯. 最多有點兒點心、水果, 所以我們必得在家吃飯."

15. 有一個人要上火車, 火車就快要開了, 他還是走的很慢. 有人說:"你應當跑的快一點兒, 不然火車就開了." 他說:"要是這次火車開了, 我就坐下次的火車."

16. 我研究中國古典文學. 要買二十多本中國古書. 因為書價太貴了, 只好先買六七本. 有人告訴我, 買中國古書, 不一定要買古版的. 如果不買古版的, 價錢就不貴了.

17. 我因為要知道「五四」、「七七」、「九
一八」是在那一年，我到書店去買
一張中國大事年表．書店的店員告
訴我，最近出版的書有原子能簡易
5 用法、民間文學、簡寫的字，內容
都不錯．我說，我都買一本看看．

18. 方縣長最喜歡會客．他說會客可以
知道民間很多的事，可以知道別人
的意見．有的事當時就可以說定，
有的事很快就可以去作，所以他每
5 天用很多時間會客．

19. 白先生出門到外國去．他去買車票
跟船票．賣票員告訴他，客船、飛機
票價都是三百塊錢．他心裏想飛機
票價不比客船票價貴，比如天氣好，
5 不如坐飛機．但是他又想要是飛機
有意外呢，不如不坐飛機．他想來
想去，最後還是買的車票跟船票．

20. 我天天坐校車上學. 去年就想買車,
今天果然買車了. 我姐姐説:"你今
天如意了, 可是我要告訴你不能開
快車, 開快車出事的機會多. 還有,
5 你買車的定錢是我給的, 你也不用
給我了." 我説:"不要客氣. 買車的
定錢應該我給." 我姐姐説:"我不是
客氣. 我説的是真話."

21. 中國人常説,「路是人走出來的」. 這
就是説, 一個人要想有出路必得往
前走, 就一定可以走出來一條路.
比如上山, 原來山上沒有路, 可是
5 要是有人走來走去, 就走出來路了.

22. 我們學校從來没有女學生. 今天出
現了兩個女學生. 這兩個女學生在
上課的時候才走進門, 有人出主意
説應該請那兩個女學生吃飯. 可是
5 没機會跟他們説. 我想出主意來了,

我就把兩本書拿給這兩個女學生.
這兩個女學生問我："這兩本書要出
錢買嗎?"我說："不用買. 這兩本書
是我的. 你們才來，還沒有書，可
5 以先用這兩本. 今天晚上我們幾個
人請你們兩個人吃飯去."那兩個女
學生說："你們太客氣了. 我們沒工
夫."

23. 近來很多國家的人民時常說出的口
號是「我們要民主」.可是這個口號
能不能實現就很難說了.

24. 我教書已經有二年了，我今年八月
要出國. 在過去的二年裏我一直的
教高中一的學生. 他們對我很好，
我也很喜歡他們. 我想離開這裏以
5 後，最少是一年以內不能回國，我
一定很想他們. 所以我就買了一本
小冊子，今天上課點名以後我請他

們每一個學生把名字寫在冊子上.
以後我雖然在外國看不見他們，可
以在名冊上看見他們寫的名字.

25. 我是作進出口生意的. 我每天必得
開車到很多地方買賣東西. 我的車
最近常出毛病. 有一次在路上又出
了毛病，毛病在那兒我看不出來.
5 没法子. 我只好走路了.

Exercise 4. Illustrative Sentences (English)

1. Originally I had no intention of buying the old edition of that book.
2. Go straight north for three miles, and you'll get there.
3. All that the Progressive Bookstore publishes are books used in (studying) science.
4. I didn't [at all] know that Mr. Bian was a famous writer.
5. You certainly can't go wrong if you buy the first edition.
6. If a novel is read as a textbook, it will certainly be interesting.
7. Those engaged in business now are really wealthy.
8. Teacher, I simply can't remember how to write the character fēi in fēijī.
9. Please see if the essay I've written has any mistakes.
10. The first edition was published in Shanghai. Was the second edition also published in Shanghai?
11. Are there both Chinese and foreign language editions of your book?
12. What's [written] in the catalogue (is that) Vol. I is $ 6.20 and Vol. II, $ 4.80.

13. Scientific workers will hold a big meeting tomorrow.

14. The man in the bookstore said that there aren't many copies left of the first edition but that the second edition is about to be published.

15. Those who are servants must work hard doing things for others.

16. I hadn't intended to study today, but we're having an exam tomorrow, so there's nothing I can do about it.

17. The second edition is better [in contents] than the first edition, so it's a dollar more.

18. Several writers are having a birthday celebration tomorrow for the publisher, Mr. Zhang.

19. I misread that character. I took the character zhí to be the character zhēn.

20. When he was head of the school, the teachers and students all liked him.

21. The teacher wrote my name wrong on the roll.

22. He will certainly get a hundred on this Chinese literature examination. There wasn't even one mistake in the characters that he wrote.

23. Although that book is a famous work, it has a lot of wrong characters.

24. Mr. Ma is now engaged in business. He's engaged in both the export and the import business.

25. He's been working here for three years already. He never makes a mistake.

26. You say you won't even be able to attend middle school any more. Is that the truth? ···It's really so.

27. Mrs. Lu discussed ways of cooking Chinese food for us.

28. Why do you go out of the city every day?

29. Do you know who the author of Handbook of Literature is?

30. Mr. Mao came to our home today. I hurried back home from school, but he had already left.

31. Don't drive fast. If you drive fast, it's very easy to have an accident.

32. His way of doing things isn't right. Without telling me, he took my books away.

33. Mr. Hua has gone away from home. His wife makes all the decisions regarding family matters.

34. What time is it now? My watch is slow.

35. The export-import business consists in buying and selling things.

Lesson 33

	1	2	3	4	5
	借	介	紹	始	完

	6	7	8	9	10
	朋	友	共	音	社

1. 借 jiè (1) borrow; (2) lend
2. 介 jiè* introduce
3. 紹 shào* introduce
4. 始 shǐ* begin
5. 完 wán finished, completed
6. 朋 péng* friend
7. 友 yǒu* friend
8. 共 gòng* (1) together; (2) altogether, in all
9. 音 yīn* sound, noise
10. 社 shè* (1) society; (2) organization

Special Combinations

1. 出版社 chūbǎnshè publishing house, press
2. 出名 chūmíng famous
3. 共事 gòngshì work together

482

4.	共用	gòngyòng	use altogether, use in all
5.	借給	jiègěi	loan to (also: jiè A gěi B 'loan A to B')
6.	介紹	jièshao	introduce
7.	介紹人	jièshaorén	introducer, middleman, sponsor
8.	借用	jièyòng	borrow
9.	開明	kāimíng	enlightened
10.	開始	kāishǐ	begin, commence
11.	口音	kǒuyin	accent, pronunciation
12.	錄音	lù yīn	to record (sound)
		lùyīn	a recording
13.	錄音機	lùyīnjī	tape recorder
14.	馬來	Mǎlái	Malay
15.	馬來語	Mǎláiyǔ*	Malay language
16.	內地	nèidì	(1) interior territory; (2) China Proper (within the Great Wall)
17.	年代	niándài	(1) period, age, epoch; (2) generation
18.	朋友	péngyou	friend
19.	日常	rìcháng	daily
20.	社會	shèhuì	society
21.	社會工作	shèhuì gōngzuò	social work
22.	社會科學	shèhuì kēxué	social science
23.	社會小説	shèhuì xiǎoshuō	social novel
24.	社會學	shèhuìxué	sociology
25.	社員	shèyuán	member of a shè: association, commune, etc.
26.	社長	shèzhǎng	head of a shè: association, commune, etc.
27.	實用	shíyòng	practically useful, practical
28.	書社	Shūshè	Bookstore (used in specific names)
29.	土音	tǔyīn	local pronunciation
30.	文字	wénzì	characters, writing
31.	文字學	wénzixué	study of characters, etymology, philology

32.	五十年代	wǔshi niándài	(the decade of) the fifties
33.	研究社	yánjiushè	research organization
34.	一共	yígòng	altogether, in all
35.	以上	yǐshàng	above
36.	以下	yǐxià	below
37.	應用	yìngyòng	(1) actually apply, put into practice; (2) applied
38.	應用科學	yìngyòng kēxué	applied sciences
39.	原始	yuánshǐ	(1) in the beginning; (2) primeval, primitive
40.	中外	Zhōng-Wài	China and foreign countries, Sino-foreign

Exercise 1. Practice in Identifying Names of Publishing Houses

The following list contains the names of a number of publishing houses in the PRC. Note that all of the names terminate in either 出版社 chūbǎnshè 'press' or 書店 shūdiàn 'bookstore.' (The term shūdiàn sometimes refers to a place which publishes as well as sells books.) Some of the names have well-known English equivalents (e.g. Foreign Languages Press, Epoch Publishing House).

Give an appropriate translation for each of the names.

1. 人民出版社
2. 作家出版社
3. 文學出版社
4. 工人出版社
5. 科學出版社
6. 開明書店
7. 時代出版社
8. 外文出版社
9. 東方書店

10. 人民文學出版社
11. 上海人民出版社
12. 古典文學出版社
13. 湖北人民出版社
14. 上海東方書店
15. 人民日報出版社
16. 河北人民出版社
17. 五十年代出版社
18. 山東人民出版社

Exercise 2. Practice in Reading Booksellers' Catalogues

The following list contains information such as is found in booksellers' catalogues. Titles of books are presented under several categories. Other information includes the number of volumes, the name of the publisher (in somewhat abbreviated form), and the price. The titles are those of books actually published in China, and the publishers' names are also authentic, but the prices, number of volumes, and attribution of books to specific publishers are fictitious.

中文圖書目錄
文學

在海邊（三冊）	人民文學	每冊 1.00元
家	文　學	1.50元
明代文學（二冊）	古典文學	共　4.50元

語文

英語法	外　文	4.00元
馬來語日常會話	上海人民	0.75元
學生作文手冊 1960年 1965年	人　民	2.50元 3.50元
英語應用文	山東人民	1.60元
實用馬來語手冊	湖北人民	3.00元
日語會話	時　代	0.80元
實用英語語法	湖北人民	2.75元
現代字典上冊	開　明	3.00元
中冊		3.50元
下冊		4.00元
中國的語言文字	作　家	5.50元

科學

原子時代（上下）	科　學	共　11.00元
一百個為甚麼	工　人	0.70元

社會科學

中國古代社會研究（上中下）	五十年代	每冊 12.00元
甚麼是原始社會？	人民日報	1.00元

Exercise 3. Illustrative Sentences (Chinese)

1. 有機會請你給我介紹幾個中國朋友好不好?

2. 他作的那本原始社會才寫完, 還没出版呢.

3. 我跟毛先生借的那個錄音機出了毛病, 不好用了.

4. 他寫那本小説是用他的朋友作中心.

5. 我想把美國學生的生活寫出來介紹給中國學生.

6. 經過張先生的介紹我就跟毛先生作朋友了.

7. 他們都是中國文字學會的會員.

8. 請你看中國大事年表五十年代都有甚麼事?

9. 張小姐跟萬先生是好朋友. 我給他們作的介紹人.

10. 我跟張有文從一九五二年開始在三
友書店就共事．我到書店就是他給
我往書店介紹的．

11. 毛太太做出來的飯比飯館兒做的都
好吃．

12. 語言研究社裏有錄音機．我們可以
跟社裏去借．

13. 研究應用科學的學生比研究社會科
學的學生多的多．

14. 那個錄音機要是一百塊錢以下我就
買．要是一百塊錢以上我買不了．

15. 東北不在中國內地．

16. 我這本社會學是在開明書社買的．

17. 語言研究社借用中外出版社的地方
開會．

18. 他一共借給我五十塊錢．

19. 我才知道，原來他寫的社會小說很
    出名．

20. 他說話又慢又是山東口音，最好不
    叫他錄音．

21. 我念社會學的原因是想以後作社會
    工作．

22. 我在五十年代出版社工作．是一個
    社員介紹我去的．

23. 前天我們到西山去．三個人共用了
    十塊錢．

24. 我的日常生活很簡單．

25. 他說的國語還有一點兒土音．

26. 我下個月要是有工夫一定要開始學
    中文了．

27. 你說中文的文法難，還是英文的文
    法難？

28. 張先生在中西書社買了一本實用馬來語.

29. 從這裏一直往南走就是中國語文研究社.

30. 這本教科書上有「魚」字從古代到現在的寫法.

31. 他會說馬來話是真的嗎?

32. 張先生錄的音你懂不懂?

33. 我學中文從開始到現在也不過五個月.

34. 念大學的時候才學文字學.

35. 我們社長的朋友差不多都是作家.

Exercise 4. Dialogues

1. 簡: 你給我介紹兩個中國朋友好不好?

   文: 好的. 有機會我給你介紹.

簡： 我要是常跟中國朋友在一塊兒
談談，我的中國話一定可以好
一點兒．

2. 邊： 你寫的那本<u>社會學</u>為甚麼還没
出版呢？

張： 我才寫完．

邊： 你寫了很多日子了是不是？

5 張： 没有．我從開始寫到現在一共
寫了還不到五個月呢．

3. 錢： <u>毛大為</u>，把你的錄音機借給我
用用可以嗎？

毛： 可以．你要錄音嗎？

錢： 是的．我想把我們學過的都錄
5 下來，可是我的錄音機出毛病
了，不好用了．我錄完了以後，
馬上就給你拿回來．

4. 田： 你上那兒去？

高：我到實用科學出版社看<u>張</u>社長去．

田：他每天這個時候都不在社裏．

高：如果他不在那兒我就跟社員談

5　　談，因為有個朋友，是馬來人，以前跟我共事十幾年了，他最近寫了一本書<u>實用馬來語</u>，我想介紹他，跟社裏的人談談出版的事．

10 田：你這個朋友還寫別的書了嗎？

高：他還寫了一本<u>馬來原始時代的社會</u>．

5. 馬：我想請語言研究社的<u>簡</u>先生去吃飯．你說在那兒好呢？

文：有個大華館兒，又好吃又不貴．我每次請客都在那兒．

5 馬：我知道大華館兒很出名．

文：是．可以說中外出名．有很多

外國人也常到那兒去吃.

馬： 如果四五個人去吃要不要二十
塊錢以上？

文： 用不了. 十五塊錢以下可以吃
的很好.

6. 華： 你寫這本社會小說共用多少時
候？

常： 我寫了差不多有一年.

華： 這本小說的內容是甚麼？

常： 我寫的大意是社會上人的生活，
還有甚麼是社會工作.

華： 你寫這本書用甚麼人作中心？

常： 我拿一個工人作中心. 我寫的
都是社會生活的事實. 我把工
人的日常生活寫出來介紹給大
家.

7. 南： 你是湖北人？

張： 我是山東人.

南：你説話是湖北口音.

張：因為我在湖北當教員很多年,
所以説湖北話. 可是有的時候
我還有山東土音.

8. 連：你到那兒去了?

馬：我到大華書社去買社會科學的
書. 他們没有.

連：你到六十年代出版社去買. 他
們那兒書最多.

9. 毛：你跟張先生借錢,介紹人是誰?

文：是文人書社的社員毛大文.

毛：錢借來了嗎?

文：借來了.

10. 白：錢先生來了. 好嗎?

錢：好. 白太太, 你好? 白先生在
家嗎?

白：才出去. 他到開明書店買書去
了.

錢：我來借東西．我想把白先生的
　　錄音機借用一次．

白：錄音機前幾天毛先生借去了．

錢：好．我再跟張法天去借．

11. 連：那幾個馬來學生他們才到內地
　　　來是不是？

路：是的，他們才從東三省來．

連：他們會說中國話嗎？

5 路：會說．他們跟我們說中國話．
　　他們幾個人在一塊兒就說馬來
　　話．

連：他們來學甚麼？

路：一個研究中國文字學，一個學
10　應用科學．還有幾個學科學還
　　是學文學，我不知道．

12. 學生：先生，甚麼叫五十年代、六
　　　　十年代？

先生：十年就是一年代．一九五〇

年到一九五九這十年裏頭就
叫五十年代. 一九六〇開始
就是六十年代.

Exercise 5. Narratives

1. 我是研究社會科學的. 我開始作事
是在出版社. 這個出版社很出名,
出版的書很多. 有中文的, 也有外
文的. 外文的書多半兒是英文, 也
5 有不少日文的. 出版社的社長從前
是一個作家,他寫了很多社會小說,
他最喜歡出版工作. 現在他是有名
的出版家, 也是名作者. 我本來沒
見過他, 經過一個朋友的介紹, 我
10 才見到他. 我們頭一次談話以後,
他就請我到出版社工作. 他説出版
社雖然也是作買賣, 但是這是社會
事業. 他還説研究社會學的人最好
是在社會上作社會工作. 出版工作

也是社會工作，所以他一定叫我到
社裏去工作.

2. 我在中外書社買了一本書，書名是
從原始社會到現代社會. 這本書的
內容很好. 書裏大意是說社會是前
進的，我們生活在這個時代也應該
5 前進.

3. 語文研究社裏有一個錄音機. 如果
社員喜歡錄音,就可以在那裏錄音.
我前天錄了一次國語. 大家都說我
的口音很好，就是話說得太慢了.
5 還有一個人也錄的國語，大家說他
有點兒東北土音. 最後一個人，錄
的是中文課本. 他的音，錄的最好,
因為他是研究社裏國語教員. 我們
三個人一共錄了兩個小時才完.

4. 張先生最會做飯. 他說他作甚麼事

都不喜歡，從小的時候就一直喜歡
做飯．他的作法，別人也學不上來．
有一天，我的朋友作生日，就是<u>張</u>
先生做的飯．所有的客人都說，<u>張</u>
5 先生飯做的真的不錯，簡直的比飯
館兒做的都好．

5. 我在圖書目錄上看見一本社會學．
作者是有名的學者，我就跑到書店
去買這本社會學．書店裏的人說：
"這本書是名作．初版的已經賣完
5 了，再版的快出版了．請你過五六
天再來看看．"

6. 大家在一塊兒作事的時候，有難作
的事，你要先去作．有容易作的事，
你要請別人去作．這個作法，人家
一定喜歡跟你共事．要不然，沒有
5 人喜歡跟你共事．

7. 看書要先看目錄. 目錄看過以後就
知道書的內容了. 但是有的書有的
時候没有目錄, 只好就看書的內容
了.

8. 我最喜歡開快車. 我姐姐叫我不要
開快車, 他説:"車常出毛病, 都是
因為開快車. 每次出了毛病, 都得
用錢, 都是我給錢. 前後共用二百
多塊錢了.如果再開快車出了毛病,
我不出錢了."

9. 中國從前內地的人口多, 東北的人
口少, 所以有很多內地的人喜歡去
東北. 他們到了東北多半兒是先給
人家做工, 或者做用人. 後來有的
是地主了, 有的還是給人家做工.

10. 我知道語文研究社有錄音機. 我想
借用一次, 可是研究社的社長我没

見過，我不知道能不能借給我．我
有一個朋友是研究社的社員．我先
去問那個朋友．那個朋友説研究社
的社長是他的朋友，要是他作介紹
5 人，一定能借來．

11. 張大為念大學的時候，日用的東西
都没錢買，連念的書也没錢買．他
有一個朋友，借錢給他買書，借東
西給他用．大家都説這個朋友真是
5 好朋友．

12. 田紹文作文常寫錯字．先生告訴他：
"你每次作文的時候必得小心，就不
會常出錯了．"

13. 我有一本古版的書，不知道是甚麽
年代的．我就去問朋友．有人説可能
是元朝時代的原版，也有人説不是
原版．

14. 我在五十年代出版社工作．社裏
　　的工人要是在社裏借錢，都要對我
　　說．有一個工人，他的女兒病了，
　　要跟社裏借一百二十塊錢．我說：
5 "社長說過，如果工人借錢在一百塊
　　以下的，可以借給，在一百塊以上
　　的，就不能借了．你要借一百二十
　　塊錢，本來我不能作主，可是我看
　　你說的是真話，就借給你一百二十
10 塊錢．"

15. 馬先生最近寫了一本書，書名是原
　　始的人．有一個出版家對馬先生說：
　　"你的大作太好了，實在是名作．要
　　不要出版？如果要出版，我給你出
5 版．"

16. 研究應用科學在日常生活上馬上就
　　可以實用，所以近來的大學生有很
　　多人喜歡研究應用科學．研究社會

科學的人就不太多了.

17. 有一個馬來人喜歡研究中國文字,
要跟我學中文. 我也想學馬來話,
我也請他教給我馬來話. 我們兩個
人到三友書店去買書. 我告訴他買
一本中國古代文字學, 他叫我買一
本簡易馬來語. 這兩本書都是開明
書店出版的.

18. 在五四時代以前田先生的思想就很
開明. 當時的女人多半不能到外頭
去念書, 可是田先生的女兒就在大
學念書. 他常對別人說兒女都應該
有學問, 為甚麼就叫兒子念書, 不
叫女兒出去念書呢?

19. 我在外國大學念書的時候, 校長跟
校長太太很喜歡我. 每年過年或者
我過生日都叫我到他們家裏去, 給

我做很好吃的東西. 他們對我真好,
簡直把我當作他們的兒子了.

20. 前天晚上我坐八點半的慢車到上海
去，可是到了上海八點的快車還没
到呢. 原因是快車在半路上出事了.

21. 馬長木先生是一個考古學家，他最
近要到河南省去. 他去的目的是到
那裏去考古. 因為有人告訴他河南
近來出現了很多古代的東西，所以
⁵馬長木先生要到河南去.

22. 文先生是作社會工作的，他工作能
力很好. 他作事從來都不出錯，真
是一個好的工作者. 很多人説他思
想很前進. 不知道是不是真的.

23. 毛先生在一個學校教書，家裏人口
多，所以生活很不好. 他有一個很
好的朋友姓文是作鐘表生意的. 有

一次<u>毛</u>先生對他說也要作生意去.
那個朋友說作生意很難,不如教書.
<u>毛</u>先生說他一定要試試, 所以他就
開始作生意. 經過二年的工夫, 生
5 意一點兒也不如意. <u>毛</u>先生想作甚
麼也不容易, 朋友說的是真話. <u>毛</u>
先生又回到學校去教書.

24. <u>錢更生</u>是一個畫家. 他有很多古今
名人的畫兒. 有一天他作生日,請我
們到他家裏吃飯. 吃了飯以後, 他
把所有的畫兒還有畫冊都拿給我們
5 看. 有一本畫冊我很喜歡, 上頭畫
的是馬跟牛, 畫的真好.

25. 前天<u>馬</u>先生介紹我到<u>白</u>先生那裏去
借書. 我說我九點到<u>白</u>先生家. 因
為路上人多車多, 車走的很慢, 我
到<u>白</u>先生家已經十點了. <u>白</u>先生、
5 <u>白</u>太太都很客氣. 他們還有一個小

兒子跑來跑去很有意思. 我在那裏
跟白先生談了一會兒，白先生把我
要借的書給我，我就走了.

Exercise 6. Illustrative Sentences (English)

1. If you have a chance, how about introducing me to some Chinese friends?

2. His book <u>Primitive Society</u> has just been finished. It hasn't been published yet.

3. That tape recorder I borrowed from Mr. Mao has something wrong with it and can't be used.

4. In writing that novel, he used a friend of his as the central figure.

5. I plan to write about student life in America to introduce it to Chinese students.

6. After having been introduced by Mr. Zhang, I became friends with Mr. Mao.

7. They're all members of the Association for the Study of Chinese Writing.

8. Please look up the events of the fifties in <u>Chinese Historical Table of Great Events.</u>

9. Miss Zhang and Mr. Wan are good friends. It was I who introduced them.

10. Zhang Youwen and I have been working together at the Three Friends Bookstore since [lit. beginning from] 1952. As for my going to the Bookstore, it was he who introduced me [to the Bookstore].

11. The food cooked by Mrs. Mao is even more delicious than restaurant food.

12. The Linguistics Research Institute has a tape recorder. We can go and borrow it from the Institute.

13. There are a lot more students studying the applied sciences than there are studying the social sciences.

14. I'll buy that tape recorder if it's less than $100. I can't afford to buy it if it's over $100.

15. Manchuria is not within China proper.

16. This sociology book [of mine] was bought in the Kaiming Bookstore.

17. The Linguistic Research Institute borrowed the Sino-Foreign Press's place for a meeting.

18. He loaned me $50 in all.

19. It's just come to my knowledge that the social novels he's written are actually quite famous.

20. In his speaking, he's slow and has a Shantung pronunciation. It would be best not to ask him to record.

21. The reason I'm studying sociology is that I plan to do social work later.

22. I work at the Fifties Press. I was introduced [to go] by a person at the press.

23. Day before yesterday we went to the Western Hills. The three of us spent ten dollars in all.

24. My [daily] life is very simple.

25. In speaking the National Language, he still has a bit of the local pronunciation.

26. Next month if I have time, I certainly will begin to study Chinese.

27. Which do you think is more difficult, Chinese or English grammar?

28. Mr. Zhang bought a copy of Practical Malay at the Sino-Western Bookstore.

29. Go straight south from here, and there's the Chinese Language Research Institute.

30. In this textbook there's the way of writing the character 'fish' from ancient times to the present.

31. Is it true that he can speak Malay?

32. Do you understand what Mr. Zhang has recorded?

33. It hasn't been more than five months from the beginning of my studying Chinese to the present.

34. Etymology isn't studied until the first year of college.

35. The friends of the director of our institute are almost all writers.